Research Data Sharing and Valorization

SCIENCES

Scientific Knowledge Management, Field Director – Renaud Fabre

Transformation Dynamics of Tools and Practices,
Subject Head – Joachim Schöpfel

Research Data Sharing and Valorization

Developments, Tendencies, Models

Coordinated by
Joachim Schöpfel
Violaine Rebouillat

WILEY

First published 2022 in Great Britain and the United States by ISTE Ltd and John Wiley & Sons, Inc.

ISTE Ltd
27-37 St George's Road
London SW19 4EU
UK

www.iste.co.uk

John Wiley & Sons, Inc.
111 River Street
Hoboken, NJ 07030
USA

www.wiley.com

Library of Congress Control Number: 2021953220

British Library Cataloguing-in-Publication Data
A CIP record for this book is available from the British Library
ISBN 978-1-78945-073-6

ERC code:
PE6 Computer Science and Informatics
 PE6_10 Web and information systems, database systems, information retrieval and digital libraries, data fusion

Contents

Chapter 3. The International Community: The Strasbourg Astronomical Data Centre (CDS).

Françoise GENOVA and Mark G. ALLEN

Chapter 4. Data INRAE – The Networked Repository.

Esther DZALÉ YEUMO

Chapter 5. SEANOE – A Thematic Repository

Frédéric MERCEUR, Loic PETIT DE LA VILLEON and Sybille VAN ISEGHEM

Chapter 6. Nakala – A Data Publishing Service.

Stéphane POUYLLAU

Chapter 7. The National Repository Option

Louki-Géronimo RICHOU and Joachim SCHÖPFEL

Chapter 8. Comparative Study of National Research Services 135
Hugo CATHERINE

Chapter 9. Mendeley Data 153
Wouter HAAK, Juan GARCÍA MORGADO, Jennifer RUTTER, Alberto ZIGONI
and David TUCKER

Foreword

Renaud FABRE

Professor Emeritus, Université Paris 8 Vincennes-Saint-Denis, France

Today, the foundations of true scientific data policies have become visible to researchers and users alike. It seems to be an opportune moment to propose an English and French version of a reference book for research work, as well as for higher education, which takes stock of the principles, projects and achievements in progress, by applying once again the editorial policy of the SCIENCES Encyclopedia, in this Collection dedicated to "Knowledge Management". This book is intended to occupy a central place in the models of basic and continuing education of Higher Education, where a "data strategy" is currently being developed by all stakeholders[1].

In this context, the main interest of the book is twofold:

– it presents a timely opportunity to discover the reference projects and understand the set-up;

– it outlines, across a wide range of disciplines and situations, the characteristic facets of the goal of data policy, and of all the work of data science, or "data scholarship" as it has come to be called (Borgman 2020).

The book provides both of these insights in a relevant and complete manner, by and for those who build these data policies and who are both the primary actors and

---

1 See, for example, the adult learning course at Sorbonne University; available at: https://www.data-strategie.sorbonne-universite.fr/.

Research Data Sharing and Valorization,
coordinated by Joachim SCHÖPFEL and Violaine REBOUILLAT. © ISTE Ltd 2022.

users: disciplinary or thematic structuring projects, current and future national sharing formulas and mechanisms are reviewed, as are the problems of data sharing, both for scientific uses and development. Recommendations for the future are formulated, and we can see that this book takes us to the heart of the new challenges of scientific work, where knowledge sharing and the enrichment of its methods are being renewed simultaneously.

The book's emphasis on research data archiving should be well understood from the outset. The function of the repository is indeed an essential one in every respect in the process of constructing data sharing: there can be no visibility, comparison, positioning, curation, sampling, stock management and replication without repositories. It is well understood that the repository is the current canonical form, global or local, of any constructed data policy process. Because of its obvious functional importance, the data repository is also the very place for researchers to learn collectively in favor of sharing: indeed, what would the perspective be if each experience of sharing, each practice, were to be confined by the walls of an approach partitioned to each laboratory and each use? It is clear that the repository is the vehicle for a new scientific practice, hence the utmost importance given to the practices of registering and managing repositories, as demonstrated by the recent publication on this subject (Downs 2021). We will return to this later in this introduction.

A few remarks on the context of the publication of this work and a look at its scope will help to illustrate this point.

The context in which this book was published is that of a "French-style" data policy that is rich in a public science dynamic, itself driven by the spirit of sharing and opening up scientific data, addressed to all of the beneficiaries and users of science.

In this sense, many steps have already been taken or are in the process of being taken, with the construction of analyses and mechanisms on the possibility of sharing, the need to do so and the need to share and exchange standards. This reflects major legislative changes, such as the law of July 17, 1978, which deems the output of public authorities and that under their control as "public data", along with data which are likely to be communicated on request, with certain limited exceptions. The principle of accessibility, the primary characteristic of Open Data, makes communication obligatory and bases open science on access to the common good which is, from the outset, a right to access the data.

France remains in this matter marked by the simplicity and universality of its data access regime, based, it may be recalled, on Article 15 of the Declaration of the Rights of Man and of the Citizen (right to communicate public data), and on the 2003 European Parliament Directive on the reuse of public sector information[2]. The French national experience has recently been enriched by a comprehensive legislative framework for structuring Open Data: The Valter Act of December 28, 2015 on free access and reuse of public sector data, and subsequently, Articles 30 and 38 of the Act for a Digital Republic of October 2016, to name but a few of the many recent European and national texts on this topic.

A stimulating conception of science in the digital age has thus been set in motion, sometimes starting from afar, with pioneers and precursors sometimes 20 years ahead of their time, and all driven by the same conviction: data are singular objects. Data, in fact, are both singular and multiple in that they contain an observation, recorded in a context and may simultaneously belong to larger or simply parallel sets, where they take on another meaning and participate in another observable reality. The data are also singular in that they can partly fall within the scope of Open Data practices and partly, in a contractual sense, fall within the scope of systems of valorization by the company or by the non-commercial associative fabric. This plasticity of data and their use shapes the ways in which they are made available.

Of course, all of these scientific sharing operations have their own meaning, which is that of the protocol to which this data sharing is linked, but this sharing is also an opportunity to expose, verify and reproduce operations, which corresponds to the growing need for reproducibility and replicability (Fineberg 2020).

We are beginning to reflect on the idea of a national networked service or services for data (Catherine 2020), and this book makes a rich and positive contribution to it.

Storing is the easiest operation in the world in physical terms, but scientifically it is one of the most complex. This is true for any deposit of information of any kind, but it is even more difficult to devise for data: it is a demanding and vigilant attitude that is required here, the rules of which are more and more clearly shared and accepted (Jeffery et al. 2021).

---

2 Available at: 2003/98/EC https://eur-lex.europa.eu/legal-content/EN/TXT/PDF/?uri=CELEX: 32003L0098&from=en.

What differentiates a data repository from complete chaos (well-known as a "Spanish inn" in French – sorry to our Spanish neighbors!) is the presence or absence of services and in-depth support for the researcher's needs. Here too, many reflections are progressing with a level of requirement that guarantees clear progress toward the maturity of projects (Suhr *et al.* 2020), which must all count with the uneven progress of open access (Hahnel *et al.* 2020) and training in digital tools (Klebel *et al.* 2020).

In conclusion, the panoramic virtue of the book promises to examine progression toward maturity, in a field where all science is solicited and questioned by multiple entries today. Of course, as Schöpfel *et al.* remarked in a very valuable previous publication, what answer can be given to the question: "how can we think of these 'data documents' which are part of the science in the making and which therefore quite naturally 'blur the boundaries'" (Schöpfel *et al.* 2020)?

However, let us be reassured and find excellent reasons to hope in the current dynamics: this blurring is only the temporary effect of a recomposition of the scientific information landscape, in which, across the board, data repositories occupy a strategic founding place, at the forefront of the organized sources of a new way of doing science. In our recent joint article devoted to the scientific information platforms in the making at the European and international levels, we emphasize the various forms that the requirement for data traceability and the structuring of their flow takes (Fabre *et al.* 2021). It is true that it is time, as observed by the European Commission[3], to deepen the approaches to open science that bring all of the actors and users of scientific information to the same table, in an approach that reconciles all of the uses and thus brings to life all of the aspects of open science in a deployment of data science that remains a critical phase (Davenport and Malone 2021).

This phase is all the more critical as the development of "multi-user" scientific projects is now extremely vigorous, as is that of collective learning projects (He *et al.* 2020), which are being used more and more widely in a growing number of disciplines. This development is also in line with that of sharing and storage tools such as knowledge graphs, which are developing extremely rapidly in the scientific field, and are oriented above all toward the shared use of heterogeneous data, thus combining various sources of documents and data.

January 2022

---

3 Available at: https://projectescape.eu/news/launch-initial-escape-esfri-science-analysis-platform-discovery-data-staging.

References

Borgman, C.L. (2020). *Qu'est-ce que le travail scientifique des données ? Big Data, Little Data, No Data.* OpenEdition Press, Marseille.

Catherine, H. (2020). Etude comparative des services nationaux de données de recherche : facteurs de réussite. MESRI comité pour la science ouverte [Online]. Available at: https://www.ouvrirlascience.fr/etude-comparative-des-services-nationaux-de-donnees-de-recherche-facteurs-de-reussite/.

Davenport, T. and Malone, K. (2021). Deployment as a critical business data science discipline. Harvard Data Science Review [Online]. Available at: https://doi.org/10.1162/99608f92.90814c32.

Downs, R.R. (2021). Improving opportunities for new value of open data: Assessing and certifying research data repositories. *Data Science Journal*, 20(1), 1.

Fabre, R., Egret, D., Schöpfel, J., Azeroual, O. (2021). Evaluating scientific impact of research infrastructures: The role of current research information systems. *Quantitative Science Studies*, 1–25 [Online]. Available at: https://doi.org/10.1162/qss_a_00111.

Fineberg, H., Stodden, V., Meng, X.-L. (2020). Highlights of the US National Academies Report on "Reproducibility and Replicability in Science". *Harvard Data Science Review*, 2(4) [Online]. Available at: https://doi.org/10.1162/99608f92.cb310198.

Hahnel, M., McIntosh, L.D., Hyndman, A., Baynes, G., Crosas, M., Nosek, B., Shearer, K., van Selm, M., Goodey, G. (2020). The State of Open Data 2020. Digital Science Report [Online]. Available at: https://doi.org/10.6084/m9.figshare.13227875.v2.

He, C., Li, S., So, J., Zeng, X., Zhang, M., Wang, H., Wang, X., Vepakomma, P., Singh, A., Qiu, H. *et al.* (2020). *FedML: A Research Library and Benchmark for Federated Machine Learning.* Preprint. ArXiv [Online]. Available at: https://arxiv.org/abs/2007.13518.

Jeffery, K., Wittenburg, P., Lannom, L., Strawn, G., Biniossek, C., Betz, D., Blanchi, C. (2021). Not ready for convergence in data infrastructures. *Data Intelligence*, 3(1), 116–135.

Klebel, T., Reichmann, S., Polka, J., McDowell, G., Penfold, N., Hindle, S., Ross-Hellauer, T. (2020). Peer review and preprint policies are unclear at most major journals. *PLoS ONE*, 15(10), e0239518.

Schöpfel, J., Farace, D., Prost, H., Zane, A., Hjørland, B. (2020). Data documents. *Encyclopedia of Knowledge Organization*, 48(4), 307–328 [Online]. Available at: https://www.isko.org/cyclo/data_documents.

Suhr, B., Dungl, J., Stocker, A. (2020). Search, reuse and sharing of research data in materials science and engineering – A qualitative interview study. *PLoS ONE*, 15(9), e0239216.

1

The Research Data Repository Facility

Violaine REBOUILLAT[1] and Joachim SCHÖPFEL[2]

[1] Claude Bernard University Lyon 1, Villeurbanne, France
[2] University of Lille, Villeneuve d'Ascq, France

1.1. Introduction

What is a research data repository? Where does this term come from? How can we describe this facility? This chapter attempts to answer all of these questions, even though the landscape of data repositories is very varied and heterogeneous. The issue of trust is at the heart of the development of research data repositories – trust in both the content and the quality of the facility. The issue of repository certification is closely related to the issue of trust.

1.2. The term repository in the context of open access

The term repository comes from the field of computer science. "In computing, a repository is a centralized and organized store of data. It can be one or more databases where files are located for distribution over the network or a place directly accessible to users"[1]. There are repositories for source code, software, data... the list goes on.

---

1 Available at: https://en.wikipedia.org/wiki/Software_repository.

Research Data Sharing and Valorization,
coordinated by Joachim SCHÖPFEL and Violaine REBOUILLAT. © ISTE Ltd 2022.

In the early 2000s, the term repository found a specific use in the context of *open access*. It can be found in the acronyms ROAR (for *Registry of Open Access Repository*) and OpenDOAR (for *Directory of Open Access Repositories*), which are both directories of open access repositories that make scientific content (journal articles, conference papers, research data, etc.) available.

In the context of open access, repositories are defined as follows by JISC[2]: "A repository is a set of services that a research organization offers to the members of its community for the management and dissemination of digital materials created by its community members" (Hubbard 2016).

According to this definition, the primary function of repositories is therefore the management and communication of digital content. These are based on a number of basic services including the storage of content, the creation of associated metadata, the indexing, dissemination and preservation of this content under predefined conditions of access and use, and the ongoing maintenance of these services. The open access policy also directs the dissemination of content toward "open" dissemination, with a minimum number of barriers to access (whether financial or technical).

The term research data repository originated from the open science movement, which gradually extended to research data (with the Berlin Declaration[3] in 2003 and the OECD Declaration[4] in 2004). It has been used to designate infrastructures specifically dedicated to the storage and sharing of scientific data.

In open science policies, data have therefore been progressively dissociated from publications: we have begun to speak of specific "data repositories", whereas initially we were talking about repositories common to both data and publications (which have notably become known as open archives). In 2007, the European Research Council (ERC) recommended the storage of publications and data in an

---

2 Available at: https://www.jisc.ac.uk.

3 *Berlin Declaration on Open Access to Knowledge in the Sciences and Humanities* (2003). Available at: http://openaccess.mpg.de/Berlin-Declaration.

4 *OECD Statement on Access to Publicly Funded Research Data* (2004). Annex 1 to the Final Communiqué of the Meeting of the OECD Committee for Science and Technology Policy at Ministerial Level, 29–30 January 2004. Available at: https://www.oecd.org/sti/sciencetechnologyandinnovationforthe21stcenturymeetingoftheoecdcommitteeforscientificandtechnologicalpolicyatministeriallevel29-30january2004-finalcommunique.htm.

undifferentiated manner in "open access repositories"[5], while 10 years later, in 2017, the European Commission distinguished between *research data repositories* (for data) and *repositories for scientific publications* (for publications)[6].

During this period, dedicated repositories were developed at the request of research funders. Among the best known are:

– *4TU.ResearchData*[7], a multidisciplinary repository created in 2008 on the initiative of three Dutch universities;

– *Dryad*[8], in the field of biology, launched in 2008 and maintained by a non-profit organization made up of publishers, scientific societies, research institutions, libraries and research funding agencies;

– *Figshare*[9] in 2011, a generic repository hosting all types of research products (preprints, posters, research data, etc.) and funded by the company Digital Science;

– *Zenodo*[10] in 2013, also a generic repository, hosted by CERN and developed within the framework of the European project OpenAIREplus.

The *re3data*[11] directory currently (as of February 2021) lists over 2,600 data repositories.

While data repositories are an integral part of open science policies, they are not a new product. Long before this openness movement, several research communities had set up more or less extensive data structuring and communication infrastructures, for example, in astronomy (Borgman *et al.* 2016), crystallography (Bruno *et al.* 2017) and genomics (International Human Genome Sequencing Consortium 2001). A common feature of these disciplines is the use of large equipment for data generation. The cost of this equipment has led research communities to collaborate

---

5 European Research Council (2007). European Research Council-Scientific Council Guidelines for Open Access. Available at: https://erc.europa.eu/sites/default/files/document/file/erc_scc_guidelines_open_access.pdf.

6 European Commission (2017b). H2020 Programme: Guidelines to the Rules on Open Access to Scientific Publications and Open Access to Research Data in Horizon 2020. Version 3.2. Available at: https://ec.europa.eu/research/participants/data/ref/h2020/grants_manual/hi/oa_pilot/h2020-hi-oa-pilot-guide_en.pdf.

7 Available at: https://researchdata.4tu.nl/.

8 Available at: https://datadryad.org/.

9 Available at: https://figshare.com/.

10 Available at: https://zenodo.org/.

11 Available at: https://www.re3data.org.

around data collection and thus to set up a system of data standardization and dissemination (Rebouillat 2019). The ability of these large facilities to generate large volumes of data has also been a driving force in the decision to pool data through international research networks responsible for their analysis (André 2015).

The diversity of these systems, both prior to and in accordance with contemporary open research data policies, explains why a very large number of repositories are listed as such in *re3data*.

In a CNRS working paper, they have been related to the category of online platforms (DIST-CNRS 2017). Defined in the Act for a Digital Republic (Article 49)[12], this concept refers to

> an online public communication service based on:
>
> 1) the classification or referencing, by means of computer algorithms, of content, goods or services offered or put online by third parties;
>
> 2) or the bringing together of several parties with a view to the sale of a good, the provision of a service or the exchange or sharing of content, goods or services.

The platform concept thus encompasses very heterogeneous services, ranging from GAFAM to scientific journal platforms such as JSTOR, Érudit and SciELO and documentary platforms such as those of the CNRS.

The CNRS therefore proposes to define a sub-category of "science platforms", which would include research data repositories. The term "science platform" would designate informational devices "with multiple functionalities [including a] repository of scientific data and work, access to scientific documentation and publications, and value-added information processing services [...]" (DIST-CNRS 2017).

Bringing together a "complicated mix of software, hardware, operations, and networks" (Kenney and Zysman 2016), including, in particular, discovery, repository and access rights management tools, the concept of a platform is nevertheless still very broad.

In this chapter, we propose a reflection on the concept of the research data repository. How are data repositories characterized? Are there any criteria for defining them?

---

12 LAW No. 2016-1321 of 7 October 2016 for a digital Republic. Available at: https://www.legifrance.gouv.fr/eli/loi/2016/10/7/ECFI1524250L/jo/texte.

We will deploy the concept of a facility, which will allow us to study repositories from both a technical and social perspective. We will first present the scope and functionalities of repositories, before focusing on the user dimension, which we will link to the notion of trust and related criteria. We will conclude by proposing some ideas for a definition.

1.3. How to define a research data repository

Data repositories contribute to the mechanism of *research data publishing*. Despite all the connotations that the notion of "publication" may have, especially in the field of scientific communication, where it is often associated with peer-reviewing, etc., *publishing* here means "making public".

Austin *et al.* (2017) propose the following definition:

> Research data publishing is the release of research data, associated metadata, accompanying documentation, and software code (in cases where the raw data have been processed or manipulated) for re-use and analysis in such a manner that they can be discovered on the Web and referred to in a unique and persistent way. Data publishing occurs via dedicated data repositories and/or (data) journals which ensure that the published research objects are well documented, curated, archived for the long term, interoperable, citable, quality assured and discoverable – all aspects of data publishing that are important for future reuse of data by third party end-users.

This definition outlines four functions that appear to be essential to data publishing devices: describing, archiving, identifying and making available (Figure 1.1).

We find these functions in the definition given by Cocaud and Aventurier (2017): a data repository is an "online service allowing the collection, description, conservation, search and dissemination of datasets". Cocaud and Aventurier cite as examples the repositories *Pangaea*[13], *Dryad, Zenodo, Archeology Data Service*[14], the Strasbourg Astronomical Data Center[15]or the Ifremer marine data portal[16].

---

13 Available at: https://www.pangaea.de/.

14 Available at: https://archaeologydataservice.ac.uk/.

15 Available at: https://cds.unistra.fr/.

16 Available at: https://data.ifremer.fr/.

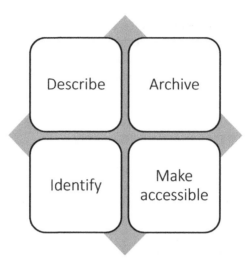

Figure 1.1. *Four key functions of data repositories*

While this definition may seem exact and straightforward, it nevertheless covers a complex reality. There are many definitions of the repository concept and they do not all focus on the same functionalities. As an example, we can compare the definitions proposed by the Network of the National Library of Medicine (NNLM, NIH, USA) and by the *re3data* directory. One might notice that these definitions are significantly different. The *re3data* repository describes research data repositories as "a subtype of a sustainable information infrastructure which provides long-term storage and access to research data" (Rücknagel *et al.* 2015). This definition presents repositories as infrastructures that enable data discovery and use, while the NNLM, on the other hand, proposes a definition that places more emphasis on data repository functionalities: "A data repository can be defined as a place that holds data, makes data available for use, and organizes data in a logical manner. A data repository may also be defined as an appropriate, subject-specific location where researchers can submit their data"[17].

While it is difficult to describe what a data repository is, it is possible to say what it is not. In particular, the term repository is distinct from archive. Even if data repositories borrow methods from archival science in terms of data preservation and documentation, the main issue is the reuse of this data in the short, medium or long term. Repository data are therefore preserved more for their scientific value than for their heritage value, unlike archival data.

---

17 Source: https://nnlm.gov/data/thesaurus/data-repository.

This chapter proposes that we consider data repositories as digital devices, that is, as tools (or services of tools) for mediating scientific information between producers and users (Prost and Schöpfel 2019). The originality of this approach is that it allows us to study repositories not only in their technical but also social dimensions (Larroche 2019).

1.4. Variable geometry devices

Considering data repositories as digital devices means, first of all, getting the measure of the variables that comprise them. What makes a repository unique depends on:

– hosted content (i.e. the nature of the data made available);

– the scope (there are institutional, national, disciplinary and publisher-specific repositories);

– the proposed features.

We will come back to these three parameters in more detail in the following subsections.

1.4.1. *Heterogeneous content*

One of the peculiarities that repositories have to deal with is the almost infinite typology of entities that can be considered as research data (Pampel *et al.* 2013).

The notion of research data is a complex one to define, as it encompasses very different realities. Borgman (2015) considers that "an observation, an object, a document or any other entity becomes research data once it is used as evidence of a phenomenon, i.e., collected, analyzed and interpreted".

Several works have highlighted the contextual nature of research data. According to Leonelli (2015), there is no such thing as data per se. What a scientist considers "data" is always relative to a specific research question. Data are not defined according to their intrinsic properties but according to their function within particular research processes. The question "what is data?" can only be answered in reference to concrete research situations.

This is why data cannot be considered as a fixed entity (it can be, but only if observed at a given moment in a particular context). Data are malleable objects that adapt to research trends, hence the notion of the "lifecycle" of data (Higgins 2012).

Schöpfel *et al.* (2017) have isolated four parameters of variation of scientific data: its factual nature, its recording, the community that generates and/or uses it and its purpose.

These four dimensions therefore have an impact on the way a repository is designed. We find repositories specialized in the dissemination of data generated by large research infrastructures, such as the *ILL Data Portal*[18], which hosts data from the spectrometers of the Institut Laue-Langevin. On the other hand, other repositories such as *Figshare* (see Chapter 10) have chosen to host so-called orphan data, for which there is no dedicated publication system. There are also specificities among repositories between simple data and complex data, big data and long tail data. The malleable nature of data nevertheless makes any attempt at typology imperfect (Rebouillat 2019) and, in fact, multiplies the number of possible specializations of repositories.

1.4.2. *A variable scope*

In addition to this data complexity, there is the question of the scope of the repository. The design of a data repository can be done at different levels. A research institution may decide to develop a repository to house the data produced by its researchers (INRAE, for example, with its *Data INRAE*[19] repository, see Chapter 4). A publisher may propose a repository as part of its policy of making the data underlying the journal articles it publishes available (*Mendeley Data*[20] from Elsevier, for example, see Chapter 9). A research consortium may choose to create a repository for the data of a particular discipline or type (this is the case of *Pangaea*).

The *re3data* directory has chosen to classify the different forms of existing repositories according to the following typology (Rücknagel *et al.* 2015):

– Government repositories: these are data collections maintained and managed by government institutions, whose repository arrangements generally exclude external contributions.

– Institutional repositories: these are repositories linked to a particular institution, usually covering several research disciplines. These institutions may have obligations regarding the storage and dissemination of data.

---

18 Available at: https://www.ill.eu/users/ill-data-policy/.

19 Available at: https://data.inra.fr/.

20 Available at: https://data.mendeley.com/.

– Disciplinary repositories: they gather research results related to a particular discipline. Often, they cover a general discipline, with contributors from different institutions. They are likely to be funded by one or more entities within the thematic community.

– Multidisciplinary repositories: these are repositories that cover several research disciplines and meet multidisciplinary needs.

– Project-based repositories: they focus on data resulting from specific research projects.

– Other types of repositories (e.g. a specific repository for a research funder).

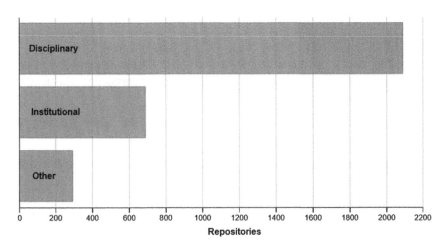

Figure 1.2. *Typology of data repositories listed in (source: re3data.org, survey of May 4, 2021, licensed under a Creative Commons Attribution 4.0 International License)*

At present, the majority of repositories listed in *re3data* are disciplinary repositories (Figure 1.2)[21]. As of May 4, 2021, there were 2,089 out of a total of 2,677 (78%), although each repository can fall into several categories. This is one of the complexities of the data repository landscape. The scope of a repository can be measured at different levels: that of the institution(s) that provide(s) its governance; that of the institution(s) that fund(s) it; or that of the discipline(s) it covers. One example is the *Gene*[22] repository, which specializes in genomic data. This repository

---

21 Source: https://www.re3data.org/metrics/types.
22 Available at: https://www.ncbi.nlm.nih.gov/gene?db=gene.

is maintained by the National Center for Biotechnology Information (NCBI) and is funded by the US federal government.

1.4.3. *More or less standardized functionalities*

Data repositories are also characterized by a set of basic functionalities, which revolve around the four verbs mentioned above: describing, archiving, identifying and making available. Here, we borrow up the analytical framework of Assante *et al.* (2016), who study repositories from the following eight axes: formatting; documenting; licensing; publication costs; validation; availability; discoverability and access and citation.

1.4.3.1. *Data formatting*

Formatting data is, in the words of Assante *et al.* (2016), organizing a dataset according to a certain format with the aim of ensuring its reusability. This involves two types of formatting:

– the formatting of the content, which guides the understanding and interpretation of the data (see section 1.4.5);

– the formatting of the container, which conditions the reading of the data with a software.

Formatting the data container is like choosing a file format. A repository can choose to accept all file formats or choose to accept only a few. For example, the *4TU.ResearchData* repository's *Preferred formats* guide provides a list of file formats considered optimal for the long-term preservation of data (Table 1.1)[23].

Some repositories, especially disciplinary ones, host file formats specific to the discipline they cover. Marcial and Hemminger cited the following examples in 2010: FITS for astronomical data; GO/FASTA/Contig annotations for bioinformatics data; statistical formats (SAS, SPSS, R, Stata) for social science data; and GIS formats for earth science data and some biological science data. Other repositories, such as generic repositories, instead give precedence to non-proprietary formats (such as html tables or comma-delimited csv files).

---

23 Source: https://data.4tu.nl/info//fileadmin/user_upload/Documenten/preffered_file_formats.pdf.

Text file	Plain text, XML, HTML, PDF (PDF/A-1), JSON, PDB (Protein Data Bank), XYZ *(All formats must be encoded in UTF-8)*
Spreadsheet	CSV (Comma-separated values), Tab-delimited values
Image	JPEG, TIFF, PNG, SVG
Geospatial file	GML (Geographical Mark-up Language), KML (Keyhole Mark-up Language), ESRI Shapefile, GeoTIFF
Digital file	NetCDF, CSV, JSON
Video file	*No sustainable format established*
Audio file	WAVE (Waveform Audio File Format)
Database	Delimited Flat File w/DDL
Archives	ZIP, TAR, GZIP, 7Z

Table 1.1. *Sustainable file formats recommended
by the 4TU.ResearchData repository*

1.4.3.2. *Documentation*

One of the added values of data repositories is the documentation of data, that is, the addition of information to facilitate its discovery, understanding and reuse, both by humans and by machines. This information is also called metadata. It describes both the data and the context in which it was produced, that is, when, where, how and by whom it was collected.

For repositories, the issue lies in the metadata model to be used. To be as close as possible to the data, a customized model may be a wise choice. Conversely, for interoperability with other information systems, the use of a metadata standard such as Dublin Core or DataCite may be more legitimate.

In a 2015 study of 32 Canadian and international repositories, Austin *et al.* (2015) found that 69% of the platforms surveyed (22 out of 32) used an internally designed metadata schema to describe hosted data, while 38% (12 out of 32) used a standard metadata schema or at least mapped their metadata schema to a standard schema.

Many standards coexist. The Research Data Alliance has attempted to bring them together in a directory, the *Metadata Directory*[24], to make them more visible and easier to use (Ball *et al.* 2014).

---

24 Available at: https://rd-alliance.github.io/metadata-directory/.

The choice of metadata model depends in part on how the data will be used by its secondary users. The way in which the data is described sets the boundaries for how it can be used. However, it is questionable to what extent it is really possible to anticipate all reuses of a dataset.

Two methods are being tested to try to improve a potential reuser's understanding of the data:

– the publication of *data papers*, that is, "authored, peer reviewed and citable articles in academic or scholarly journals, whose main content is a description of published research datasets, along with contextual information about the production and the acquisition of the datasets, with the purpose of facilitating the findability, availability and reuse of research data" (Schöpfel *et al.* 2019);

– the addition of links to other online resources in the metadata, such as the *data paper* of the dataset, the associated publication(s) and the bibliography of its author(s), etc.

1.4.3.3. *Terms of use*

From a legal perspective, repositories have a responsibility to inform users of the terms of use that apply to the data so as to enable appropriate and informed reuse.

In the context of open data, the trend is to assign free licenses to datasets such as Creative Commons[25] and Open Data Commons licenses[26]. However, studies by Kindling *et al.* (2017) and Austin *et al.* (2015) show that a majority of repositories also compose licenses tailored to their specificities, not meeting any standard.

Some repositories impose a single license, like *Figshare*, which uses the CC0 license. Other repositories allow depositors to choose between a set of several licenses (this is the case of *Gene, Ortolang*[27], *HEPData*[28], etc.).

The *re3data* directory provides an online overview of the licenses used by the repositories it lists in the form of an updated histogram (Figure 1.3)[29].

---

25 Available at: https://creativecommons.org/.

26 Available at: https://opendatacommons.org/.

27 Available at: https://www.ortolang.fr/.

28 Available at: https://www.hepdata.net/.

29 Source: https://www.re3data.org/metrics/dataLicenses.

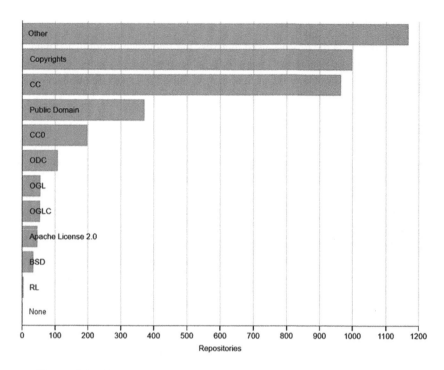

Figure 1.3. *Licenses of use offered by the repositories listed in (source: re3data.org, survey of May 3, 2021, licensed under a Creative Commons Attribution 4.0 International License)*

1.4.3.4. Publication costs

Maintaining a repository has a cost. This includes the preparation of datasets, their storage and their online availability. These investments are sometimes passed on to depositors who are asked to make a financial contribution to publish a dataset. Nevertheless, this business model turns out to be relatively rare, as shown by the study of Kindling *et al.* (2017), based on the *re3data* directory: out of a total of 1,381 data repositories, only 0.7% require the payment of submission fees.

This finding probably stems from the openness of scientific results. To achieve an increase in the amount of published data, open science policies need to rely on easily accessible infrastructures with low or no publication costs, so as not to discourage researchers from publishing their data (Roche *et al.* 2013). Another reason for the absence of publication costs for many data repositories is that they are attached to a public research organization, especially those located in Europe. Their business model is often based on public grants.

1.4.3.5. *Validation*

Data validation is the process used to assess the relevance of published data. It is a process that is still far from being fully characterized. To date, there are no common criteria on how to conduct this review, unlike in scientific publications, for example, with peer reviewing.

The underlying question is that of data quality: what determines the quality of data? Should it be evaluated on a scientific and/or technical level? Since data deposited in repositories can potentially be reused for various purposes, it is still difficult to define scientific conformity criteria. The validation of data by repositories is therefore currently limited to checking the consistency of metadata and file content. This is what the *Dryad* repository does, for example. Its data curation staff performs a series of checks, which are technical (they check that the files can be opened, that they are not corrupted and do not contain viruses, etc.) and administrative (in particular, they ensure that the metadata is technically correct). However, they do not check the data from a scientific point of view.

1.4.3.6. *Availability*

Publishing data means that data repositories must ensure that the data are preserved in the short, medium and long term. The objective is to ensure that the datasets are available to users. To achieve this, two mechanisms are used: a mechanism for immediate availability of the data sets and a mechanism for future availability, which guarantees the availability of the data over time. From a technical point of view, the secure archiving of the data involves storing multiple copies of the data files, either on the repository's own servers (this is the case for *Zenodo*, whose data are stored at CERN) or with third-party service providers (e.g. *Figshare* uses the University of California's Chronopolis service[30]). Making data available over the long term also sometimes requires repositories to migrate file formats as technology evolves.

1.4.3.7. *Discovery and access*

In a repository, data discovery and access is the function that allows users to become aware of the existence of a dataset and to access it. This service includes user-oriented functions such as navigation and the ability to search by keywords or filters. In addition, repositories can provide programmatic access to their content through data and metadata exchange interfaces (APIs). These APIs are either based

---

30 Available at: http://libraries.ucsd.edu/chronopolis/.

on proprietary developments or on standard protocols such as File Transfer Protocol (FTP) or OAI-PMH[31].

1.4.3.8. *Citation*

Finally, one of the key issues in data sharing is citation, which allows for both tracking the reuse of datasets and crediting their producer with some form of recognition. This aspect has been developed in particular by Force11 (Data Citation Synthesis Group 2014) and the Research Data Alliance (Rauber *et al.* 2015).

For repositories, the citation functionality consists of adding a reference to a dataset in order to allow the attribution, discovery and interconnection of these data, as well as access to them. This translates into the attribution of an identifier, whether it is a code specific to the repositories or a persistent identifier such as URN, DOI, Handle, etc.

In most repositories, the citation itself is in the form of a bibliographic reference (including the name of the author(s), the year of publication, the title of the dataset, its identifier, etc.) to be copied/pasted or exported in generic formats such as RIS, BibTex, DataCite or Dublin Core.

In addition to the eight primary functionalities described above, other value-added services such as data analysis and visualization tools can be added. Repositories are therefore very rich in terms of functionalities, but also complex, as they must deal with the diversity of disciplinary practices and institutional mechanisms.

1.5. The question of trust

The actual use of a new device or technology is affected by several factors, including perceived usefulness, ease of use, quality of services and results, and the brand image of the device[32]. For an information system to be accepted, it must be credible in the eyes of users, with reliable performance in terms of functionality and service delivery. Data quality plays a particular role (Azeroual *et al.* 2020).

---

31 *Open Archives Initiative Protocol for Metadata Harvesting*, see https://www.openarchives. org/pmh/.

32 As an example of a rich literature on the technology acceptance model, Davis (1989), Venkatesh and Davis (2000), and Xu *et al.* (2013) can be cited.

In relation to data repositories, it is important to distinguish between two types of use, even though users will often come from the same communities or organizations: the use of repositories to store, preserve and share research data (repository), and the use of repositories to verify published results, merge datasets, perform new analyses, etc. (reuse). In the first case, the focus will be on the facility, the reliability and security of the system, the promise of service (e.g. long-term preservation), the ease of deposit, the amount of storage used by other researchers, etc. In the second case, credibility is also and above all affected by the content and the resources stored, and it will be a question of quality variables (the quality of the data and the quality and richness of the metadata), the right to reuse (licenses) and interoperability with other operating systems.

This link between users' trust in curation devices and trust in the digital content of these devices has been modeled for digital archives in general (Donaldson 2019); it has been formalized as an ISO standard[33]. Empirical studies, such as those by Yakel *et al.* (2013) or Yoon (2014), have led to a better understanding of some key factors of trust or distrust in data repositories. Among these factors, three seem particularly important:

– transparency of the system;

– the guarantee (promise) of long-term preservation (sustainability);

– the reputation of the institution that manages and/or hosts the device.

In addition to these factors, there are other criteria, such as the perception and experience of the functionalities and services and the quality of the data and the measures implemented to control, guarantee and improve this quality, in terms of data sources and selection upstream and "cleansing" downstream.

The institutional aspect plays a separate role. Part of the trust afforded to a platform of this type is linked to the characteristics of the institution responsible for and in charge of the platform. What is its reputation? Is it a model in this field? What is its field of activity and does it have authority in this field? Who does it work with, what are its own reference points and who trusts it? Studies have also shown how acceptance and use are influenced by colleagues, other researchers, engineers, etc., a finding that highlights the community aspect of these devices.

---

33 Open Archival Information System (OAIS), ISO 14721:2012. *The reference model: The OAIS* on the CINES. Available at: https://www.cines.fr/archivage/un-concept-des-problematiques/le-modele-de-reference-loais/.

In 2019, Science Europe published a "Practical Guide to International Harmonization in Research Data Management". In it, Science Europe presents a list of minimum criteria for how to select a trusted repository. These criteria are organized around four major themes which all trusted depositories should meet:

– assignment of unique and persistent identifiers;

– metadata;

– data access and licensing;

– preservation.

For each theme, Science Europe describes more or less specific recommendations, such as using recognizable, community-based metadata (standards) or ensuring data integrity and authenticity (see Science Europe 2019).

In 2020, a working group proposed a catalog of principles that make research data depositories *trustworthy* and credible (Lin *et al.* 2020). These are the five TRUST principles that can be summarized as follows (Table 1.2).

T	*Transparency*	Conditions of use, shelf life, promise of service, etc.
R	*Responsibility*	Norms, standards, rights, etc.
U	*User focus*	Community practices, search process, data lifecycle, etc.
S	*Sustainability*	Durability, sustainability
T	*Technology*	Hardware, software, services

Table 1.2. *The TRUST Principles (Lin* et al. *2020)*

Transparency: for the authors of this catalog, transparency is a prerequisite for a repository to be considered reliable, credible and trustworthy. Transparency means that the repository must provide transparent, honest and verifiable evidence of practices and procedures to convince users that it is able to ensure the integrity, authenticity, accuracy, reliability and accessibility of data over a long period of time. Transparency also means providing accurate information about the scope, target user community, mission and policy and technical capabilities of the repository. This includes the terms of use, both for the repository and for the datasets, the minimum retention period, and other complementary services, such as the ability to responsibly manage sensitive data.

Responsibility: trusted repositories take responsibility for the management of their data holdings and service to the user community. Accountability is demonstrated through adherence to designated community standards for metadata and preservation, as well as the management of stored datasets, such as technical validation, documentation, quality control, authenticity protection and long-term preservation. Accountability also includes the ability to manage the intellectual property rights of data producers, the protection of sensitive information resources and the security of the system and its contents. Accountability may be clarified through legal means (retention rights) or may take the form of voluntary compliance with a standard (ethical standards).

User focus: according to the authors of the TRUST catalog, a data repository must provide services that are consistent with the practices and needs of the target user community, which may vary from community to community, depending, in part, on the "maturity" of the community in managing and sharing data. A *trustworthy* repository is embedded in the data management practices of the target user community and can therefore meet the evolving needs of the community. Respecting this principle means knowing and respecting the norms and standards of the target user community, because conformity facilitates interoperability and data reuse. We will come back to this later.

Sustainability: the authors emphasize the need for sustainability to ensure uninterrupted access to data. In practical terms, this means two things in particular:

– knowing how to manage risks: based on a risk analysis, implementing actions and procedures to mitigate risks and ensure business continuity, disaster recovery and succession;

– establishing a sustainable business model: finding a way of financing the system to guarantee its functioning and quality in the long term.

In addition, there is the interest in creating a form of governance that can guarantee the long-term preservation of the data deposited.

Technology: the repository must have reliable and efficient technology, that is, appropriate software, hardware and technical services that are up to the challenge. The technological dimension includes compliance with standards and the implementation of measures to ensure the physical and IT security of the device and the data.

1.6. Certification

Lin *et al.* (2020) argue that the appropriate resources and actions required to meet each of the five TRUST principles must be put in place, and that this is the prerequisite for a research data repository that can be trusted and accepted by researchers and their institutions. However, they emphasize that this cannot (and should not) be a one-time effort, but must be sustained over time. It is a constant and continuous endeavor. Regular audits or even certification are one way to support this effort.

Certification is not a new approach in the environment of IT devices, especially digital archives and data repositories. Wikipedia describes certification as a process of conformity assessment (with a specification) that results in written assurance that an organization meets certain requirements. Often the verification is done by an independent certifying body (or expert), but it is possible for certification to be done on the basis of a self-declaration by the organization itself. With respect to data repositories, certification means conducting an independent (external) audit of a data repository against a catalog of performance criteria established by experts and recognized by the responsible structures, supervisory and funding agencies, and the scientific communities. The key word is "trust". To develop data infrastructures and to encourage researchers to store and publish their data via data repositories, it is necessary to reassure them about the quality, integrity, traceability, etc. of the data and their description, but, above all, about the sustainability, coherence, accessibility and interoperability of the repositories.

There are several certificates for research data repositories, including the *World Data System* (WDS) certificate, supported by the International Council for Science (ICSU), and the *Data Seal of Approval* (DSA), developed by the Dutch organization DANS from 2008. In 2018, both procedures converged to the *CoreTrustSeal* (CTS)[34], which is now the most recognized international certificate and the one advocated by the French Ministry, the CNRS and the Research Data Alliance (RDA).

The CTS certificate contains sixteen themes with specific requirements (CTS 2019, Table 1.3). Each theme is mandatory and must be assessed individually and separately from a guidance text describing the information and evidence to be provided.

---

34 CoreTrustSeal; available at: https://www.coretrustseal.org/.

1	*Mission/scope*	The repository has an explicit mission to disseminate and preserve data.	T, R
2	*Licenses*	The repository distributes the data with appropriate licenses.	T
3	*Continuity of access*	The repository is able to ensure continuous accessibility and permanent preservation of data.	S
4	*Confidentiality/ethics*	The repository ensures, as far as possible, that data are produced and managed in accordance with disciplinary and ethical standards.	R, U
5	*Organizational infrastructure*	The repository has sufficient human and financial resources, with transparent governance, to carry out its mission effectively.	T, S
6	*Expert guidance*	The repository has established a scientific council or other form of guidance and expert advice.	R, U
7	*Data integrity and authenticity*	The repository guarantees the integrity and authenticity of the data.	R
8	*Appraisal*	The repository implements an explicit policy for the evaluation and selection of data to be integrated and their metadata.	T, R
9	*Documented storage procedures*	The repository has documented procedures for data storage and long-term retention.	T, S
10	*Preservation plan*	The repository assumes responsibility for the long-term preservation of the data and has the technical capacity to do so.	R, S
11	*Data quality*	The repository has a quality policy for data and metadata (control, cleansing, etc.).	R
12	*Workflows*	The repository implements transparent, documented and efficient production flows (ingestion, management, dissemination, conservation, etc.) (OAIS standard).	T, Tech
13	*Data discovery and identification*	The repository provides rich, standardized metadata (including persistent identifiers) that are essential for referencing, identifying and discovering data.	R
14	*Data reuse*	The repository takes steps to facilitate longer term reuse (formats, metadata).	S
15	*Technical infrastructure*	The repository operates on a reliable and stable core infrastructure, appropriate to the practices and expectations of the target community.	R, S, Tech
16	*Security*	The technical infrastructure of the repository ensures the protection of the structure and its data, products, services and users.	S, Tech

Table 1.3. *The 16 CoreTrustSeal themes (CTS 2019)*

Themes 1–6 are in the area of organizational infrastructure, themes 7–14 are in the area of digital object management and themes 15–16 are in the area of repository technology. The themes partially overlap. In the last column of the table, we have tried to link to the five TRUST principles. The above table also shows that a theme or criterion of the CTS can contribute to the realization of several TRUST principles, and that a TRUST principle, be it transparency (T), sustainability (S) or technology (Tech), always depends on the implementation of a number of criteria or requirements.

The certification process involves two steps. First, the repository conducts a self-assessment, indicating for each topic the level of compliance on a five-point scale (not taken into account, in the implementation phase, etc.) and providing evidence and documentation. In the second step, the results of the self-assessment are re-examined by independent experts, and their analysis may lead to recommendations or certification of the system.

Such a procedure requires a considerable effort in terms of self-assessment, but also, subsequently, of long-term action, monitoring, maintenance and constant improvement. Nevertheless, at the time of writing, 90 data repositories have gone through the process and obtained the CTS certificate, including 59 sites in Europe[35].

1.7. The FAIR principles

Making repositories *trustworthy* is a process that is primarily aimed at human users. But it's not just about human use. As digital devices, data repositories communicate with other machines, both upstream, for the ingestion of data produced by research equipment and infrastructures, and downstream, with search engines, analysis and exploitation tools, aggregation platforms and other repositories, among other things. We must remember that data repositories have sometimes been criticized, especially in the United States, for being decentralized, unconnected and isolated "silos" linked to a particular institution, equipment or community, but without interconnection with other devices (Borgman 2018).

In addition, to develop the interoperability of research data devices, an international committee has drafted another catalog of principles, formalized as the FAIR Guiding Principles (Wilkinson *et al.* 2016)[36]. The aim is to improve the

---

35 List of CTS certified repositories; available at: https://www.coretrustseal.org/why-certification/certified-repositories/.
36 See also the European initiative GO FAIR; available at: https://www.go-fair.org/go-fair-initiative/.

infrastructures that support the reuse of research data, with a focus on improving the ability of machines to automatically find and use data, as a complement to reuse by researchers. Specifically, there are four principles that encompass 10 technical criteria (Table 1.4).

Findability	F1	The (meta)data are given a unique and globally persistent identifier.
	F2	The data are described with rich metadata.
	F3	Metadata clearly and explicitly include the identifier of the data they describe.
	F4	The (meta)data are stored or indexed in a searchable resource.
Accessibility	A1	The (meta)data can be retrieved by their identifier using a standardized communication protocol.
	A2	The metadata are accessible even when the data are no longer available.
Interoperability	I1	(Meta)data use a formal, accessible, shared and widely applicable language for knowledge representation.
	I2	The (meta)data use vocabulary that adheres to the FAIR principles.
	I3	(Meta)data contain qualified references to other (meta)data.
Reusability	R1	The (meta)data are richly described with a plurality of precise and relevant attributes.

Table 1.4. *The FAIR principles*

The application of these technical criteria must make research data easy to find (findable), accessible, interoperable and reusable. The FAIRization of data repositories places metadata at the heart of the system, insofar as its standardization, richness, quality, accuracy, relevance and durability, as well as its representativeness and acceptance by the scientific communities, are essential for its *machine readability* and its interconnection with other systems and infrastructures. It is important to keep in mind the vision of this approach, which aims to promote the coherent development of the global Internet of FAIR data and services, particularly in the context of the European Research Area and the European Open Science Cloud (EOSC) infrastructures[37].

This standardization action has an impact on data repositories and their development. It provides a set of expected functionalities for repositories that wish

---

37 See GO FAIR; available at: https://www.go-fair.org/go-fair-initiative/vision-and-strategy/.

to be part of the open science movement. The development of data repositories is therefore now guided by the quest to comply with the FAIR principles. A report by the Research Data Alliance (RDA), for example, sets out a list of best practices for improving the findability of data in repositories (Wu and Khalsa 2017). However, the FAIR principles do not currently aim to:

– ensure (guarantee) the quality of research data;

– contribute to the legal interoperability of devices and their use;

– develop a sustainable business model.

1.8. Lifecycle and facility

The definition of data repositories as a particular category of data services, based on some fundamental characteristics and common functionalities, allows us to distinguish and describe a new family of systems. Nevertheless, this approach limits the analysis to the technical dimension and excludes the other dimensions of the concept of the device, its nature of "framework in which techniques and humans are arranged to enable repetitive and distributed activities", and the "collective" dimension, with skills, know-how and practices (Larroche 2019).

In talking about the role of trust and the TRUST principles, we mentioned the importance of "user focus", that is, the crucial interest of placing the practices and needs of users at the center of the development and operation of data repositories. Eun-joo Carré-Na from EHESS specifies this aspect of data in HSS: "The object of management by the research data repository is data as objects produced by and for a scientific project, i.e., elaborated or derived data ready for storage" (2018, p. 9). In this way, she emphasizes the link to the research process and the data lifecycle:

> In its raw state, stored in a private space (the data) is not the object of repository management. The change of state between "raw" and "processed" does not necessarily mean the modification of the content, let alone the modification of its factual nature, but simply a change of status, depending on the attachment to a scientific objective, with or without transformation of the form of the content.

This link involves two aspects: On the one hand, repositories play a particular role in what is usually called the "research data lifecycle" and which is, in fact, a dynamic, variable and not necessarily linear or circular process in a scientific ecosystem (see Figure 1.4).

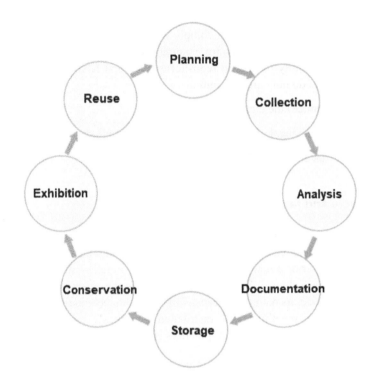

Figure 1.4. *Research data lifecycle (source: Cat-OPIDoR, CC0)*

When analyzing the position of repositories in this process, a characteristic profile emerges, different from other data services. Repositories essentially cover the last three stages of the lifecycle (preservation, exposure, reuse), with half of them having storage and documentation functionalities (Figure 1.4).

Compared to other types of services, such as management tools or acquisition, calculation or access platforms, repositories generally do not offer collection or analysis functionalities. Another peculiarity is their "two-sided" nature: the conservation of data deposited by researchers, and the exposure, oriented toward the reuse of these same data by other researchers (or machines). This two-sided nature (which also means two types of users and uses) distinguishes repositories from other platforms that are more oriented toward analysis and temporary storage or toward collection, exposure and reuse, both of which often have no guarantee of longer term preservation.

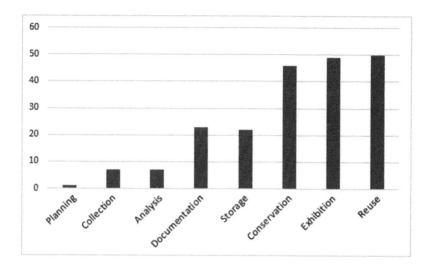

Figure 1.5. *Data repositories and their lifecycle*
(source: Cat-OPIDoR, N = 53, September 2019)

However, this close link with the research process, this *"user focus"*, has another implication. Contrary to what the figure of the data lifecycle may suggest, there is no standard process. What a scientific community does with its data depends on its equipment, methodologies, themes, infrastructures, resources, constraints, ethical values, etc. It is in this sense that a 2019 ITHAKA S+R study described a data community as a "fluid and informal network of researchers who share and use a certain type of data"[38] that is not necessarily disciplinary, with three characteristics: bottom-up development, lack of technical barriers and community standards regarding the conditions of data sharing.

These data communities can be linked to a piece of equipment (observatory, particle accelerator, MRI, etc.), to a methodology (surveys, archaeological excavations, cohort studies, etc.), to a domain (oceanography, health, psychology, etc.) or to a type of data (images, sound recordings, etc.). A study on data repositories in information and communication sciences attempted to identify these links between community and devices (Prost and Schöpfel 2019). This study also showed how the landscape of repositories can reflect certain disciplinary characteristics.

---

38 Available at: https://sr.ithaka.org/publications/data-communities/.

In the words of Lin *et al.* (2020), the use and reuse of research data is an integral part of the scientific process, and thus trusted repositories should enable their communities to find, explore and understand stored data with respect to its potential (re)use. To this end, users depositing data should be encouraged to describe the data in a comprehensive and rich manner at the time of deposit, and attention will need to be paid to any issues that may arise during exposure and reuse. Lin *et al.* (2020) refer to metadata schema, data file formats, controlled vocabularies, ontologies and other semantics where they exist in the user community, as well as usage indicators and community catalogues to facilitate data discovery, and call for repositories to be attentive and responsive to evolving community practices and expectations

This makes it easier to understand the interest and the limits of standardization, FAIRization and interoperability initiatives: to serve upstream communities, for preservation and, to a lesser degree, for storage and documentation, a specific approach is needed, closely linked to the particularities of the communities; at most, a "silo" would be sufficient. However, to expose these data to a wider audience and to facilitate their reuse by other researchers, by industry and/or by machines, more standardization and interoperability are needed, which will always be at the expense of community specificities.

1.9. References

André, F. (2015). Déluge des données de la recherche ? In *Big Data : nouvelles partitions de l'information. Actes du Séminaire IST Inria, octobre 2014*, Calderan, L., Laurent, P., Lowinger, H., Millet, J. (eds). Louvain-la- Neuve, De Boeck.

Assante, M., Candela, L., Castelli, D., Tani, A. (2016). Are scientific data repositories coping with research data publishing? *Data Science Journal*, 15, 6.

Austin, C.C., Brown, S., Fong, N., Humphrey, C., Leahey, A., Webster, P. (2015). Research data repositories: Review of current features, gap analysis, and recommendations for minimum requirements. *IASSIST Quarterly*, 39(4), 24–28.

Austin, C.C., Bloom, T., Dallmeier-Tiessen, S., Khodiyar, V.K., Murphy, F., Nurnberger, A., Raymond, L., Stockhause, M., Tedds, J., Vardigan, M., Whyte, A. (2017). Key components of data publishing: Using current best practices to develop a reference model for data publishing. *International Journal on Digital Libraries*, 18(2), 77–92.

Azeroual, O., Saake, G., Abuosba, M., Schöpfel, J. (2020). Data quality as a critical success factor for user acceptance of research information systems. *Data*, 5(2), 35.

Ball, A., Chen, S., Greenberg, J., Perez, C., Jeffery, K., Koskela, R. (2014). Building a disciplinary metadata standards directory. *International Journal of Digital Curation*, 9(1), 142–151.

Borgman, C.L. (2015). *Big Data, Little Data, No Data: Scholarship in the Networked World.* MIT Press, Cambridge.

Borgman, C.L. (2018). Research data alliance in the data sharing landscape. *JNSO 2018. Premières Journées Nationales de la Science Ouverte "De la stratégie à l'action"*, December 4–6, Paris, France [Online]. Available at: https://webcast.in2p3.fr/video/research-data-alliance-in-the-science-data-sharing-landscape.

Borgman, C.L., Sands, A.E., Darch, P.T., Golshan, M.S. (2016). The durability and fragility of knowledge infrastructures: Lessons learned from astronomy. *Proceedings of the Association for Information Science and Technology*, 53(1), 1–10.

Bruno, I., Gražulis, S., Helliwell, J.R., Kabekkodu, S.N., McMahon, B., Westbrook, J. (2017). Crystallography and databases. *Data Science Journal*, 16 [Online]. Available at: https://doi.org/10.5334/dsj-2017-038.

Carré-Na, E.-J. (2018). Entrepôt de données de la recherche en SHS : un modèle de description pour l'autogestion. *Overseas Korean Studies Librarian Workshop*, Bibliothèque Nationale de Corée, Seoul, South Korea [Online]. Available at: https://hal.archives-ouvertes.fr/halshs-01884386.

Cocaud, S. and Aventurier, P. (2017). Participer à l'organisation du management des données de la recherche, gestion de contenu et documentation des données. *Action Nationale de Formation Organisée Par Les Réseaux Renatis et Médici*, Centre National de La Recherche Scientifique (CNRS). FRA, Vandoeuvre-Les-Nancy, France.

CTS (2019). CoreTrustSeal Trustworthy Data Repositories Requirements 2020–2022 (Version v02.00-2020-2022). CoreTrustSeal Standards and Certification Board [Online]. Available at: https://doi.org/10.5281/zenodo.3638211.

Data Citation Synthesis Group (2014). *Joint Declaration of Data Citation Principles.* FORCE11, San Diego.

Davis, F.D. (1989). Perceived usefulness, perceived ease of use, and user acceptance of information technology. *MIS Quarterly*, 13(3), 319.

DIST-CNRS (2017). Le travail de la science et le numérique – Données, publications, plateformes. Une analyse systémique de la loi pour une République numérique [Online]. Available at: http://www.science-ouverte.cnrs.fr/wp-content/uploads/2019/07/Analyse-syst%C3%A9mique-fevrier-2017.pdf.

Donaldson, D.R. (2019). Trust in archives – Trust in digital archival content framework. *Archivaria*, 88(Fall), 50–83.

Higgins, S. (2012). The lifecycle of data management. In *Managing Research Data*, Pryor, G. (ed.). Facet, London [Online]. Available at: https://doi.org/10.29085/9781856048910.003.

Hubbard, B. (2016). In the context of Open Access policies in the UK, what is a "repository"? *JISC Scholarly Communications* [Online]. Available at: https://scholarlycommunications.jiscinvolve.org/wp/2016/10/14/in-the-context-of-open-access-policies-in-the-uk-what-is-a-repository/.

International Human Genome Sequencing Consortium (2001). Initial sequencing and analysis of the human genome. *Nature*, 409(6822), 860–921.

Kindling, M., Pampel, H., van de Sandt, S., Rücknagel, J., Vierkant, P., Kloska, G., Witt, M., Schirmbacher, P., Bertelmann, R., Scholze, F. (2017). The landscape of research data repositories in 2015: A re3data analysis. *D-Lib Magazine*, 23(3–4) [Online]. Available at: http://www.dlib.org/dlib/march17/kindling/03kindling.html.

Kenney, M. and Zysman, J. (2016). The rise of the platform economy. *Issues in Science and Technology*, Spring, 61–69.

Larroche, V. (2019). *The Dispositif: A Concept for Information and Communication Sciences.* ISTE Ltd, London, and John Wiley & Sons, New York.

Leonelli, S. (2015). What counts as scientific data? A relational framework. *Philosophy of Science*, 82(5), 810–821.

Lin, D., Crabtree, J., Dillo, I., Downs, R.R., Edmunds, R., Giaretta, D., De Giusti, M., L'Hours, H., Hugo, W., Jenkyns, R. *et al.* (2020). The TRUST principles for digital repositories. *Scientific Data*, 7(1), 144.

Marcial, L.H. and Hemminger, B.M. (2010). Scientific data repositories on the Web: An initial survey. *Journal of the American Society for Information Science and Technology*, 61(10), 2029–2048.

Pampel, H., Vierkant, P., Scholze, F., Bertelmann, R., Kindling, M., Klump, J., Goebelbecker, H.J., Gundlach, J., Schirmbacher, P., Dierolf, U. (2013). Making research data repositories visible: The re3data.org registry. *PLoS ONE*, 8(11), e78080.

Prost, H. and Schöpfel, J. (2019). Les entrepôts de données en sciences de l'information et de la communication (SIC). Une étude empirique. *Études de Communication*, (52), 71–98.

Rauber, A., Asmi, A., van Uytvanck, D., Proell, S. (2015). Data citation of evolving data: Recommendations of the Working Group on Data Citation (WGDC) [Online]. Available at: https://doi.org/10.15497/RDA00016.

Rebouillat V. (2019). Ouverture des données de la recherche. De la vision politique aux pratiques des chercheurs. Thesis on Information and Communication Sciences, Conservatoire national des arts et métiers [Online]. Available at: https://tel.archives-ouvertes.fr/tel-02447653.

Roche, D.G., Jennions, M.D., Binning, S.A. (2013). Fees could damage public data archives. *Nature*, 502(7470), 171–171.

Rücknagel, J., Vierkant, P., Ulrich, R., Kloska, G., Schnepf, E., Fichtmüller, D., Reuter, E., Semrau, A., Kindling, M., Pampel, H. *et al.* (2015). Metadata schema for the description of research data repositories: Version 3.0 [Online]. Available at: https://doi.org/10.2312/re3.008.

Schöpfel, J., Kergosien, E., Prost, H. (2017). Pour commencer, pourriez-vous définir "données de la recherche" ? Une tentative de réponse. *Atelier VADOR : Valorisation et Analyse Des Données de La Recherche, INFORSID 2017*, 31 May, Toulouse, France [Online]. Available at: http://dblp.uni-trier.de/db/conf/inforsid/vador2017.html.

Schöpfel, J., Farace, D., Prost, H., Zane, A. (2019). Data papers as a new form of knowledge organization in the field of research data. *Knowledge Organization*, 46(8), 622–638.

Science Europe (2019). Practical guide to the international alignment of research data management. Science Europe Working Group on Research Data, Brussels [Online]. Available at: https://www.scienceeurope.org/media/jezkhnoo/se_rdm_practical_guide_final.pdf.

Venkatesh, V. and Davis, F.D. (2000). A theoretical extension of the technology acceptance model: Four longitudinal field studies. *Management Science*, 46(2), 186–204.

Wilkinson, M.D., Dumontier, M., Aalbersberg, I.J., Appleton, G., Axton, M., Baak, A., Blomberg, N., Boiten, J.W., Bonino da Silva Santos, L., Bourne, P.E. *et al.* (2016). The FAIR guiding principles for scientific data management and stewardship. *Scientific Data*, 3(1), 160018.

Wu, M. and Khalsa, S.J. (2017). Best Practice for Data Discovery: Data Repositories and Portals. RDA Interest Group "Data Discovery Paradigms", Etterbeek [Online]. Available at: https://www.rd-alliance.org/group/data-discovery-paradigms-ig/wiki/best-practices-making-data-findable-task-force-wiki.

Xu, J., Benbasat, I., Cenfetelli, R.T. (2013). Integrating service quality with system and information quality: An empirical test in the E-service context. *MIS Quarterly*, 37(3), 777–794.

Yakel, E., Faniel, I.M., Kriesberg, A., Yoon, A. (2013). Trust in digital repositories. *International Journal of Digital Curation*, 8(1), 143–156.

Yoon, A. (2014). End users' trust in data repositories: Definition and influences on trust development. *Archival Science*, 14(1), 17–34.

2

The Landscape of Research Data Repositories in France

Joachim SCHÖPFEL

University of Lille, Villeneuve d'Ascq, France

2.1. Introduction

How many research data repositories are there in France? In this chapter, we attempt to provide an answer to this question, with an analysis of the typology of repositories, their scientific domains and their quality. Yet what does "in France" mean in such a highly internationalized landscape?

2.2. Context

In 2015, most data repositories were located in four countries, namely the United States, Germany, the UK and Canada, which then accounted for 70% of the institutions in the international *re3data* directory (Kindling *et al.* 2017). Five years later, in June 2020, the situation had not changed; on the contrary, this concentration increased, with these four countries now representing 80% of the 2,516 repositories listed. France followed in the fifth position, but lagged quite far behind with only 107 sites, which corresponds to less than 5% on the international level (see Figure 2.1)[1].

---

1 Source: https://www.re3data.org/metrics/institutionCountry.

Research Data Sharing and Valorization,
coordinated by Joachim SCHÖPFEL and Violaine REBOUILLAT. © ISTE Ltd 2022.

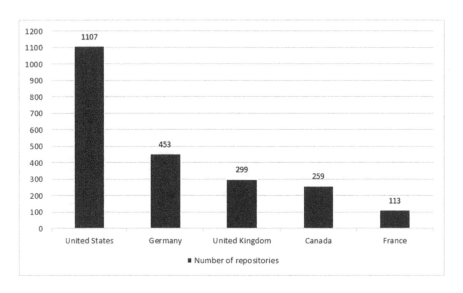

Figure 2.1. *Most represented countries among institutions responsible for data repositories (source: re3data, survey of May 4, 2021)*

Rebouillat (2017) has described the French landscape of research data services as emerging, heterogeneous. They are also facing two major challenges: sustainability (economic model), especially for long-term preservation and accessibility, and usage by scientific communities. In her March 2017 inventory, Rebouillat counted 60 data services, including 13 repositories.

How many research data repositories were actually in France in 2020? It is a simple question, but the answer is not so straightforward, for three reasons.

The first reason is that there is no up-to-date, reliable, comprehensive directory, list or database. There are certainly some useful sites, such as *Cat-OPIDoR*[2], hosted by INIST-CNRS, and *re3data*[3] by DataCite, hosted by the Karlsruhe Institute of Technology. But these directories have neither the same content nor the same objective, and they are of uneven quality and not always coherent, since they mainly rely on statements and information provided by the sites themselves.

The second reason is that the repositories do not share the same design. *re3data* defines a data repository as a subtype of information infrastructure that ensures the

2 Available at: https://cat.opidor.fr/.
3 Available at: https://www.re3data.org/.

long-term (sustainable) preservation and accessibility of the research data that forms the basis of a scientific publication. *Cat-OPIDoR*, on the other hand, simply states that a data repository is a platform where researchers can deposit and share the data they have produced in the course of their research.

The third concern is related to the scope. What does "repository in France" mean? A device hosted on a server located in France? A device under the legal responsibility of a French operator, public or private? A multinational or international system in which one or more French operators participate(s)? Or a service available to the French research community?

These three problems limit the reliability and relevance of any attempt at indexing. Therefore, instead of conducting a new field survey, we assessed the situation based on the contents of the *re3data* and *Cat-OPIDoR* directories (as of June 4, 2020), comparing, correcting if necessary[4], and enriching the information on repositories, especially with respect to the disciplines covered and the type and status of repositories.

2.3. Number

From the information in both the *Cat-OPIDoR* and *re3data* directories in June 2020, we were able to identify 135 research data repositories in France. Thirty-one sites are indexed by both directories, 28 are indexed solely by *Cat-OPIDoR* and 76 repositories (56%) are indexed solely by *re3data* (see Figure 2.2).

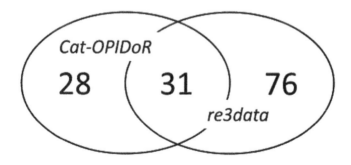

Figure 2.2. *Data repositories in both directories (N = 135, June 2020)*

---

4 One example is that *re3data* indexes EDF and Lufthansa as non-profit organizations.

At the time of our study – early June 2020 – the CNRS *Cat-OPIDoR* catalog contained 59 data repositories, of which 47 repositories (80%) are coordinated and hosted by one or more French organizations, without international cooperation.

The international *re3data* directory contained 107 repositories for France, in the sense of French involvement, including 63 sites with an international consortium (59%) and 44 sites without foreign partners (41%).

So, what does "French repository" mean? Comparing the two directories, we have two main categories as follows:

– on the one hand, 71 repositories with one or more French organizations (52%), coordinated, hosted and funded by 100% French universities, laboratories, agencies, companies, etc.;

– on the other hand, 64 repositories with one or more French organizations, but also with one or more foreign or international partners (48%). Half of these international consortia seem to be coordinated by a French organization; for the other half, French organizations are members of a consortium in the same capacity as other partners, without a leadership role (see Figure 2.3).

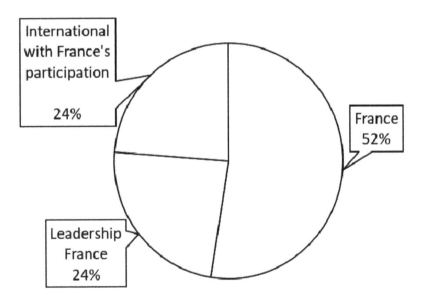

Figure 2.3. *International character of French repositories (N = 135)*

Some examples are as follows:

– *ESTHER database*, an experimental database in the field of enzymes (ESTerases, alpha/beta-hydrolase enzymes and relatives) is a 100% French repository, with a consortium of two joint research units, INRA and CNRS, with two funding sources, ANR and AFM-Téléthon. There is no foreign partner;

– the *Ortolang* (Tools and Resources for Optimized Language Processing) repository, a facility of excellence, is coordinated and hosted by ATILF, a joint research unit of the University of Lorraine and the CNRS, which is open to the international community via the European CLARIN-ERIC infrastructure. Here, there is clear French scientific and technical leadership;

– a third case is *TropFlux*, an oceanographic repository that provides data on the surface heat and kinetic energy flux of the tropical oceans. This is a Franco-Indian partnership, with the Institut Pierre Simon Laplace of Sorbonne University on the French side, supported by the IRD, but coordinated and hosted by an Indian organization, Earth System Science Organization-Indian National Centre for Ocean Information Services (ESSO-INCOIS). It is indeed a research data repository with French participation, but the leadership is abroad.

The OECD and CERN repositories represent two special, borderline cases. The *re3data* directory considers the three facilities of the Organisation for Economic Co-operation and Development (OECD), *OECD iLibrary Statistics*, *NEA Data Bank Computer Program Services* and *Thermochemical Database*, as French research data repositories because they are located in France or rather, under the responsibility of an international organization whose headquarters is located in Paris. A second special case is *Zenodo*, the CERN data repository, the only international device listed by *Cat-OPIDoR* among French data services. The OECD and CERN repositories clearly raise the question of the meaning of the term "repository in France" or "French repository". Perhaps, also, this question itself does not make much sense, given the increasing internationalization of scientific communities and infrastructures.

One final remark on this point: language is not a distinguishing criterion (anymore). Of the 107 *re3data* repositories, 39 offer French interfaces (36%) but almost all – 99 – are also or only accessible in English (93%).

2.4. Types of repositories

Several types of repositories can be distinguished, depending on their content, subject matter, governance or institutional affiliation. For example, the

CoreTrustSeal certificate (see below) makes a distinction between thematic, national, institutional, publication, library, museum or archive repositories, or research project repositories, although the distinction is not always easy to make; a repository can be both disciplinary, that is, devoted to a single theme, and institutional, that is, reserved for the results of a single research unit.

Among the French repositories, discipline-based facilities are by far the most numerous, with 105 sites (see Figure 2.4).

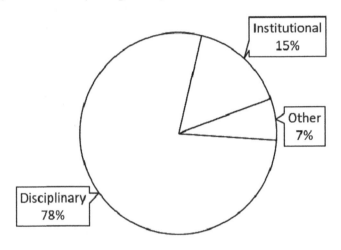

Figure 2.4. *Repository typology (N = 135)*

Three quarters of the repositories (78%) are explicitly related to a scientific field or discipline, or cover a particular theme, which may be multidisciplinary or interdisciplinary. Research data are produced by a facility or infrastructure (observatory, etc.), a consortium or network, or as part of a scientific project or research program. A typical example is *ArkeoGIS* of the University of Strasbourg, a multilingual geographic information system, initially developed to pool the archeological and paleo-environmental data of the Rhine valley. Another example, also from the humanities, is the *CoCoON* platform (*Collections de Corpus Oraux Numériques*), a data service hosted by Huma-Num and piloted by two mixed research units to create, structure, share and archive audio or video recordings, possibly accompanied by textual annotations. A third example is the *International Argo Project* oceanographic data repository, in which Ifremer participates. What these three sites have in common is their focus on a particular field or theme, by pooling the scientific production of several organizations, institutions, etc.

Only 21 data repositories (15%) have an institutional character, that is, they are linked to a particular structure. These include university (Gustave Eiffel, Paris-Saclay) or school (Sciences Po Paris, EHESS) data repositories, research organizations or institutes (INRAE, CIRAD, IRD, INED, etc.), or even EPICs (BRGM) or infrastructures (Strasbourg Astronomical Observatory). For example, *Didómena*, the EHESS research data repository[5], is a platform that allows EHESS research units to organize, share and perpetuate the data used or produced in the course of their work; as of June 2020, the repository contained 1,754 datasets, mainly still images but also some texts, digitized archives and quantitative data. In all cases, the main mission of these institutional repositories is the preservation and dissemination of data produced by the research teams of the institution in question. This does not exclude a thematic character or even partial sharing with other actors.

The third "other" category includes nine repositories that are neither institutional nor thematic, but are defined differently by a category of data or specific scope. For example, there is *MédiHAL* from the CNRS, dedicated to scientific photographs and images, *CENHTOR* from the MSH Lorraine, a platform for researchers whose research project is focused on Lorraine as its field or object of study, or *Software Heritage*, a repository developed by INRIA in partnership with UNESCO to collect, organize, preserve, share and enable the reuse of open-source software.

The relative supremacy of disciplinary repositories is neither a new phenomenon nor a French peculiarity. An analysis of the 1,381 sites listed by *re3data* in 2015 revealed an even higher percentage (86%) of disciplinary devices (Kindling *et al.* 2017). But by 2020, this percentage had slightly decreased and now corresponds to the situation in France with 79%.

Finally, *re3data* distinguishes between two types of devices: the data provider if it offers research data and its metadata (ideally exposing the metadata via interfaces), and/or the service provider (e.g. a portal) if it harvests the metadata of the research data from the data providers in order to create value-added services. Among the French sites studied, the vast majority correspond to the first category, that is, providing data (90) or offering data with some additional services (33). Only 12 sites (9%) position themselves primarily as providers of services to the research community, such as aggregation, indexing, metadata enrichment, etc., and it is questionable whether these services are being provided to the research community. The question is whether these sites are still to be considered as data repositories in the strict sense.

---

5 Available at: https://didomena.ehess.fr/.

2.5. Institutions and partners

Few data repositories are under the control of a single organization or institution. With the exception of five of the 107 sites listed by *re3data*, all of the repositories are multi-institutional, with several partners and shared responsibilities.

Two-thirds of French repositories depend on three, four or five institutions, at least one of which (but often several) is in France. However, there are much larger consortia. For example, the *Kinsources.net* website, a platform for sharing data on family relationships, brings together 11 partner institutions and organizations, including the ANR for funding, the TGIR Huma-Num as technical operator and the Collège de France, Sorbonne University, the Université Paris Ouest Nanterre La Défense, the CNRS, the EHESS and others as scientific partners.

At the other end of the spectrum, the Institut Max Von Laue-Paul Langevin's data repository, the *Institut Laue Langevin (ILL) Data Portal*, has no other partner or operator; however, in this case, it should be remembered that the Institut Laue-Langevin (ILL) is itself a multi-institutional institution, funded and managed by France, Germany and the United Kingdom, in partnership with 10 other European countries.

Sixty-three repositories (47%) depend on an international consortium, with two or more institutions, half of which are in France and half in another country. *EBRAINS*, for example, a brain research data repository, is funded by the European Union and brings together French (CNRS), German, Norwegian and Swiss partners. The multidisciplinary *BAOBAB* (Base Afrique de l'Ouest Beyond AMMA Base) is coordinated by a French institution, the Observatoire Midi-Pyrénées and includes an international research programme, AMMA (Analyses Multidisciplinaires de la Mousson Africaine).

The vast majority of partners are public institutions, laboratories, universities, research bodies, funding agencies, infrastructures, etc. Only nine repositories (7%) have one or more private companies as members of their consortium. These private partners include French and foreign companies such as EDF, Engie (formerly GDF Suez), Danone, BNP Paribas, Unilever, Nestlé and Deutsche Lufthansa. Their role appears to be primarily "sponsorship", sometimes with a funding agency, and their presence does not necessarily imply a commercial business model (see below). The *Gazel* cohort, for example, coordinated by INSERM, receives funding from several health insurance funds and is sponsored and supported by EDF and Engie. But in the French data repository landscape, this remains an exception.

2.6. Domains

Generally speaking, French repositories cover all scientific fields. However, most repositories are dedicated to science and technology (48%) and/or life sciences and health (28%). Only 21% cover the humanities, with the fields of arts, letters and languages, and only 2% concern the disciplines of law, economics and management. Note that 10% of the repositories have a generic, multidisciplinary character (see Figure 2.5).

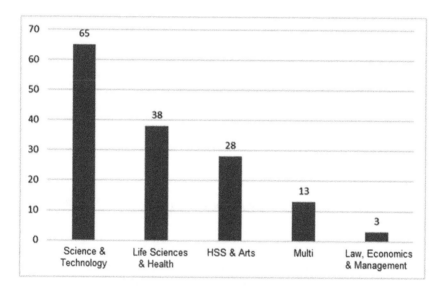

Figure 2.5. *Data repository domains (N = 135)*

The sum is higher than 100% because nine repositories are positioned at the interface between science/technology and life science/health, while the three law, economics and management repositories also contain other humanities data.

A more detailed indexation of disciplines, using the nomenclature of the French National Directory of Research Structures (*répertoire national des structures de recherche* (RNSR)), confirms this unequal distribution between the major fields, but also reveals the disciplinary interconnections (Figure 2.6).

Among the data repositories, earth and space sciences are the most represented disciplines (39%), followed by biology, medicine and health (28%), physics (20%) and humanities (16%). However, 45 repositories cover two or three disciplinary fields. Thus, 29 repositories with data from earth and space sciences contain chemical, physical, biological and/or medical data. In addition to these, there are the 13 generic, multidisciplinary repositories already mentioned.

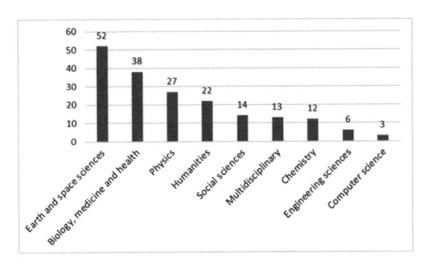

Figure 2.6. *Disciplinary distribution of data repositories (N = 135)*

These 58 repositories with two, three or more disciplines represent 43% of data repositories in France. This percentage is much higher than the findings by Kindling *et al.* (2017), who found that at the international level, 74% of repositories specialized in a single discipline or domain. This multi-disciplinarity and interdisciplinarity, with the relative importance of the earth and universe sciences domain, is perhaps one of the characteristics of the data repository landscape in France.

Does this disciplinary distribution match the needs and practices of scientific communities? Our study on repositories in information and communication sciences (Prost and Schöpfel 2019) suggests that the degree (or lack thereof) of organization and "maturation" of a discipline partly explains the development of data repositories, including at the level of metadata standardization. However, another explanation is undoubtedly the impact of large research infrastructures as massive producers of data, which are very present in the fields of science, technology and medicine (STM), but rather rare in the humanities, where it is more a question of a long tail of research data, or even so-called "orphan" data, not attached to a specific facility or infrastructure.

2.7. FAIR principles

The ambition of the National Plan for Open Science is "to ensure that the data produced by French public research is progressively structured in accordance with the FAIR principles (Findable, Accessible, Interoperable, Reusable; see Chapter 1), preserved and, when possible, opened" (MESRI 2018, p. 6). For the implementation of the FAIR principles (Wilkinson *et al.* 2016) when implementing data repositories, several strong recommendations have been made, including, in particular, the assignment of a unique and persistent identifier, open and long-term accessibility, the dissemination of data under license and the use of standardized and rich metadata[6]. The situation of French repositories is mixed, and the sites are more or less "FAIR" (see Figure 2.7).

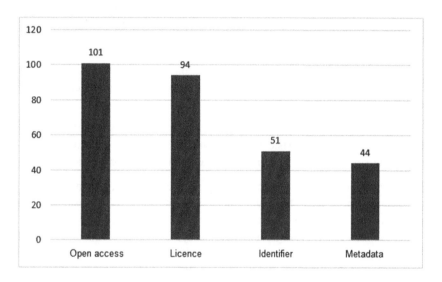

Figure 2.7. *Compliance with FAIR principles (N = 135)*

According to the information in the directories, most of the repositories release their data without restriction and under license. In practical terms, this means that about 75% of the repositories have an open access policy for at least part of the data, although this does not exclude other data being embargoed or restricted to authorized users.

---

6 FAIR Principles, by GO FAIR; available at: https://www.go-fair.org/fair-principles/.

Almost as many repositories offer one or more licenses for data dissemination. These are often specific licenses, such as the VizieR license for the use of the *SIMBAD* database of the *Centre de Données astronomiques de Strasbourg* (CDS)[7]. Forty sites offer one or more Creative Commons licenses, sometimes with other licenses. A small minority of only six repositories show a public domain distribution, such as the database of the *Aerosol Robotic Network* (AERONET) program of NASA's Goddard Space Flight Center, in which CNES, CNRS and the University of Lille participate.

However, in terms of metadata and identifiers, French repositories seem to be less advanced. Again, according to the information from the repositories, only two out of five use a unique and persistent identifier for their data. For the most part, this is a Digital Object Identifier (DOI) recommended and promoted by the DataCite[8] consortium, and less often this is a handle, an Archival Resource Key (ARK) or a Uniform Resource Name (URN).

As for metadata, all repositories describe and index their data in some way, but only one-third explicitly display one or more standards, often generic, sometimes community or disciplinary.

– Generic: this is primarily the Dublin Core format which is not specific to research data, but provides basic standardization. Only eight repositories report using DataCite's recommendations[9] for a standardized description of research data.

– Specific: several repositories apply more specific standards, such as ISO 19115 for geographic data, the Data Documentation Initiative (DDI) standard for humanities surveys, the CF (Climate and Forecast) format for climate and weather research or the ISA-Tab (Investigation-Study-Array) format for biomedical research.

Some examples are included as follows: the BRGM repository has implemented the format recommended by the DataCite consortium; *MédiHAL*, the open archive of scientific photographs and images on the HAL platform, is compatible with the Dublin Core; and CF is used by *HyMeX*, the repository of the Observatoire Midi-Pyrénées, and by Ifremer's *SISMER* portal, which also applies the DataCite format and the ISO 19115 standard. As for the DDI format, it is used by the *BeQuali* (qualitative surveys) and *NESSTAR* (INED surveys) sites, and by the portal for accessing French data in SHS, *Quetelet PROGEDO Diffusion*.

---

7 CDS VizieR license; available at: http://cds.u-strasbg.fr/vizier-org/licences_vizier.html.

8 As a member of the DataCite consortium, INIST-CNRS is the designated DOI agency in France for research data.

9 DataCite Metadata Schema; available at: https://schema.datacite.org/.

Of course, the directories do not tell us whether data indexing is done in a consistent and rich way, nor do they tell us how much data are actually released under license and open access. A detailed field survey would be required to determine the degree and profile of each repository's compliance with the FAIR principles. It is likely that such a survey would reveal a higher rate of "FAIRization" than our analysis from the repositories, particularly with regard to the use of standard identifiers and metadata. Nevertheless, these few elements of analysis suggest that the situation can be described as follows:

– It is a heterogeneous, dynamic situation in transition.

– Progress in dissemination and accessibility is more tangible than in that of the identification and description of data.

There is still some way to go. Moreover, the ANR's 2019 Flash Open Science Call and the first call for projects of the French National Open Science Fund 2020 (*Fonds National pour la Science Ouverte 2020*) have both insisted on the need to develop data services compliant with the FAIR principles, in order to "accelerate the maturation of the various disciplinary communities in the face of the challenges of structuring, accessing, reusing, interoperating, citing, sharing, and opening up research data"[10].

The role of the organizations and institutions responsible for these repositories is certainly a key factor in making this transition. Among the 23 data repositories that meet the four conditions of accessibility, licenses, identifiers and metadata are CDS, CIRAD, INRAE, IFSTTAR, CCSD (with *MédiHAL*) and Huma-Num (for the *Ortolang* consortium), structures and organizations that have been pursuing an explicit and voluntary policy in the field of open science and research data for years.

2.8. Certification

The National Plan for Open Science advocates, among other structuring measures, initiating a "data infrastructure certification process" (MESRI 2018). The CNRS has taken up this idea in its roadmap for open science (CNRS 2019), and the French national Research Data Alliance (RDA) hub has made the certification of data services and data repositories an information and training priority.

---

10 Agence Nationale de la Recherche : Appel Flash science ouverte 2019; available at: https://anr.fr/fr/detail/call/appel-flash-science-ouverte-pratiques-de-recherche-et-donnees-ouvertes/.

The previous chapter presented the certification process and the most important certificates for research data repositories. To date, few French repositories have undergone the certification process. According to the *CoreTrustSeal*[11] website and directories, there are 10 sites, two of which have obtained the CTS certificate (*CDS* and *Ifremer-SISMER*) (see Table 2.1).

Certificate	Repositories (all countries)	French repositories
World Data System WDS	48	3
Data Seal of Approval DSA	20	1
CoreTrustSeal CTS	90	2
Other	Not determined	4

Table 2.1. *Certified repositories (June 2020)*

So, we are at the very beginning in France. RDA France organizes certification seminars, runs a survey to better identify needs and projects and tries to encourage and coordinate the certification process. At least two ANR-funded projects are moving in the same direction: the CEDRE project (toward the certification of French solid earth data repositories) and the COPiLOtE project (Certification des Centres de Données et de Services du Pôle de Données Océan – Odatis), both coordinated by the *Ecole et Observatoire des Sciences de la Terre* (University of Strasbourg and CNRS). The number of certified data repositories is expected to increase in the coming years, contributing to the emergence of a world-class, *trustworthy* ecosystem of data infrastructures.

2.9. Perspectives

Our analysis of research data repositories in France shows a dynamic landscape, which is in rapid transition, but is also complex, heterogeneous and uneven. Internationally, the number of listed repositories has doubled in five years, from 1,318 in 2015 to 2,516 in 2020. In France, according to figures from the *Cat-OPIDoR* website, they quadrupled in number between 2017 and 2020, from 13 to 59. We have come a long way. But it seems clear that there is some catching up to do, both in terms of site reporting and visibility and consolidation of the supply on the ground (Figure 2.8).

---

11 CTS-certified repositories; available at: https://www.coretrustseal.org/why-certification/certified-repositories/.

Figure 2.8. *French keyword cloud of Cat-OPIDoR indexing (59 repositories)*

The 2018 National Plan for Open Science has certainly contributed to the development of repositories at the level of institutions, organizations and other research structures, without being able to speak, to date, of a real model, federation or real mutualization. The current trend seems to be bringing the systems into line with international recommendations and standards, above all the FAIR principles. Thus, more than half of the projects funded under the ANR FLASH 2019 program aim to create FAIR data services or further "FAIRize" existing services.

The analysis of the repositories shows inequalities across fields and disciplines. Some communities are more advanced than others in the management, preservation and publication of their data. A white paper produced by the CNRS on the "Computation-Data" mission suggests that some fields remain, for the moment, less concerned by the opening of data and FAIR principles than others (CNRS 2018). However, notably because of the development of infrastructures and the internationalization of research, this finding of inequality is probably itself an indication of transition rather than an obstacle to be removed.

Certainly, questions remain. One issue is the nature of the data to be preserved and disseminated. The National Plan introduces a distinction between "simple" data in a generic data service for reception and dissemination, and more complex data in more specific repositories, limited to a field of research, equipment or methodology. The analysis of the repositories also shows great diversity; some sites contain a single type of data, simple or complex (texts, images, software, etc.) while others are "multi-data", with a wider diversity. The question of the nature of the data has two dimensions: one, upstream, is the link with equipment, infrastructures, instruments and themes; the other, downstream, is the quality of the description (metadata) and dissemination (licenses); in other words, whether or not it complies with the FAIR principles and, in particular, its potential to be reused. This question remains, along with others.

– The long tail: despite a number of multidisciplinary repositories, no site to date corresponds to a platform such as *Figshare*, *Mendeley Data* or *DRYAD*, that is, to a device that the National Plan describes as a "generic data hosting and dissemination service" for "simple" or even "orphan" data produced by small teams or individual researchers in the context of scientific studies or projects, outside of major facilities and infrastructures. Even if the CERN *Zenodo* platform is referenced by Cat-OPIDoR, it is not a generic data repository under the responsibility of a French organization or consortium. We will come back to this issue in Chapter 7.

– Sustainability: following his 2015 survey, Rebouillat (2017) identified "*sustainability*" as a central issue for repository development. According to his results, more than one-third of the schemes (37%) were not sustainable, in that they lacked financial, technical and/or human resources. Often, these services were under-equipped, had only two or three posts, lacked sustainable funding and were seeking project budgets, for a short duration, incompatible with their long-term mission and contrary to the service promise of preservation beyond 5–10 years. Our analysis did not assess the size and quality of the resources available to the repositories. Two elements, however, suggest that the situation has not fundamentally changed. On the one hand, is the importance of funding agencies and other sponsors in setting up consortia; at least one-third of the repositories, and probably more, seem to have recourse to non-recurring sources of funding (source: *re3data*). On the other hand, is the lack of a sustainable business model for these repositories, which depend, with a few exceptions, essentially or exclusively on public subsidies (human resources, operations, equipment, projects). On the other hand, an in-depth study is needed to assess the interest and sustainability of an alternative, mixed business model with several sources of financing, including the sale of services, as is the case for *Gazel*, *OmicTool*, *Pro-Act* and *CARIBIC*.

– Reliability: we have already mentioned that the reliability of repositories, in the sense of "*trustworthiness*" and in terms of a promise or guarantee of their service level, is a key factor for acceptance by the scientific communities. The certification process is a means to develop and enhance this trustworthiness. The Ministry, the CNRS and the Research Data Alliance (RDA) are rightly promoting the CTS certificate and encouraging repositories to undertake this process. This certification will also reveal the real contribution of each site, in the sense of added value, for the description of the data: if it is a simple distribution of the deposited data, if there is a basic "curation" with a quick check and the addition of some elementary metadata, or if the site proposes an in-depth curation service with data reformatting, enriched documentation, standardized metadata, the attribution of an identifier, quality control for each data deposit, etc. In the future, it will be the richness and quality of the metadata that will distinguish the different sites.

In conclusion, we ask a final question, the same one as Rebouillat (2017): are these services really used by researchers? Do researchers know about these sites? Do they upload their data there? Do they reuse other researchers' data? To date, there is very little evidence to answer this question. Rebouillat's (2019) PhD thesis gives a mixed impression. Further studies will be required to assess the actual utility and function of these devices for researchers, institutions, organizations, information services and innovation within industry research and development departments.

2.10. References

CNRS (2018). Livre blanc sur les données au CNRS. État des lieux et pratiques. Mission "Calcul Données" MICADO. Centre National de la Recherche Scientifique – Comité d'Orientation pour le Calcul INtensif (COCIN), Paris [Online]. Available at: http://www. cocin.cnrs.fr/spip.php?article8.

CNRS (2019). Feuille de route pour la science ouverte. Centre National de la Recherche Scientifique, Paris [Online]. Available at: http://www.cnrs.fr/fr/le-cnrs-se-dote-dune-feuille-de-route-pour-la-science-ouverte.

Kindling, M., Pampel, H., van de Sandt, S., Rücknagel, J., Vierkant, P., Kloska, G., Witt, M., Schirmbacher, P., Bertelmann, R., Scholze, F. (2017). The landscape of research data repositories in 2015: A re3data analysis. *D-Lib Magazine*, 23(3/4) [Online]. Available at: http://www.dlib.org/dlib/march17/kindling/03kindling.html.

MESRI (2018). Plan national pour la science ouverte. Ministère de l'Enseignement Supérieur, de la Recherche et de l'Innovation, Paris [Online]. Available at: http://www.enseignementsup-recherche.gouv.fr/cid132529/le-plan-national-pour-la-science-ouverte-les-resultats-de-la-recherche-scientifique-ouverts-a-tous-sans-entrave-sans-delai-sans-paiement.html.

Prost, H. and Schöpfel, J. (2019). Les entrepôts de données en sciences de l'information et de la communication (SIC). Une étude empirique. *Etudes de Communication*, 52(1), 71–98 [Online]. Available at: https://www.cairn.info/revue-etudes-de-communication-2019-1-page-71.htm.

Rebouillat, V. (2017). Inventory of research data management services in France. In *Expanding Perspectives on Open Science: Communities, Cultures and Diversity in Concepts and Practices*, Chan, L. and Loizides, F. (eds). IOS Press, Amsterdam.

Rebouillat, V. (2019). Ouverture des données de la recherche : de la vision politique aux pratiques des chercheurs. PhD Thesis, Conservatoire National des Arts et Métiers (CNAM), Paris.

Wilkinson, M.D., Dumontier, M., Aalbersberg, I.J., Appleton, G., Axton, M., Baak, A., Blomberg, N., Boiten, J.-W., da Silva Santos, L.B., Bourne, P.E. *et al.* (2016). The FAIR guiding principles for scientific data management and stewardship. *Scientific Data*, 3, 160018.

3

The International Community: The Strasbourg Astronomical Data Centre (CDS)

Françoise GENOVA and Mark G. ALLEN
Strasbourg Astronomical Observatory, CNRS, University of Strasbourg, France

3.1. Introduction

Astronomy has been, and remains, a pioneering discipline for the sharing of scientific data. This chapter discusses the development of the Strasbourg Astronomical Data Centre (*Centre de Données astronomiques de Strasbourg* (CDS)) since its creation in 1972. The CDS is exemplary in several respects, including through its CTS certification, FAIRization of data, proximity to research and international role. It is facing several challenges, such as the rapid evolution of research with new tools, equipment and types of data, the volume of data to be managed and integration within the European infrastructure cloud.

3.2. The Strasbourg Astronomical Data Centre

The Strasbourg Astronomical Data Centre (CDS)[1] provides reference data and services to the international scientific community.

---

1 Available at: http://cds.unistra.fr/.

Research Data Sharing and Valorization,
coordinated by Joachim SCHÖPFEL and Violaine REBOUILLAT. © ISTE Ltd 2022.

It was created in 1972, within the *Observatoire Astronomique de Strasbourg*[2], by the *Institut National d'Astronomie et de Géophysique* (INAG, the French National Institute of Astronomy and Geophysics) and the Université Louis Pasteur, and is still under the responsibility of their successors, the *Institut National des Sciences de l'Univers* (INSU, National Institute for Earth Sciences and Astronomy) of the CNRS[3] and the Université de Strasbourg[4].

The CDS is a team that is part of the *Observatoire Astronomique*, which includes astronomers, documentalists and computer engineers, along with administrative support staff. Its director is appointed by the INSU in agreement with the University of Strasbourg. It is a certified research infrastructure according to the French National Roadmap for Research Infrastructures[5], established in 2008. The bulk of its funding, which amounts to around €3.2 million over the course of a year, includes the salaries of the permanent staff assigned to it by the CNRS and the University of Strasbourg, and also contracts linked to its participation in European projects, among others.

The CDS is one of the major players in international astronomy data sharing and in the development of the disciplinary data sharing framework, known as the astronomical Virtual Observatory (VO). In 2019, CDS services generated on average more than 1,500,000 queries *per day*, nearly 20 queries per second.

3.3. The mission and organization of the CDS

The CDS was one of the first data centers in the world dedicated to the management of digital data. Its creation by INAG in 1972 shows a remarkable anticipation of the importance of data sharing, well before the emergence of the Open Science concept and when the use of computers was just beginning to develop. At that time, French astronomy had only one computer in France, which was located on the Meudon campus of the *Observatoire de Paris*. This is where the CDS services were originally installed.

---

2 Available at: http://astro.unistra.fr/.

3 Available at: https://www.insu.cnrs.fr/.

4 Available at: https://www.unistra.fr/.

5 *La Feuille de Route Nationale des Infrastructures de Recherche* (see: https://www.enseignementsup-recherche.gouv.fr/cid70554/la-feuille-de-route-nationale-des-infrastructures-de-recherche.html) is regularly updated by the Ministry of Higher Education, Research and Innovation. The version published in 2018 includes 99 infrastructures that cover all scientific fields.

The mission of the CDS was described in the following terms at its inception in 1972:

– collect useful data on astronomical objects in electronic form;

– improve them by critically evaluating and combining them;

– distribute the results to the international community;

– conduct research using the data.

The modernity of the CDS charter is also remarkable, and it has served as the foundation of the data center by defining the essential aspects of its role and activities from the outset. Even back in 1972, it emphasized data curation, with the objective of reuse by researchers, rather than simply storage and preservation, which requires an excellent knowledge of the scientific field and has a profound influence on the way data are managed and documented. These principles are now at the heart of the Open Science paradigm, but they were far from being shared by all, or even identified, in 1972. They led to the creation of the CDS within a research structure, the *Observatoire Astronomique de Strasbourg*, to ensure the presence of the necessary scientific expertise and the link with research. They also underpinned the organization of the CDS into an integrated team of researchers, documentalists and computer engineers, who work together on a daily basis by combining their complementary skills, with their different points of view contributing to the definition of the development strategy.

The international role of the CDS was also present from the very beginning for the French authorities who created it; astronomy is a discipline where international collaborations play a major role. From the outset, the CDS has had a scientific council of 12 members, half of whom are foreigners. This council, which evaluates the strategy and activities of the CDS and issues recommendations, is one of the elements of its international base; in particular, it includes representatives of the major agencies in charge of astronomy, the European Southern Observatory (ESO)[6], the *Centre National d'Études Spatiales* (CNES)[7], the European Space Agency (ESA)[8] and NASA[9].

Over time, the CDS has built a network of international collaborations with all of the major players in the production and sharing of astronomical data, the observatories that operate the large telescopes on the ground and in space, and the academic journals of the discipline. It participates very actively in defining and maintaining the International Virtual Observatory Alliance (IVOA) standards.

---

6 Available at: https://www.eso.org/.

7 Available at: https://cnes.fr/.

8 Available at: https://www.esa.int/.

9 Available at: https://www.nasa.gov/.

3.4. The evolution and services of the CDS

The CDS was originally created as a *Centre de Données Stellaires* to look after data on stars, facilitating the study of the structure of the Galaxy. Its mission was extended in 1983 to all astronomical data, and it became the Strasbourg Astronomical Data Centre, a name change that allowed it to keep its acronym, which was already well known at the time.

The CDS was in charge of the *Bibliographical Star Index* (BSI; Ochsenbein and Spite 1977), developed in collaboration with the *Observatoire de Paris*, and the *Catalogue of Stellar Identifications* (CSI; Ochsenbein *et al.* 1981), which were merged to create the SIMBAD database, the first interactive version of which became operational in 1981. SIMBAD is the international reference database for the identification and bibliography of astronomical objects outside the solar system. As of August 2020, it contained more than 11 million objects and more than 370,000 bibliographic references. It lists more than 22 million links between articles and the objects they cite.

The CDS has also collected and distributed astronomical catalogs since its inception and has collaborated with international partners to digitize large historical catalogs that could include hundreds of thousands of objects. This collection also included tables published in academic journals, which were ingested more systematically from 1993 onwards, when collaborations with major journals began to be established in this field. The journal *Astronomy & Astrophysics*[10] stopped printing the "long tables"[11] of its articles and made them available online in a CDS FTP service from that date. This was a paradigm shift: the figures printed on paper in the journal became reusable data. The VizieR service, which provides access to the CDS table collection and also allows criteria-based queries on the entire table content, was launched in 1996. It also includes data attached to publications that are not tabular data, such as images or time series. As of August 2020, VizieR had more than 20,000 "catalogs", catalogs or publication-related data. Some catalogs have over a billion items. Catalogs can also contain a lot of information. For example, a catalog that contains 300,000 items might have more than 500 columns.

The appearance of the web has led to data linked to articles being published online, as well as to the development of the VizieR service for searching for data within catalogs. The new possibilities it offered have also guided the development of

10 Available at: https://www.aanda.org/; *Astronomy & Astrophysics* is one of the major journals in the discipline and is unique in that it has a number of member states – initially European countries, which have since been joined by South American countries.

11 Tables with more than 100 rows, or shorter tables that contain a lot of data.

the interactive sky atlas Aladin, which makes it possible to visualize sky images kept at the CDS or in remote services – for example, the archives of the large ground and space observatories – to compare them and superimpose the contents of catalogs or databases on to them. Aladin is also a reference image database managed by CDS, which as of August 2020 included more than 800 sky surveys, representing a volume of more than 320 TB.

In addition to SIMBAD, VizieR and Aladin, the CDS is developing a catalog cross-identification service – that is, an operation that compares two catalogs to identify items that they have in common. The CDS service is particularly efficient at cross-identifying very large catalogs. The Data Centre is also responsible for the Dictionary of Nomenclature of Astronomical Objects Outside the Solar System. The Dictionary lists the acronyms that can be used to designate objects, composed from the initials of the words that make up their names. It contained almost 25,000 acronyms as of August 2020. The CDS portal provides access to all services.

The CDS services are accessible via their web interface (Figure 3.1), and also programmatically via numerous application programming interfaces. These are used by programs developed by the CDS or its users, which may be other data centers. Observatory archives have long used CDS services to allow their users to search for data based on the name of an astronomical object, while they organize their data according to the position of observations in the sky. A query to the CDS services transforms the object name provided by the user into its position. The first program module to perform these queries was made available by the CDS in 1993. The possibilities for accessing services have continued to take advantage of new capabilities made possible by technological developments. One example is the provision of Python library modules, a system increasingly used by researchers. The vast majority of requests received by the CDS are machine-to-machine by program. Accesses via Python now constitute a significant proportion of the queries.

Data centers, such as the CDS, are in a constantly changing environment. Astronomy is evolving, which influences both the content of the services and the expectations of users. It is imperative that the team's disciplinary skills remain in step with these scientific developments. The context of the activity is also evolving, with new telescopes, instruments and actors; it is therefore necessary to establish new collaborations or make changes to the collaborations already established. Finally, the evolution of the techniques used in a data center can be rapid and fundamental: recall, for example, the emergence of the web in the early 1990s, which made all of the previous developments of dedicated interfaces obsolete.

Figure 3.1. *CDS web interface. For a color version of
this figure, see www.iste.co.uk/schopfel/datasharing.zip*

CDS services were available remotely before the web. Astronomers could send a
letter requesting a copy of a catalog on magnetic tape, or a printout of the catalog on
paper or microfiche. The tape or printout was sent by mail. They could also submit
requests via a packet of punch cards over computer networks. The very first Internet
connection in France[12], on July 28, 1988, was to allow American astronomers to
access SIMBAD during a session of the General Assembly of the International
Astronomical Union held in Baltimore at the beginning of August that year. Before
that date, they had to pay more than 100 dollars each time they wanted to connect to
the international network.

The services that were operational in the early 1990s, SIMBAD and the catalogs
service, were gradually moved to the web. New services or functionalities taking
advantage of the new possibilities offered by the web were developed, such as
VizieR and Aladin. The web's ability to create links between services was also fully
utilized early on, based on internationally shared metadata. The collaboration
between the CDS and the *Astrophysics Data System* (ADS)[13], the reference
bibliographic service for the discipline, is an excellent example. The ADS database
was created as a proof of concept in 1988 and was connected to SIMBAD as soon as

---

12 Available at: https://interstices.info/au-coeur-de-la-premiere-connexion-francaise-a-larpanet/;
the web page describes the first French connection to the ARPAnet network, a precursor of the
Internet as we know it today.

13 Available at: https://ui.adsabs.harvard.edu/; ADS is produced by the *Harvard-Smithsonian
Center for Astrophysics* on behalf of NASA.

the service was installed on the web in 1994. The links between the CDS and ADS have continued to grow, allowing users to navigate between data found in publications and bibliographic information with a single click on a web page. Another example is the CDS's collaboration with NED[14], in particular for the nomenclature of astronomical objects and the International Astronomical Union working group on designations. The CDS has also been, and continues to be, actively involved in the development of the disciplinary data sharing framework, the astronomical VO, which is the subject of the next section.

3.5. FAIR principles in astronomy: the astronomical virtual observatory

Astronomy has been, and continues to be, a pioneering discipline in the sharing of scientific data. The international agreement on the Flexible Image Transport System (FITS) format, which allows any astronomer to use data from any telescope and develop common tools, was published in 1981 and has been maintained ever since[15]. The IVOA[16], which is in charge of the development of the VO standards, was established in 2002.

The VO allows data to be found, accessed and interoperable, and was operational long before the publication of the paper by Wilkinson *et al.* (2016) that defines the FAIR principles. It provides access to archive data from most ground and space-based telescopes. A single query based on a position in the sky can, for example, find and facilitate access to all available observational data in that area. The CDS services are accessible in the VO, and the same query allows the requester to find and obtain the data available in this area in SIMBAD, VizieR and Aladin. The position in the sky is only one of the many query parameters in the VO. For example, the VO allows users to perform complex multi-criteria queries based on the VizieR data.

The CDS largely anticipated the need to develop the interoperability of astronomical data. As early as 1998, Aladin was able to visualize data from observatory archives thanks to a register of web addresses of remote resources. By 2000, the CDS had defined *Unified Content Descriptors* (UCDs), metadata describing the quantities used by astronomers, from the 100,000 columns in the VizieR catalogs. UCDs have been adapted to become one of the IVOA standards in the field of semantics.

---

14 Available at: https://ned.ipac.caltech.edu NASA/IPAC Extragalactic Database.

15 Available at: https://fits.gsfc.nasa.gov/.

16 Available at: http://www.ivoa.net/.

The CDS was very actively involved in the development of the VO even before its official launch. It led the group that conducted the first international discussions on interoperability in astronomy, a European network working group, who defined the first VO standard in 2002, a few months before the creation of IVOA. IVOA then took over the coordination of standards development.

The CDS has been the cornerstone of the creation of a French community around VO, which brings together individuals who are involved in defining standards and those who use them in their services or in the applications they develop (Genova 2019). It has participated in all of the European projects that have supported and coordinated the development of VO in Europe from 2001 onwards, and it has led four of them between 2006 and 2014. Since then, it has been involved in the European projects ASTERICS[17] (2015–2019) and ESCAPE[18] (2019–2022), which coordinate activities among large research infrastructures. For ASTERICS, these activities related to astronomy and astroparticles, while the field of particle physics has been added to ESCAPE. In addition to the leading role played by the CDS in organizing the development of the VO, its members have piloted, or been co-authors, of almost half of the standards (21 out of 46 in August 2020).

3.6. The use of CDS services

CDS services are "reference services" and are used as such by different user groups.

Researchers use the services during all phases of the research process, from working on an observation proposal to analyzing the data, visualizing it, comparing it with other data and publishing the resulting data, which leads to the creation of new reference data.

In the preparation stage of an observation, for example, an astronomer will consult SIMBAD to find and analyze what has been previously published about an astronomical object, and use the basic information about the object available in this service. When creating a sample of astronomical objects for an observing proposal, VizieR's 20,000 catalogs (over 30 billion rows of tables) can be used to extract properties provided by published measurements of the objects or build a sample based on complex criteria from multiple starting catalogs. The preparation of the

17 Astronomy ESFRI and Research Infrastructure Cluster; available at: https://www. asterics2020.eu/.

18 European Science Cluster of Astronomy and Particle Physics ESFRI Research Infrastructures; available at: https://projectescape.eu/.

observation can include the production of a "finding chart" with the Aladin visualization tool and its database of sky images, plus the distributed data to which Aladin provides access through the VO.

Once the observations have been obtained, the data – either images or tabulated data – can be compared with existing data, for example, by comparing and overlaying images in Aladin, or by using the cross-identification service to cross-identify the resulting catalog with existing catalogs.

One of the major uses of the CDS is of course by authors, who use the services to publish data associated with a new publication, in coordination with the journal's editorial board and its publisher.

The use of CDS services for research goes well beyond the direct researcher use scenarios described above: these services are used by other astronomical services through programmatic access mechanisms. For example, as explained above, the CDS "name resolver" is used by many astronomical data archives to convert a user-supplied object name to its position in the sky, which is then used to query the archive. The Aladin visualization client has been used as the basis for observing preparation tools made available to their users by observatories. More recently, there has been a rapid growth in the implementation of "Aladin Lite", a web client that is easily integrated into a web interface. CDS services are also used by amateur astronomers and in the teaching and dissemination of scientific information.

The CDS services are widely used: usage statistics show an average of 1.7 million queries per day in 2019. Some queries are simple and quick, such as "resolving" a name as coordinates. Others involve complex criteria queries and can take several minutes or even an hour. Services are sometimes heavily loaded when a major data set is released, or when a project launches a major operation that involves CDS services.

Usage statistics are the main tool for monitoring the use of services, but they are also cited in articles published in academic journals. Each year, for example, VizieR publishes data from some 1,500 catalogs. There are also about 1200 mentions of "SIMBAD", "VizieR" or "Aladin" referring to CDS services in related articles each year. In the year 2019, the ADS had 672 mentions of SIMBAD, 436 mentions of VizieR and 85 mentions of Aladin. These citations are in some ways just the tip of the "iceberg" that is the massive use of the services.

3.7. Overview

The CDS is one of the major components of the international astronomy data system, which is distributed worldwide but which, because of the effective FAIRisation of data, services and tools, appears to the user as a unique data infrastructure in support of its research. Its services are used on a daily basis by the research community, and also by (not insignificant and rapidly growing) other groups who use it for teaching, amateur astronomy and general interest purposes, in the form of tools for members of the public interested in astronomy. It is one of the Research Infrastructures of the National Roadmap, a recognition of its role, impact and the quality of its work and services; in astronomy, the other infrastructures of the National Roadmap are large ground-based telescopes managed by international organizations and partnerships.

The large number of requests it receives every day shows that the CDS is trusted by its community. It has also been awarded the *Data Seal of Approval*[19], and subsequently the *CoreTrustSeal*[20], making it a trustworthy data center, following an evaluation by external experts of the way it is organized and how it manages the data and technical aspects of its work to fulfill its mission of serving its community.

The CDS has been a forerunner in data sharing in astronomy, a discipline that has been a pioneer in Open Science. Its success and longevity show the value of its model, which involves the different profiles, researchers and documentalists who manage the content, and computer engineers who develop the services, in close collaboration within an integrated team. It defines an evolutionary strategy focused on the current and future needs of the scientific community in its discipline, seeking to make the most of technological developments. It participates fully in the methodological and technological developments of the discipline in the field of data sharing. And it has established a vast network of international collaborations with major players in the discipline.

3.8. Perspectives

3.8.1. *Current and future challenges*

Reference data services in astronomy will remain an important part of the discipline's research system. Researchers continue to rely on them to find the data

---

19 Available at: https://www.coretrustseal.org/about/history/data-seal-of-approval-synopsis-2008-2018/.

20 Available at: https://www.coretrustseal.org/.

they need, access it, reuse it and interoperate, as they did before the FAIR principles were defined in support of Open Science.

Some of the current and future challenges are in line with those that the CDS has faced since its creation: adapting to scientific and technological developments and developments in its environment, and managing the growth in the volume and complexity of data, while maintaining the content of the databases and the tools made available to users at the highest level of quality.

Astronomy, like all sciences, is continuously evolving. New areas of research must be fully taken into account in terms of content (support of new data types, definition of new metadata, etc.), as well as technical capabilities. Multi-wavelength astronomy, which combines data from several instruments operating in different wavelength ranges of the electromagnetic spectrum, is now well established. We have witnessed the birth of multi-messenger astronomy, particularly with the emblematic discovery of gravitational waves and the search for and discovery of the astronomical objects from which they originate. The inclusion in the VO of data from astroparticle observatories, which include gravitational wave observatories, is one of the objectives of the ASTERICS and ESCAPE projects.

The rapid development of time-domain astronomy is creating a new perspective on the transient and variable universe; most astronomical objects are variable, on time scales ranging from microseconds to tens of billions of years. New large surveys are being prepared to monitor the sky. They will generate streams of data that will need to be filtered to extract events and objects for study.

An obvious challenge is that the data is becoming increasingly massive, both in volume and in terms of the number of astronomical objects. The Rubin Observatory[21] will produce 20 TB of data each night and will accumulate 60 PB of data over its planned 10 years of operation, which should begin in 2022. The Square Kilometre Array (SKA)[22], which is scheduled to begin producing routine scientific observations in the late 2020s, will produce 5 TB per second. Astronomy has already entered the era of Big Data. Take, for example, the catalog of observations from the Gaia satellite[23], the second version of which was published in 2018 and contains 1.7 billion objects. We need to adapt the methods for handling and distributing data to these very large volumes. We must also learn to make the best use of the new possibilities offered by artificial intelligence and deep learning. In

21 The Rubin Observatory, formerly known as the Large Synoptic Survey Telescope (LSST), is optimized to detect transient phenomena. Available at: https://www.lsst.org/.

22 Available at: https://www.skatelescope.org/.

23 Available at: https://sci.esa.int/web/gaia.

particular, the CDS uses the hierarchical data structure (Fernique *et al.* 2015) it has developed to implement the management of the massive data it is in charge of, as will be explained in the next section.

Other challenges related to the changing landscape of scientific data sharing are completely new. One important development in the context in which the CDS operates is the development of the European Open Science Cloud (EOSC)[24]. The vision of the EOSC as "the Web of FAIR data" resonates with the well-established role of the CDS and the way astronomy shares its data. The CDS should be a thematic data center within the EOSC, and the ESCAPE project is working to interface the VO with it. The evolution of scientific publications in the context of Open Science is also a fundamental element for the CDS, in particular, the way in which data associated with publications are taken into account and managed, and of course, the way in which data curation is recognized and supported by institutional, national and international authorities.

3.8.2. *Future developments*

One of the major development axes of the CDS is related to the spatiotemporal indexing of data. The first step was to define a hierarchical scheme for the description of large sky surveys, allowing large data to be stored in a simple file system and accessed efficiently by zooming in progressively. This is the purpose of the IVOA *Hierarchical Progressive Survey (*HIPS) standard[25], along with the *Multi-Order Coverage Map* (MOC) method[26] for specifying the sky regions to be accessed. This sky indexing was then used in the temporal domain, and the CDS is now extending it to other dimensions of high-volume data. These hierarchical methods are the basis for CDS's management of large volumes of data. They are ready to be scaled up, but of course the CDS needs access to the massive storage capacity required.

The CDS provides access to a large amount of reference data (FAIR's A) that users can find (F), reuse (R) and use in an interoperable way (I). Another focus of service development is to provide users with the ability to analyze the data obtained from the CDS to strengthen the I and R facets of FAIR. This is in line with the general move toward the implementation of platforms for scientific data analysis, and one of the first steps in practice is to facilitate the simple use of CDS data in *Jupyter notebooks*.

---

24 Available at: https://ec.europa.eu/research/openscience/index.cfm?pg=open-science-cloud.
25 Available at: http://www.ivoa.net/documents/HiPS/20170519/index.html.
26 Available at: http://www.ivoa.net/documents/MOC/20191007/index.html.

Many developments concern the internal architecture and organization of CDS services, while others concern the scientific and technical interface of CDS with major journals and astronomical data producers. For example, one of the recent developments in the tools that allow the CDS to process journal articles to extract the names of astronomical objects has led to the use of the XML version of articles instead of the PDF version. This opens up many possibilities for finer and more efficient ingestion of data into CDS services, as well as for the establishment of more links between articles and data.

3.8.3. *What will the CDS look like in 5 or 10 years?*

The CDS will always be a reference data center for the international astronomical community, a partner to other major players in the field at the forefront of new and evolving ways of sharing and using scientific information. It will continue to contribute to major projects in the field of astronomy.

Its activities and evolution will always be driven by the needs of scientists. The CDS will celebrate its 50th year in 2022 and, while its original missions remain fully relevant, the challenges and expectations of users will continue to evolve and it will need to remain at the forefront of technological innovation.

We also hope that the Open Science paradigm will be understood and accepted by all, and that the roles played by all those who make it possible, including researchers, engineers and technicians, will be fully identified and recognized.

3.9. Acknowledgments

The authors would like to thank Daniel Egret for his careful review of the text.

3.10. References

Genova, F. (2019). The Action Spécifique Observatoires Virtuels France (Virtual Observatory France Specific Action) in the open science context. In *Proceedings 2019 SF2A*, 27–31 [Online]. Available at: https://ui.adsabs.harvard.edu/abs/2019sf2a.conf...27G.

Fernique, P., Allen, M.G., Boch, T., Oberto, A., Pineau, F.X., Durand, D., Bot, C., Cambresy, L., Derriere, S., Genova, F., Bonnarel, F. (2015). Hierarchical progressive surveys. Multi-resolution HEALPix data structures for astronomical images, catalogues, and 3-dimensional data cubes. *Astronomy & Astrophysics*, 578, A114.

Ochsenbein, F. and Spite, F. (1977). Main features of the stellar bibliographic file. *International Astronomical Union Colloquium*, 35, 175–177.

Ochsenbein, F., Bischoff, M., Egret, D. (1981). Microfiche edition of CSI. *Astronomy and Astrophysics, Suppl. Ser.*, 43, 259–264.

Wilkinson, M.D., Dumontier, M., Aalbersberg, I.J., Appleton, G., Axton, M., Baak, A., Blomberg, N., Boiten, J.W., Bonino da Silva Santos, L., Bourne, P.E *et al.* (2016). The FAIR guiding principles for scientific data management and stewardship. *Scientific Data*, 3(1), 160018.

4

Data INRAE – The Networked Repository

Esther DZALÉ YEUMO

INRAE, Paris, France

Introduction

Since 2018, the French National Research Institute for Agriculture, Food and the Environment (*Institut national de recherche pour l'agriculture, l'alimentation et l'environnement* [INRAE]) has made a repository for reporting and depositing research data available to its researchers. This repository, called Data INRAE[1], is based on the open-source application Dataverse[2]. We asked Esther Dzalé Yeumo, head of the "Digital Science" unit within the Directorate for Open Science (*Direction pour la Science Ouverte*, DipSO), about the choice of this solution, its advantages for an institute such as INRAE and, more generally, its functionalities and uses.

Interview conducted by Violaine REBOUILLAT, September 29, 2020 and January 21, 2021.

For a color version of all the figures in this chapter, see www.iste.co.uk/schopfel/datasharing.zip.

1 Available at: https://data.INRAE.fr.

2 "The Dataverse Project is housed and developed by the Dataverse Team at the Institute for Quantitative Social Science (IQSS) at Harvard University. A Dataverse repository hosts multiple databases. Each dataverse contains dataset(s) or other dataverses, and each dataset contains descriptive metadata and data files (including documentation and code that accompany the data)". Source: https://en.wikipedia.org/wiki/Dataverse.

Research Data Sharing and Valorization,
coordinated by Joachim SCHÖPFEL and Violaine REBOUILLAT. © ISTE Ltd 2022.

What is the purpose of the Data INRAE repository?

Data INRAE is one of the major components of the institution's e-infrastructure and as such contributes to the management, dissemination and reuse of the institution's data, as stipulated in the INRA Charter (INRA 2016) and the more recent document on principles for Data INRAE governance (INRAE 2020).

The Data INRAE portal thus helps to:

– complete and strengthen the service offered to the research teams of the institute and their partners in order to facilitate the management and sharing of scientific data;

– meet French regulatory obligations regarding open research data.

What are the resources dedicated to Data INRAE?

Data INRAE is administered by a team of five people from the DipSO (*Direction pour la Science Ouverte*) for a little less than two FTEs, who also provide support to users. The DipSO, which is in charge of Data INRAE's project management, works in close collaboration with the DSI (*Direction des Systèmes d'Information*) on the implementation and maintenance in operational conditions (MOCs) of the portal. In 2020, the team of developers mobilized consisted of four people, or 2.5 FTEs, including the equivalent of two FTEs in service. In cash, the annual budget dedicated to Data INRAE between 2018 and 2020 averaged out at €250,000 (including services and data storage).

Data INRAE is based on the Dataverse software solution. What was behind this choice?

The repository was born out of the *Datapartage* project, conducted between 2013 and 2016. Different working groups had been set up at the institutional level with the aim of contributing to a reflection on the management and sharing of INRA's data. One of the groups was devoted to tools. It drew attention to two needs for:

– a directory listing the data produced by INRA researchers;

– a repository to manage and share long tail data and data underlying scientific publications, in a context where scientific journals are increasingly demanding access to the data supporting the articles (Figure 4.1).

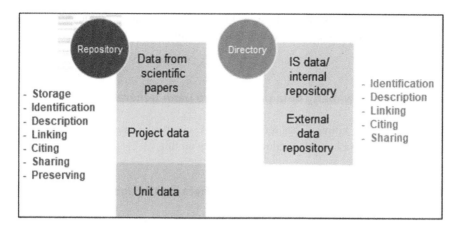

Figure 4.1. *The directory and repository functions of Data INRAE (Dzalé Yeumo 2019)*

A benchmarking exercise was then conducted to determine which tool could best meet these needs. The Dataverse software solution proved to be the one that offered the best compromise to meet the collected needs and non-functional requirements. The organization of data into collections, which can be managed by each collective in charge of it, as well as the possibility of parameterizing each collection in terms of metadata and workflows was particularly well suited to our needs. Moreover, this solution allowed us to quickly implement a solution with a reasonable budget.

Did the initial specifications change afterwards?

The project was managed in an agile manner with minimal initial specifications. Overall, Dataverse evolutions met most of the needs collected from users, probably because these evolutions are based on the expression of the needs of a large scientific community.

Additional modules have nevertheless been developed. Among them, there is the option of generating data paper templates from DOIs of datasets deposited in Data INRAE. Two data paper templates have been proposed:

– the template of Data in Brief, the data journal in which the majority of data papers have been published by INRAE researchers to date;

– a model specific to INRAE, intended to be an agnostic journal (in that it synthesizes the various existing data paper models).

The generated data paper template is a draft document based on the information available in the dataset metadata, which can be completed and refined to produce the final data paper.

Do you know how many data papers have been generated so far?

No, we don't know. The tool does not count the number of templates downloaded. And we haven't conducted a survey on this.

Do you have any feedback from researchers on the use of this module?

Several people who tested it said it was easy. The template provides a first draft with the metadata that has been entered in Dataverse in the chosen format, which saves time. It would be interesting to have more detailed feedback from users of this tool who have actually published data papers and who have quantified the time saved by using the Data INRAE template.

What is the workflow when depositing or reporting data in Data INRAE?

Data INRAE is organized in collections. The collections created at the request of scientists or groups (units, projects, etc.) are administered by the applicants. The workflow and the access and deposit rights in these collections therefore depend on their choices. However, any user logged into their INRAE account can deposit data at the root of the repository, in three generic collections, depending on the data production mode: Experimental-Observation-Simulation Dataverse, Omics Dataverse and Survey and Texts Dataverse (Figure 4.2). The data deposited in these three generic collections can be published by their depositors. The DipSO support team then carries out *a posteriori* curation, which focuses on the metadata (verification of the completeness and quality of the metadata) and on the files (identification of formatting problems). The team can also offer its support to the administrators of a collection to help them curate its content.

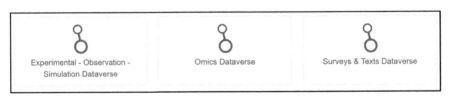

Figure 4.2. *Data INRAE generic collections*

Does each scientific department of INRAE have a *de facto* collection in Data INRAE?

No, the organization of data in Data INRAE is not dependent on the administrative organization of the institution. Each structure (department, unit, collective scientific infrastructure or research infrastructure) is free to create a collection to organize the management of its data if it so wishes (Figure 4.3).

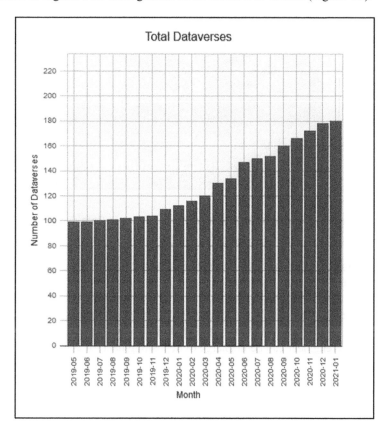

Figure 4.3. *Evolution of the number of collections in Data INRAE between 2019 and 2021*

Collections allow scientists to highlight the dynamics of a structure or a project (Figure 4.4). This does not prevent researchers whose structures do not have a collection from depositing and publishing data in Data INRAE. This flexibility is appreciated by users. It should be noted that deposited data can be attached to collections at a later date.

Figure 4.4. *Distribution of collections by type in Data INRAE*

Can you quantify the number of INRAE researchers who deposit data in the repository?

To date, there are 1,022 user accounts, but this number is not necessarily representative, because often depositing of data is done in a collective way: a researcher or an engineer can be in charge of depositing data for a group.

Does the repository comply with the FAIR principles?

By design, the Dataverse tool offers functionalities that allow the data to meet the FAIR principles to a certain extent. Beyond these functionalities, there will always be a dichotomy between the technology and the user. Technology alone is not enough to make data FAIR; user engagement is essential. For example, the ability of a dataset to be discovered or retrieved by a search largely depends on the accuracy and richness of the metadata that describes it. This is the limit of the exercise. The responsibility does not merely rest with the support team or the technology.

F: FINDABLE

– Data INRAE assigns persistent identifiers (DOI).

– It allows you to search for data using rich and standardized metadata.

– Three metadata standards are proposed: Dublin Core, DDI Light and DataCite (these are the standards initially integrated in Dataverse).

A: ACCESSIBLE

– The repository uses the HTTP protocol.

– It guarantees permanent access to the metadata, even if the data file is deleted.

I: INTEROPERABLE

– The repository offers open and machine-readable file formats.

– Some proprietary file formats are converted to open formats.

– For some metadata, the repository uses controlled lists.

R: REUSABLE

– The data are systematically assigned a user license.

– The source of the data is traced: all modifications made to the data and the metadata are listed, from the moment the data is in the repository. In addition, specific metadata and the ability to import source files are available.

Box 4.1. *FAIR principles*

What about the archiving of the data deposited in Data INRAE?

A working group was formed in early 2019 to define the framework of a workstream on the storage and long-term archiving of data deposited in Data INRAE (Sbeih *et al.* 2020). A pilot project is currently under way with CINES as part of the European project EOSC-Pillar. This pilot project will allow the realization of connections necessary to transfer data from Data INRAE to CINES for archiving. It will also mean that the selection criteria for data to be archived can start to be identified with the aid of INRAE's data governance cell, led by the Data Administrator.

Do you use web analytics tools to measure the audience of the repository?

Yes, we use XiTi[3] to measure dataset viewing. We record the number of downloads and views of a dataset by third-party tools (Figure 4.5). For example, for tabulated files, we have two tools coupled with Dataverse that allow us to visualize the data and make some statistics. The accesses to the files via these tools are counted as downloads. Indeed, these tools connect to Dataverse to download and open the file, although this is transparent to the end user.

Why is displaying the number of downloads important?

This display allows those who share their data to see if it is being viewed. I think that when you spend time preparing a dataset for sharing, knowing that others are interested in it is important.

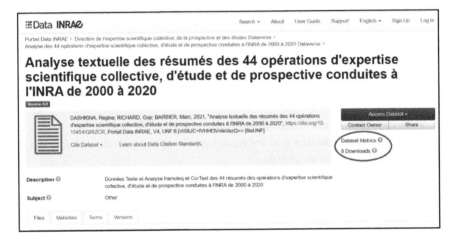

Figure 4.5. *How the number of downloads of a dataset is displayed*

Do you publicize Data INRAE? If so, how and for what purpose?

We publicized the tool at the time of its launch. At the moment, we are a bit past the publicization stage, although there is still a user mailing list and information on the *datapartage*[4] website, as well as demos when there are new features.

---

3 XiTi is a free web analytics tool; available at: https://www.xiti.com/.

4 Available at: https://datapartage.INRAE.fr.

What we offer today are short training sessions every three months, which last two hours. We offer two levels of training: training for users and training for collection administrators in Dataverse. Each training session gathers on average about 15 participants. These training sessions are conducted remotely, because it is easier for scientists to connect to a videoconference, but also because the current public health situation requires it. Moreover, as the platform is rather intuitive and easy to use, the participants in the training sessions are mainly looking to save time with regard to the finer points of the tool and to understand the tips and tricks that would have taken them a long time to discover on their own.

What are the strengths of Data INRAE?

Data INRAE has strengths in terms of tools and services.

In terms of tools, I see three strengths as follows:

– the first is that Dataverse meets the data management and sharing needs of INRAE researchers;

– the second is its flexibility;

– the third is that it provides DOIs, which allow persistent access to data and increase its visibility and traceability.

Data INRAE also has advantages in terms of services. The curation service is particularly appreciated by researchers: getting feedback in the form of suggestions for improving metadata or data formatting is indeed perceived as a plus.

What are the weaknesses of Data INRAE?

At present, Data INRAE has two weak points, which the technical team plans to address.

The first is the link with the repositories. Indeed, the only way today to control the input of certain metadata, whose values must be standardized, is to "manually set up the controlled lists" (i.e. to declare each value of the repository in the software, which does not allow us to link with external resources). We want to contribute to the development (in particular within the framework of the ANR BRIDGE project[5])

5 Bridge Research through Interoperable Data Governance and Environments (2019–2021): "By taking advantage of the favourable partnership context between IRD, INRA and CIRAD, the BRIDGE project aims to demonstrate how, by activating three levers (political,

of the possibility of connecting a metadata to a remote repository (e.g. the INRAE Thesaurus for keywords, or the INRAE LDAP directory for authors affiliated to INRAE).

The second weak point concerns the license settings. In a native way, the Dataverse tool offers a CC0 license (which is equivalent to a transfer in the public domain). We therefore systematically propose that collection administrators set up an input form that pre-fills specific conditions of use corresponding to the Etalab license (equivalent to CC-BY): the latter allows the free reuse of data, provided that their creators are cited. We plan to contribute to the evolution of Dataverse so that several licenses, including CC-BY, can be offered in the Licenses section of the tool.

How is the Dataverse community helping to evolve the software?

When you reuse a software like Dataverse, developed by others, there are three ways to make it evolve in the direction you want it to. Dataverse, in this case, is an open-source software. Its code is open. This means that you can decide to take a version of the code and adapt it however you like. In this case, we "derive" from the main branch of the software. But this is not the method we want to use for Data INRAE. The second way of doing things, when we want to make evolutions, is to make our needs known to the community and to work together with other interested members to push these evolutions along the roadmap of the developments to be carried out. In this case, we are a little more passive. Finally, the third way to make the Dataverse code evolve is to say to the community that we ourselves will develop the evolution we are interested in and then hand over the code. So, first, the community must be interested in the development we want to do. Then, you have to follow the software development standards. And finally, you have to give the code to the community and wait for them to integrate it in a future version of Dataverse. For example, on the issue of repositories, there is a development that has been done by DANS[6], but it has not yet been integrated into the main version of Dataverse. On the issue of user licenses, which I mentioned earlier, we have already tested the idea with the community. We found that there is a shared interest around this issue: several members of the community would indeed be interested. However, to date, this has not been one of the development priorities on the roadmap.

---

community and technological), we can promote the implementation of FAIR principles".
Source: https://anr.fr/Projet-ANR-19-DATA-0013.

6 Available at: https://dataverse.nl/dataverse/dans.

What is the point of being part of Dataverse?

The Dataverse community allows development needs to be discussed. In fact, there are two ways to be part of the Dataverse community. There is the community which is, let's say, informal: all those who use Dataverse are somehow part of the community. We have at our disposal a certain number of open access resources on the web. Then, there is the Global Dataverse Community Consortium[7], which can be joined for an annual membership fee of $500. INRAE joined this community in 2020. This consortium gives access to benefits in the form of support, experience sharing or participation in the governance of Dataverse.

Is Data INRAE referenced in European or international meta-catalogs?

The data are referenced in the DataCite[8] catalog. Through the assignment of DOIs, the metadata is traced back to the DataCite level and from there to other catalogs such as OpenAIRE[9]. Data INRAE data are also referenced in Google Dataset Search[10] (a Google search engine that enables datasets to be queried). They are also referenced in the European catalog B2Find[11]. This referencing is currently being improved, in particular to make the metadata at the file level (the names of the fields in column headers in a tabulated file) searchable, in addition to the metadata describing a dataset as a whole (title, keywords, authors, etc.). Indeed, Dataverse has an ingestion process that allows you to index column names in a tabulated file and record them as metadata.

INRAE is involved in one of the working groups of the Committee for Open Science (CoSO) on a feasibility study for a national research data dissemination system. Why was INRAE interested in being part of this working group?

By participating in this working group, INRAE is contributing its expertise. It is also important for INRAE to contribute to this study, so that the option of a national repository, if it is chosen, does not cancel out the work done on Data INRAE. The challenge is that it should take into account the institutional solutions

---

7 Available at: https://dataverse.org/global-dataverse-community-consortium.

8 Available at: https://search.datacite.org/.

9 Available at: https://www.openaire.eu/.

10 Available at: https://datasetsearch.research.google.com/.

11 Available at: https://www.eudat.eu/services/b2find.

that have already been developed, such as Data INRAE, and modes of compatibility should be envisaged.

What will be the challenges for Data INRAE in the years to come?

I see three challenges, as follows:

– the first is archiving (which we mentioned earlier);

– the second is to maintain (or even improve) the quality of the service, particularly the quality of curation, despite the increase in the number of deposits, which will continue to grow;

– the third challenge will be to bring the data closer to the calculation. The aim is to have appropriate infrastructures to be able to analyze data from the cloud, without having to download them first. This aspect is the subject of a proof of concept in the EOSC-Pillar project, which INRAE is participating in. More generally, our goal is to achieve an integrated repository that is part of national or European infrastructures relevant to our fields.

What will Data INRAE look like in 5 or 10 years? What needs will it have to meet and how will it be used by researchers?

The trajectory we are setting for ourselves is to have a Dataverse whose data do not remain dead and are effectively reused. To do this, we are working on making the data usable from environments that include tools and codes to process and analyze them again. Furthermore, we wish to be part of the dynamics of national (such as Data Terra[12] or IFB[13]) and European (with EOSC[14], in particular) infrastructures, by creating the necessary bridges between Data INRAE and these e-infrastructures. Finally, as mentioned above, there is a project for a national repository for research data. We are considering at least creating a bridge between Data INRAE and this future national repository, and considering integrating this repository fully in line with the idea of mutualization. It is still too early to say, but it is a possibility.

---

12 Data Terra is a research infrastructure for accessing space and *in situ* Earth system data; available at: https://www.data-terra.org/.

13 The *Institut Français de Bioinformatique* is a national service infrastructure whose mission is to provide the life sciences and bioinformatics communities with access to the resources (data, tools, training, etc.) they require for their research ; available at: https://www.france-bioinformatique.fr/.

14 Available at: https://eosc-portal.eu/.

References

Dzalé Yeumo, E. (2019). Dataverse : retour d'expérience sur la mise en œuvre à l'Inra. Réunion annuelle RDA France 2019, September 12–13, Paris, France [Online]. Available at: https://rdafrance2019.sciencesconf.org/data/pages/03_Expe_rience_dataverse_INRA. pdf [Accessed 4 May 2021].

INRA (2016). Charte pour le libre accès aux publications et aux données [Online]. Available at: https://dx.doi.org/10.15454/1.485854076583696E12 [Accessed 12 January 2021].

INRAE (2020). Principes pour la gouvernance des données [Online]. Available at: https://www6. INRAE.fr/datapartage/Gouvernance-des-donnees2/Principes-pour-la-gouvernance-des-donnees-INRAE [Accessed 21 January 2021].

Sbeih, L., Dedet, F., Moreau, P., Dzalé Yeumo, E. (2020). L'archivage des données de la recherche à l'INRA. Eléments de réflexion, démarche et perspectives. *Cahier des Techniques de l'INRA*, INRA [Online]. Available at: https://hal.INRAE.fr/hal-02861909 [Accessed 12 January 2021].

5

SEANOE – A Thematic Repository

Frédéric MERCEUR, Loic PETIT DE LA VILLEON and Sybille VAN ISEGHEM

Ifremer, Brest, France

Introduction

The French Research Institute for Exploitation of the Sea (*Institut français de recherche pour l'exploitation de la mer*, Ifremer) has developed a repository for marine research data, called SEANOE (Sea Scientific Open Data Edition). SEANOE is published in Ifremer's marine data portal. It is not an institutional repository, as it is open to all researchers in the field. What are the unique characteristics of SEANOE? What is it used for? Is it FAIR? What are the challenges and opportunities for development?

How would you describe the general mission of the SEANOE repository?

SEANOE[1] allows marine science datasets to be published easily, quickly and freely. It is open to the whole international scientific community in the field of marine research. SEANOE is solely dedicated to data from different fields of marine science, such as physical oceanography, marine geology, marine biology, etc.

Interview conducted by Joachim SCHÖPFEL, May and June 2020.

1 Available at: https://www.seanoe.org.

Research Data Sharing and Valorization,
coordinated by Joachim SCHÖPFEL and Violaine REBOUILLAT. © ISTE Ltd 2022.

Each dataset published by SEANOE has a DOI (Digital Object Identifier used as a resource identification mechanism) in which the author (the producer of the data) is clearly identified. This allows for an accurate, reliable and sustainable citation.

SEANOE thus offers a solution tailored to journals, requesting that the data used in an article will be available online (e.g. *PLoS ONE*).

The data published by SEANOE can be used under the conditions of the Creative Commons license selected by the author of the data. An embargo limited to two years on a dataset is possible (for current scientific publications).

SEANOE accepts datasets smaller than 100 GB.

What is its administrative context?

SEANOE is managed by the team through the Sismer data center[2].

In 1971, the French government entrusted CNEXO (*Centre National pour l'Exploitation des Océans*) with the mission of representing France at the IOC (Intergovernmental Oceanographic Commission) of UNESCO. At that time, only the management of data from oceanographic campaigns was assured. When Ifremer was created in 1984, as a result of a merger between the CNEXO and the *Institut Scientifique et Technique des Pêches Maritimes* (ISPTM) organizations, this mission was passed on to it.

Ifremer then set up the Sismer (*Systèmes d'Information Scientifique pour la Mer*) data center to manage the collection, processing and dissemination of these marine data. The scope of the data handled has been progressively extended since 1984. The Sismer staff now consists of a team of 28 people (21 permanent and six fixed-term contracts). Sismer manages and/or participates in a series of national and international thematic databases:

– the *Coriolis* International Physical Oceanography Base[3];

– the national *Harmonie* database of the Fisheries Information System[4] (*Système d'information halieutique*), which contains fishing data;

– the national *Quadrige* database for environmental data;

2 Available at: https://data.ifremer.fr/SISMER.

3 Available at: http://www.coriolis.eu.org/.

4 Available at: http://sih.ifremer.fr/.

– the catalogue of French oceanographic campaigns[5];

– *CATDS* and *CERSAT* spatial oceanographic databases.

The Sismer data center is supported by two other teams in its missions:

– the ISI team (14 permanent employees, seven fixed-term contracts) manages the development of these databases in a subcontracting context;

– the RIC team (20 permanent staff, four temporary staff) maintains the technical infrastructures (e.g. servers) of Ifremer. About 40% of the RIC team's activity is dedicated to the management of the infrastructures of these databases.

In 2019, the total budget for these three teams was €5.3 million. The budget is 100% funded by Ifremer.

At the national level, Sismer is now a component of the Odatis[6] ocean data center, which federates data management activities and scientific expertise in oceanography at the national level.

How does the SEANOE team work?

SEANOE (Figure 5.1) is hosted on Ifremer's central shared servers that are administered by the RIC team (*Oracle*, *ElasticSearch*, *Tomcat*, file system, archiving system). The specific cost of the SEANOE project for Ifremer, in terms of infrastructure and management of this infrastructure, is therefore marginal as it is based on existing services and shared with a large number of services.

The SEANOE project is managed by a project manager from the Sismer team. The evolutionary maintenance of the SEANOE code is currently subcontracted to a service company (Altran). In 2015, it took four months of work for *Archimer* to implement SEANOE. Since 2015, about one month of work has been needed annually to ensure its evolutionary maintenance. The management of the subcontracting is ensured by someone from the ISI team, who also ensures that the users are provided with support.

The validation of the filings is currently carried out in turn by two people from the Sismer team (including the project manager). In case of absence, the validation is ensured by the Sismer team's helpdesk. A continuous service is thus ensured.

---

5 Available at: https://campagnes.flotteoceanographique.fr/.
6 Available at: https://www.odatis-ocean.fr/.

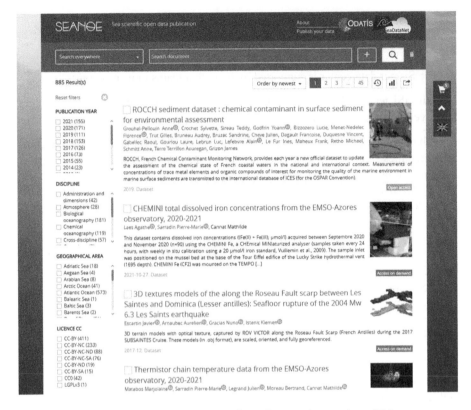

Figure 5.1. *SEANOE web interface. For a color version of this figure, see www.iste.co.uk/schopfel/datasharing.zip*

We systematically contact depositors who have initiated a deposit, but have not finalized it straight away, to offer them our help. This is often an opportunity to answer questions about versioning, for example.

From time to time we also have to help with uploading data files when the size of a data file exceeds 20–30 GB. In case of difficulty, we suggest that users make the data available on an FTP site of their organization, so that we can download and upload them in SEANOE from the Ifremer network ourselves.

In total, between half a day and one day per week is required for:

– project management;

– user support (e.g. answering questions about versioning, etc.);

– checking and updating the uploaded data;

– overseeing citations;

– soliciting new deposits from authors of papers co-authored by Ifremer;

– management of the outsourcing of computer code.

When was SEANOE launched and what were the requirements?

SEANOE was launched in November 2015.

The European and then French regulatory context with the law on the digital republic enacted in 2016, recommends open access dissemination of public research data. In addition, publishers such as PLoS require that the data used in an article be freely accessible online and cited using a DOI; the simultaneous publication of data and an article can strengthen the credibility of the study.

However, back in 2015, the Sismer data center was not organized in such a way that it could meet this need:

– Sismer managed a set of databases that covered most marine science topics. The data that fed these databases came from automated devices (e.g. Argo autonomous floats), national monitoring networks (e.g. Rephy), oceanographic campaigns, etc.

– The ingestion of a dataset into one of these databases was often done manually, with a need to transform the format of the data and qualify the data before being able to upload the data into one of the databases.

– Some of these databases were not open access (e.g. fishing data).

– The data uploaded onto these databases was anonymized and did not allow a particular author to be credited.

What were the initial specifications?

In the above context, Sismer decided to develop a dataset publishing system that offers a simple web-based repository interface, a validation system and the possibility of assigning a DOI to these datasets. The model we had then was the *Pangaea* database developed and maintained in Germany[7].

---

7 Available at: https://www.pangaea.de/.

Scientists who publish a dataset to be cited in an article often do so in a hurry, sometimes after having been refused by their publishers, because the data used was not accessible online (this is a little less true today, with some authors taking this requirement from the publishers on board, thus anticipating the publication of their data before they have submitted an article). The system should therefore allow a DOI to be assigned quickly, ideally in less than 24 hours.

The data had to be freely accessible, after a possible time-limited embargo.

For Sismer, the objective of this new service was also to broaden the scope of data collection and capture new datasets that could feed its thematic databases.

During the validation process, Sismer must simply ensure that the deposited dataset is indeed a dataset, that the theme is respected and that it is sufficiently described. In fact, only two deposits have been refused so far: an article deposited by mistake in SEANOE and a dataset insufficiently described, and whose author seemed unable to describe it correctly.

During validation, Sismer may request additional metadata (e.g. geographic range, author affiliation, etc.) and recommend, where possible, that the data be converted to another format (e.g. Excel vs. csv) or that the data be better described (e.g. adding missing units in data columns).

The size of the accepted datasets should not exceed 100 GB. This limit has been set because, beyond that, it starts to become difficult for users to download the data. It is therefore preferable to select systems backed by computing resources where the data can be used directly without having to be downloaded.

These specifications have not been modified since the launch.

What technical resources were mobilized for SEANOE?

To set up this service, two approaches were considered: using the *Sextant*[8] infrastructure, a Geographic Information System (GIS) based on the *GeoNetWork* system, or adapting *Archimer*[9], Ifremer's institutional archive. The *Archimer* solution had the advantage of offering a simple repository system, as well as a validation system, and of being very quickly operational. This is the solution that was chosen.

---

8 Available at: https://sextant.ifremer.fr/.

9 Available at: https://archimer.ifremer.fr/.

SEANOE is therefore a subset of *Archimer*, Ifremer's Institutional Archive. *Archimer is* an internal development of the documentation service based on the central servers of Ifremer (*Oracle, ElasticSearch, Tomcat*). *Archimer* has been adapted to create SEANOE. These are two versions of the same system. The code of SEANOE is more than 95% similar to that of *Archimer*. The vast majority of metadata describing a report in *Archimer* and a dataset in SEANOE are the same. Only a few specific metadata have been added to describe a dataset (e.g. temporal extent, level of data processing, geographical area, etc.). The file loading form also had to be adapted. Indeed, SEANOE accepts datasets up to 100 GB in size. To upload such large volumes of files online, special mechanisms must be implemented to manage uploads that can last several hours and reduce the risk of http "TimeOut" errors.

The data are published under the new domain name SEANOE.org. We have taken care to make SEANOE anonymous to Ifremer so as not to give the impression that Ifremer wanted to appropriate the published data.

The interface and metadata are only available in English. Even to attract datasets from French teams, we have to present ourselves as an international service.

How do you promote SEANOE to researchers? How do you communicate with them?

We have presented SEANOE in all Ifremer research units. We have also presented it to several national data collection networks.

We have contacted the publishers PLoS, Elsevier and Nature to list SEANOE in their recommended data repositories.

Finally, since 2016, we have been sending a message to the authors of all papers co-authored by authors from the UMRs with which Ifremer is associated with, offering them the opportunity to publish the data associated with their papers in SEANOE. The immediate positive response to these requests is less than 1%. On the other hand, when these authors are confronted with a request from a publisher that requires the publication of data to accept an article, they sometimes remember the service offered by SEANOE.

As we expected, and as confirmed by usage statistics, Google is the main source of access to datasets in SEANOE; in 2019, 50% of site visits came from Google. Improving the visibility of a dataset means above all working on its SEO and this is something we are working on in particular.

A good SEO rating cannot be obtained without quality metadata and among all of the metadata, the title is particularly important. When an author submits a dataset, we therefore refuse, for example, titles that are not explicit. As an example, a dataset initially published with the title "*GULF_IND_PLOS_One*" will ultimately be published under the title "Output from a 1/12-degree Global experiment with the Hybrid Coordinate Ocean Model (HYCOM), forced with NCEP Reanalysis products – Data for the Persian Gulf and Strait of Hormuz".

Technically, the HTML code of the dataset landing pages is then structured to optimize its visibility. For example, it contains metadata structured in JSON-LD schema.org format.

Finally, we aim to enrich the network with automatic cross-links between datasets published in SEANOE and external resources. Google counts the number of links to a resource in its popularity calculation.

At this stage, a dataset published in SEANOE may offer cross-links to:

– the ORCID page of its authors;

– the CV of its Ifremer authors;

– documents in *Archimer*;

– a batch of images in the Ifremer Ocean Library;

– campaigns in the catalog of French oceanographic campaigns;

– samples in the catalog of French oceanographic campaigns;

– Elsevier and Taylor & Francis articles via Scholix.

Finally, the SeaDataNet project and the Odatis data cluster, in which Ifremer is a driving force, have selected SEANOE as their DOI attribution service.

We also monitor the citations of datasets in international papers using alerts on the word SEANOE and the DOI prefix in Google Scholar, and on the websites of several publishers (e.g. Elsevier). When we find an article that cites a dataset, we add its reference to the SEANOE record. Its record is then automatically updated with the DataCite DOI/article DOI pair. These pairs are then also pushed by DataCite to the Scholix project, which is used by several publishers.

When the authors of the article are not the authors of the dataset, we report the citation to the authors of the data.

Sometimes the dataset is misquoted. The most common error is the citation of the landing page URL instead of the DOI. We then report the error to the authors of the article so that they correct the citation if it is not too late.

Finally, for some major datasets that have a name that is not too competitive on the Internet (e.g. Argo, Rephy, etc.), we have also set up an alert on the name of the dataset. If we spot an article that cites a dataset without citing the corresponding DOI, we ask the authors of the article to add the citation of the SEANOE DOI. Otherwise, when it is too late, the authors usually promise to respect the citation instruction in their subsequent articles.

What has changed since the launch?

SEANOE has evolved relatively little since its launch. From the beginning, we noticed that some metadata fields were missing. For example, in the first repositories, many scientists recorded their acknowledgments at the end of the description field. We therefore added a specific "Acknowledgment" field.

In April 2016, to meet the specific needs of the Argo[10] project, we developed the possibility of managing several versions of a dataset within the same DOI and accessing them in a differentiated way using fragmentation (#). This possibility has since been opened up to all datasets published in SEANOE.

For the Argo data, a snapshot of the dataset is frozen and stored monthly. In the initial version, a master DOI was assigned to the Argo dataset and specific DOIs were assigned to each monthly snapshot.

At the request of the scientific direction of the Argo project, a unique DOI has been assigned to the Argo data by SEANOE. This unique DOI allows the global dataset or a specific snapshot using the same DOI to be cited. In this respect, each snapshot is uploaded to SEANOE and is assigned a URL and a key. For example, the snapshot of 2016-02-08 has been assigned the key 42350.

The citation of the global dataset is done by citing the new DOI without parameters. For example:

– Argo (2000). Argo float data and metadata from Global Data Assembly Centre (Argo GDAC). SEANOE (http://doi.org/10.17882/42182).

---

10 Available at: http://www.argo.ucsd.edu/.

The citation of a specific snapshot is done by adding its key preceded by the # character to the DOI:

– Argo (2016). Argo float data and metadata from Global Data Assembly Centre (Argo GDAC) – Snapshot of Argo GDAC of February 8, 2016. SEANOE. (http://doi.org/10.17882/42182#42350).

This ability to assign a unique DOI to an evolving dataset has many advantages, in particular:

– citation instructions are simpler to give to users of the dataset. They only have one DOI to understand. This is an important point because even simple instructions are difficult to apply: for example, we see that scientists regularly ask for a DOI to cite their data in an article, and, in the end, they cite the URL of the landing page instead of the DOI;

– to improve the visibility of the DOI in search engines (e.g. Google), it is preferable to distribute a single landing page that concentrates a maximum number of citations and therefore links (backlink), rather than multiple landing pages of almost identical content;

– if a specific DOI is assigned to each version, search engines will not necessarily show the most recent version in their results lists. A user may therefore discover an obsolete version of the dataset and not realize that a more recent version exists.

Recently, we have implemented the capability of duplicating published SEANOE data in EMODnet Ingestion. EMODnet (European Marine Observation and Data Network) is a network of organizations supported by the EU Integrated Maritime Policy. The EMODnet project manages a set of thematic databases, including:

– *EMODnet Biology* (see: https://www.emodnet-biology.eu);

– *EMODnet Bathymetry* (see: https://www.emodnet-bathymetry.eu);

– *EMODnet Physics* (see: https://www.emodnet-physics.eu).

Datasets published in SEANOE can be automatically pushed into EMODnet Ingestion (see Figure 5.2). EMODnet Ingestion then assigns them to the national data center corresponding to the nationality of the "corresponding author". This national data center must then check whether the data can be ingested into one or another of these portals and, if so, format them and ingest them into the most appropriate thematic database. The Sismer team selects the datasets to be duplicated from SEANOE to EMODnet Ingestion: the datasets are duplicated when the data are qualified, when the selected distribution license allows it and when the dataset is not already exported from an international database.

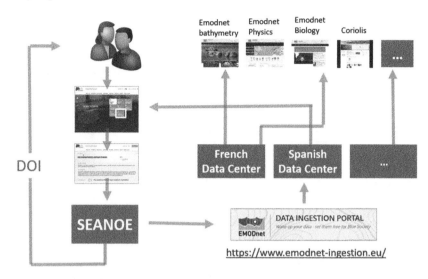

Figure 5.2. *Duplication of SEANOE data in EMODnet. For a color version of this figure, see www.iste.co.uk/schopfel/datasharing.zip*

Furthermore, the link with EMODnet is currently the only way in which SEANOE interconnects with another infrastructure.

What is the number of deposits to date?

As of May 15, 2020, 594 datasets were published in SEANOE. Since the end of 2018, two spontaneous filings have been recorded every week on average. In more detail, in 2019, 118 datasets were published by SEANOE, of which 108 were spontaneous deposits by authors and 10 were deposits related to the EGO Gliders project. Spontaneous deposits are overwhelmingly related to article publications. For several publishers (e.g. PLoS ONE, Elsevier, etc.) it is now a requirement that the data used in an article are made freely accessible online and cited with a DOI. Figure 5.3 shows the evolution of repositories.

Figure 5.4 shows the topic of the datasets deposited in 2019. A deposit can be classified in several themes. In this graph, only datasets deposited spontaneously by their authors have been taken into account. The most representative areas are physical, biological and chemical oceanography.

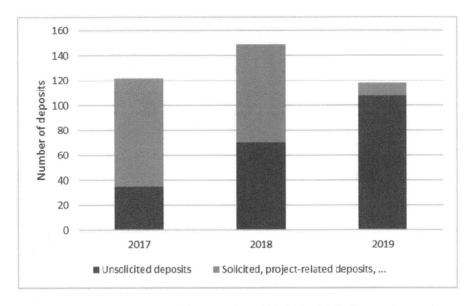

Figure 5.3. *Number of filings in SEANOE 2017–2019. For a color version of this figure, see www.iste.co.uk/schopfel/datasharing.zip*

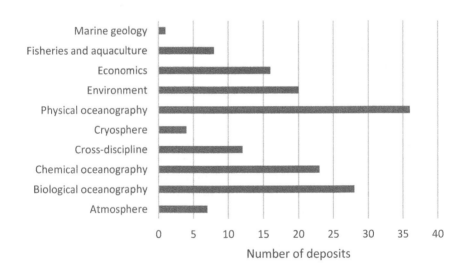

Figure 5.4. *Topics of unsolicited filings in 2019 (108)*

The total volume of data files deposited in 2019, if we include version updates (e.g. Argo, Cora, etc.), is 0.56 TB. The median size of the deposits is 10–100 MB. Figure 5.5 shows the distribution of data volume, DOI by DOI. If a dataset is published as several files, the size of the files is cumulated.

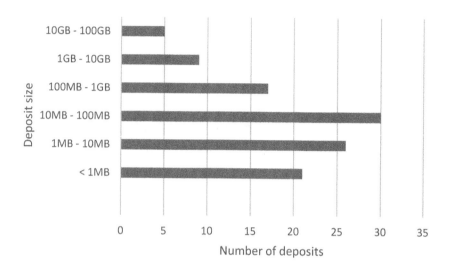

Figure 5.5. *Data file volumes by DOI for 2019 repositories*

As for the format of the repositories, NetCDF and CSV are the most commonly used formats. Files that are provided in Excel format are usually transformed into CSV before publication. However, this is not always possible when, for example, the Excel file contains presentation elements necessary to understand the data. PDF files usually contain information describing the data (format, acquisition). Some datasets are composed of a large number of files, sometimes of different formats, which are then zipped.

What are the statistics in terms of connections, user sessions, downloads and so on?

Here is some information taken from an analysis of Ifremer's Apache web server logs. In 2019, the landing pages were accessed 24,000 times from outside Ifremer (excluding robots). The data files were downloaded more than 9,700 times. The progression since 2016 has been significant; between 2017 and 2019, page visits and downloads have more than doubled (see Figure 5.6).

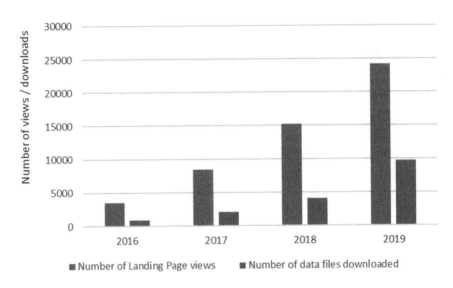

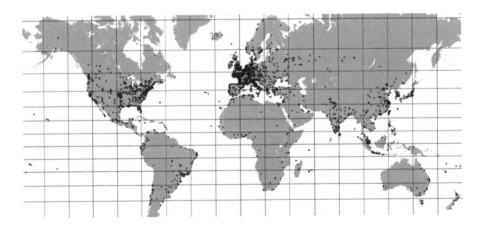

The most requested repository was downloaded 1,002 times in 2019 ("Labeled SAR imagery dataset of ten geophysical phenomena from Sentinel-1 wave mode [TenGeoP-SARwv]"); the 10 most downloaded datasets accounted for 46% of downloads in 2019. But despite this concentration, 75% of the repositories have been downloaded at least once.

Page views and downloads come from all continents (see Figure 5.7). The leading countries in terms of usage are China, France, the United States, India and Italy, followed by the United Kingdom and Germany.

What do we know about the depositors? What is the feedback from users?

Between January and May 2020, 47 new datasets were published in SEANOE. Almost all of these datasets were published by scientists or engineers with a view to citing the dataset in a draft paper. Note that 31 of these 47 datasets were published by French scientists. The other nationalities are varied (Australia, Brazil, Canada, China, Germany, Italy, Japan, Korea, Mexico, Qatar and the United States).

The feedback from scientists who publish their data is generally very positive. In fact, we regularly see the same scientists publishing new datasets. Among the positive points, the help provided during the deposit and the speed of the service come up most often.

What are the strong points of SEANOE for you?

SEANOE has benefited from the *Archimer* project's experience in publishing. For example, the mechanisms for SEO, such as Google had never been implemented before in the systems managed by Sismer. The links with ORCID, the management of authors' affiliations, the links with article DOIs and the provision of download statistics to users are other examples of the contribution of the documentary world to this data publication project.

Conversely, the management of files of several tens of GB, advice on data formats and links with the EMODnet Ingestion project are all contributions made by the Sismer team in terms of data management.

Among the strengths of SEANOE, we would mention:

– availability and involvement of support during the deposit and after the publication of the dataset;

– the sustainability of the system based on a data center that has existed since 1984;

– overview of article citations;

– the version control system using fragmentation within the same DOI;

– the SEO mechanisms in Google;

– the richness of the automatic cross-linking network;

– the readability and richness of DOI landing pages.

Does SEANOE consider the FAIR principles?

In general, yes, we strive to comply with the FAIR recommendations in SEANOE. Note that the Sismer data center, which includes SEANOE, is *CoreTrustSeal*[11] certified. Sismer has also been accredited as a national oceanographic data center by the IODE program[12].

Here is a detailed description of SEANOE's compliance with the various FAIR principles[13].

Findability

F1. (Meta)data are assigned a globally unique and persistent identifier.

This is the case; each dataset published in SEANOE has a DOI.

F2. Data are described with rich metadata (defined by R1 below).

SEANOE imposes a list of mandatory metadata (title, authors, description, etc.) and proposes a set of optional metadata. We refuse to validate repositories that we consider insufficiently described (e.g. title not explicit, etc.). But the detail of the description of a dataset differs according to the authors.

F3. Metadata clearly and explicitly include the identifier of the data they describe.

The landing page of the dataset clearly presents the DOI in both the metadata and the suggested citation. In addition, some authors ask us to reserve a DOI for

---

11 Available at: https://www.coretrustseal.org/wp-content/uploads/2019/11/IFREMER-SISMER.pdf.

12 Available at: https://archimer.ifremer.fr/doc/00389/50015/50604.pdf.

13 Available at: https://www.go-fair.org/fair-principles/.

them before deposit so that they can add it to the data files. This is a practice we should encourage in the future.

F4. (Meta) data are registered or indexed in a searchable resource.

Datasets are accessible from the SEANOE front-office. The metadata are also stored in a structured way in schema.org format in the landing pages, which allows Google to index them in its Dataset Search tool. The metadata is also accessible through SEANOE's OAI-PMH engine. The SEANOE REST API should be made available on the Internet in a future release (although we haven't had any requests for this yet).

Accessibility

A1. (Meta)data are retrievable by their identifier using a standardized communications protocol.

Metadata and data are freely accessible without authentication using HTTPS links (with the exception of embargoed data which is accessible on demand).

A2. Metadata are accessible, even when the data are no longer available.

The SEANOE Terms of Use specify that it is forbidden to request the removal of a dataset already published. It is possible to update a dataset but not to remove it. In fact, we sometimes put a dataset back under embargo at the request of an author while they release a correction when an error is detected in their dataset.

Interoperability

I1. (Meta)data use a formal, accessible, shared and broadly applicable language for knowledge representation.

The metadata are accessible in JSON LD format from the landing pages and in Dublin Core format from the OAI-PMH engine.

I2. (Meta)data use vocabularies that follow FAIR principles.

This is something we need to improve. For example, by implementing the ability to list parameters using vocabulary lists defined in the SeaDatanet project.

13. (Meta)data include qualified references to other (meta)data.

It is possible to link the dataset to other resources, using:

– ORCIDs from the authors;

– NSCIs of geological samples;

– DOIs of related articles;

– DOIs of associated datasets.

All of these SEANOE DOI/PID resource pairs are updated in the DataCite record.

On the other hand, we do not disclose the nature of the association with articles and datasets. We only use the IsAssociatedTo role. Specifying the nature of the link could be an evolution in a future version.

Reusability

R1.1. (Meta)data are released with a clear and accessible data usage license.

Datasets in SEANOE are published under a CC license.

R1.2. (Meta)data are associated with detailed provenance.

This information is often available, but is scattered in the description and in the "Sensor metadata" field. We do not propose a specific metadata field to record this information.

R1.3. (Meta)data meet domain-relevant community standards.

The metadata collected by SEANOE is compatible with the DataCite and Dublin Core schema. The addition of fields (e.g. parameters) based on SeadataNet vocabulary lists is a medium-term project.

Is SEANOE linked to EOSC or does it plan to be?

SEANOE is an EOSC data management service[14]; SeaDataNet uses SEANOE to assist researchers in publishing their datasets.

---

14 Available at: https://marketplace.eosc-portal.eu/services/seadatanet-doi-minting-service.

What are the current and future challenges?

In terms of tools, the back-office interface is aging and will need to be redesigned in the medium term. But it is above all the relative weakness of the number of deposits that could be problematic in the long term. The main challenge for SEANOE is to attract more deposits. Reaching a critical mass of repositories, which is difficult to estimate, would ensure that SEANOE has sufficient visibility at the international level, which in turn would lead to new repositories.

How will you develop SEANOE?

The filing forms in SEANOE are aging. They are based on a system that was developed in 2009. The redesign of the SEANOE back-office is envisaged from 2021. The first impression given by a data repository back office is important. Indeed, when an author has to publish the data associated with an article, they have several hundreds of general or thematic repositories at their disposal. We sometimes notice scientists passing by and quickly filling in a few fields before abandoning their deposit. We assume that they spend a few tens of seconds on a first selection of repositories before choosing one to publish their data. When an author has experienced a repository system that suits them, they usually remain faithful to it for their next repositories. For SEANOE, the lack of immediate appeal of the current repository system is a drawback.

The development of an indexing system using a list of standardized vocabularies from the SeaDataNet project (e.g. list of measured parameters, country and contact point organizations, etc.) would allow the automation of data transfers between SEANOE and EMODnet Ingestion. The description of the data sets using standardized vocabularies is also a FAIR recommendation.

What will SEANOE look like in 5 or 10 years?

At this stage, SEANOE is correctly fulfilling the role it has been assigned: to provide a simple and fast publishing interface to publish a dataset and obtain a DOI so that it can be cited in an article. In 10 years, this need should continue to exist and will probably be even stronger due to the societal demand for open access publication of research data.

In 10 years, SEANOE should therefore be substantially the same as the current version. We hope that it will offer free access to a significant number of new data sets. The datasets published by SEANOE should also be part of a larger ecosystem of interconnected international resources.

6

Nakala – A Data Publishing Service

Stéphane POUYLLAU

CNRS – TGIR Huma-Num, Paris, France

Introduction

Since 2013, the TGIR (*Très Grande Infrastructure de Recherche*, Very Large Research Infrastructure) Huma-Num has offered the humanities and social sciences (HSS) community a data publication service called Nakala. On the basis of a shared foundation, allowing the storage and organization of files, Nakala centers around modular editorial tools, which make it possible for each research project to create its own web interface for access to data. Stéphane Pouyllau explains how this particular system meets the expectations of the HSS community in France and how it is adapting to the policies aimed at opening up research data.

How would you describe Nakala to people who are not familiar with Huma-Num's services?

Nakala (Figure 6.1) is an online service that allows us to deposit, document and organize documents, datasets and files in the field of human and social sciences in order to disseminate and publish them.

Interview conducted by Violaine REBOUILLAT, January 7, 2021.

For a color version of all the figures in this chapter, see www.iste.co.uk/schopfel/datasharing.zip.

Research Data Sharing and Valorization,
coordinated by Joachim SCHÖPFEL and Violaine REBOUILLAT. © ISTE Ltd 2022.

Would you use the term data repository to describe Nakala?

The problem with the term "data repository" is that it is not really understood in the humanities and social sciences. In HSS, the notion of "data" does not exist in a standardized way. It must be defined in relation to the historical practices of the discipline we are talking about and in connection with what we plan to "put into data". Above all, there are documents, there are files and there are databases with structured information in them. And a historian, a sociologist and a geologist would all define the word "data" differently. In this sense, it is a notion that is very much linked to the practice of researchers. In HSS, researchers have files. When they have digitized these files, when they start to organize and document them, they become documents. And then when they organize them into knowledge, they become databases (I am simplifying, but that is the basic premise).

Figure 6.1. *Nakala web interface*

So, when you talk to a political scientist or a sociologist or a historian about a data repository, they don't know what it is in theoretical terms. They don't have a stable mental image of what it is. If you tell them that it's a service that allows you to deposit or archive files, to document them and then to publish them, then they'll understand. Nakala is a service for publishing documents and datasets, which involves depositing files, documenting and organizing them in a way that makes sense to the scientist, and finally publishing these documents online.

How has Nakala evolved since the initial specifications were drawn up?

Nakala is a service that has evolved enormously at Huma-Num (Figure 6.2). We launched it in 2013 as a proof of concept, which was not intended to last. We had created an initial tool, which was not Nakala, but looked a bit like it, for a particular research project. It was a history project, for which we were asked to create a tool that would allow us to document files and make collections of documents. And by the time we had four or five research programs asking us for more or less the same thing, we decided to make it a service. And we called it Nakala, because we need to copy files to preserve them. Nakala means "copy", in the sense of making a copy, in Swahili.

The first version of Nakala was very basic: there was no graphical interface. It just allowed people to transfer files via FTP into directories and have little programs they could run on their computers to document the data.

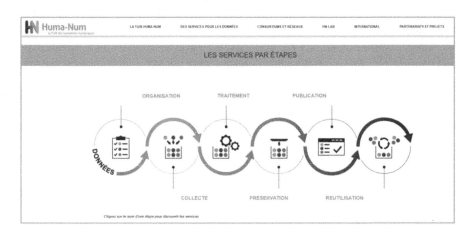

Figure 6.2. *Huma-Num services*

In 2015, we released a second version. It was a bit more organized: there was more metadata and tools; we had a small rudimentary GUI, APIs, etc. It was a tool that could be put under a DMS, for example, or under an interface that people developed themselves (with Nuxeo, for example).

The problem with Version 2 was that it was not accessible to isolated researchers who didn't have the computer skills or the financial means to have a working graphical interface developed. In 2019, we decided to rethink Nakala and come up with a third version with a real web interface, services, etc.

Could you tell us more about the latest version of Nakala?

This is a version we released in December 2020. It's a more complete version, featuring a document container, metadata, three access interfaces (a web interface, APIs, and a SPARQL Endpoint in RDF), DOIs to identify documents and datasets, and embedded data viewers to read images, Excel spreadsheets, etc.

What was behind the development of this latest version?

There were three motivations. The first motivation was that Version 2 was a bit obsolete in terms of technologies. At the time, we had chosen Java, which is a technology that is a little complicated to make work over time, a little slow, and it did not allow us to easily develop web interfaces. Also, we wanted to make Nakala and Isidore, the search engine for HSS that we have been developing since 2010, more compatible. So, we redeveloped Nakala with the same technologies that we had redeveloped Isidore with in 2018.

The second reason was that we wanted to add visualization functionalities to the documents deposited on Nakala so that we could do embedded visualization. Why did we do this? Because nowadays we're seeing that HSS journals are adamant that they want to be able to publish data papers and therefore have places to deposit the associated documents. For this, we needed to rework the data model, the connectors to the documents that are deposited, etc.

Finally, the third reason is linked to a trend that we have been observing over the past two or three years. For the past few years, we have seen the deployment of Dataverse more or less everywhere. When we did a market analysis, we realized that the institutions that make this choice often find themselves trapped in the tools they have chosen, because they don't master the code or because they are obliged to follow developments that they don't always need. The large international tools are very interesting, but only if your IT team is capable of doing updates, contributing to the tool, etc. There are also service providers, but the costs can quickly become quite high.

What we wanted was to be able to be autonomous. We believe that, as a national infrastructure, we must offer a data storage solution whose developments we control from A to Z so that we can build maximum complementarity with Isidore and the other Huma-Num services. In the past, we used Fedora (merged with DuraSpace in 2019), but it was oversized for our teams and difficult to optimize at our scale. It was a gas factory. So that was a lesson to us: we told ourselves we'd never do that again. We need to be masters of our code (while making it public and having developers create modules for us) in order to be able to respond to the needs of the humanities and social sciences.

Between Versions 2 and 3, we are moving from a system restricted to research projects to a more open system, also accessible to individual researchers. Why did you make this choice?

This was a request that came from researchers. In fact, all of 2019 was spent creating user panels. We had three panels. The first panel consisted of HSS researchers with no computer knowledge. They were asked to think about what kind of interface they would like to work with. We also did a lot of observations of how they worked. The second panel consisted of developers, engineers and documentalists, who were used to using Nakala and had often developed visualization tools on top of Nakala. Finally, the third panel came from our consortia[1] (Figure 6.3). This panel was formed spontaneously and consisted of the Nakala working group of the Huma-Num consortia. They had formed a small working group because they wanted to develop new features on Nakala. Their needs involved data visualization, corpus processing and data organization. In particular, they had been thinking about how to interface Nakala with existing tools. When they came to see us, we were starting to plan Version 3 of Nakala. So we decided to get them back to work.

Thanks to these three panels, we were able to draw up a set of specifications. Then we gave ourselves a year, starting in early 2020, to develop the new Nakala. Obviously, we were not able to deal with everything in the specifications, but these are things that we will continue to develop in the future, in particular within the

1 The Huma-Num infrastructure certifies disciplinary consortia, which bring together several research units and teams around common themes and objects for which they define shared digital procedures and standards (methods, tools, experience sharing).

framework of the Huma-Num Open Science (HNSO) program[2]. So Nakala is a service that has had a lot of input from the users. Making it possible for any researcher to deposit datasets on Nakala was what the first panel of researchers asked us for. When we showed them Version 2 of Nakala, they said: "Great, but it's not for me. I can't handle that: I don't know how to manipulate APIs. I don't have a team or developers. How do I do it?". We therefore decided to develop a graphical interface that would allow a researcher managing their own digital data to be autonomous while still complying with the FAIR principles.

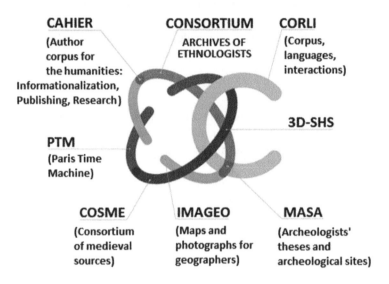

Figure 6.3. *Huma-Num labeled consortia (source: Huma-Num)*

In this new version, is the business model of Nakala still free for the user?

Yes, as a TGIR, Huma-Num receives funding from the Ministry of Higher Education, Research and Innovation. Our role is to offer the most open service possible and the easiest one to access, that is, with no direct financial impact on the projects of as many people as possible. This is the case for researchers in France, but it is obviously not the case for international collaborations. We have researchers and institutions abroad who ask us if they can use Nakala, and we are thinking about

2 The Huma-Num Open Science project is financed by the *Fonds National pour la Science Ouverte* (FNSO), initiated by the Ministry of Higher Education, Research and Innovation.

other models, because the Ministry's funding does not allow us (in terms of human resources and long-term operations) to cover the needs of researchers from foreign institutions. We can do it unofficially. We sometimes have collaborations, which are generally free of charge, but we are thinking about an economic model for outside France. It should also be noted that similar schemes exist elsewhere, especially in universities. Europe, with Zenodo and OpenAIRE, also offers schemes at the European Union level. Nowadays, it is mainly a question of proposing search and data discovery tools that encompass as many existing devices as possible. This is what we are doing with isidore.science, which provides access to data from Nakala, but also from Zenodo, Didomena, Dataverse, etc.

How many people are in charge of the development and maintenance of Nakala at Huma-Num?

Between the first and the third version of Nakala, the team evolved a lot. At the beginning, we were two people, Nicolas Larousse and myself. Then we started working with a service provider: Thomas Francart from the company Sparna. And, little by little, the team has grown. Today, it is the same team within Huma-Num, the ACCES division, which looks after Isidore and Nakala, under the direction of Laurent Capelli. There are currently five of them, including various service providers.

At present, Nakala can be considered as the reference repository for HSS in France. Is this a good thing or should there be other parallel initiatives to avoid a centralization effect?

That is a good question. It depends on what you call centralization. What is important, it seems to me, is that the scientific disciplines should be the masters and pilots of this kind of initiative. I have a very firm position on this: to have a Jacobin reading of the repositories, saying "there must be a single repository in France", in my opinion, makes no sense. On the other hand, it makes sense for historians to have a single repository in France, because it corresponds to a need of the community and that is what is important.

Researchers think more in terms of community than institution, I think, especially in France. Several of them told us: "What is important for me is that I show my community of historians, sociologists, anthropologists... that I have published my data". Centralization is interesting in that it allows us to build a national base, open to all. For example, anyone can obtain DOIs for the documents they have deposited on Nakala. It wouldn't make sense for researchers to go out and buy their DOIs individually – and that would be expensive. On the other hand, it makes sense to do it at the national level, for a community.

Nakala plays both the national card and the disciplinary card: it is a national repository for all of the HSS, which we then break down by discipline by involving our various scientific consortia, the *Maisons des Sciences de l'Homme*, the networks of partners abroad, etc. In archaeology, there are four or five platforms that are connected to Nakala, ArkéoGIS[3], for example. The same thing is happening in geography with Navigae[4], as well as in linguistics, history, etc. Our goal is to design services that researchers can use.

Is Nakala intended to serve as an interface for consulting datasets, for someone looking for data in the context of their research, for example?

Yes, increasingly so. That's something we didn't have in V2 that we put in place for V3. On the Nakala home page, you even have a little search engine. It's a search window for the data published on Nakala. As part of the HNSO2 program, we are going to work on the link with Isidore as well, which will allow for better indexing of metadata and full text in real time. Later on, we will editorialize this page a little to present the documents. We'll have tools so that we can exhibit them and other things like that. For example, Nakala will be used as a repository for archaeological documents related to the reconstruction of Notre-Dame Cathedral, so we can do something around that. The important thing is that the research communities help us with this. This is one of the roles of the HN Lab that I initiated with Huma-Num.

Have you used web analytics tools since the launch of V3 to calculate the number of views or downloads of the datasets deposited on Nakala?

We're going to look at that in late spring. Right now, we're finishing tightening the bolts on V3. We've migrated all the data. And mostly we're just overwhelmed with requests to open accounts at the moment. There has been a lot of word of mouth. The simplified graphical interface was very much expected by the HSS communities, who are very sensitive to it. Even though it is as automated as possible thanks to HumanID, the interface that centralizes the authentication of Huma-Num's Web services, we still need to study the requests on a scientific level.

---

3 Available at: https://arkeogis.org/.
4 Available at: https://www.navigae.fr.

How many datasets have been deposited on Nakala to date?

Today, there are about 300,000 datasets. We're going to do another count in the spring because we think there are more. In reality, there are probably a few more, because there are people who have probably put datasets within datasets while they were playing around with the original Nakala data model.

What do you mean by the term dataset? Does a dataset correspond to a file, a collection...?

No, they are neither files nor collections. A dataset is a scientifically coherent set of several files and metadata.

How many user accounts are there on Nakala?

Currently there are a little over 1,000 user accounts, although not all of them are used at the same time. In fact, user accounts are not very important for us. At Huma-Num, we work more at the level of the research program. There are research programs where there are only two people who have an account and there are research programs like Karnak (we host the data of the photo library of the Karnak temples in Egypt), where there are maybe 40 or 50 accounts.

What are the different depositor profiles?

There are researchers. There are information professionals from universities and research organizations (documentalists, librarians, archivists, computer scientists, etc.) who have developed a website or a scientific corpus. There are also external service providers (e.g. digitization or data processing service providers for a research project, who upload the digitized files directly into Nakala).

Why do depositors choose Nakala? Do you have any feedback on this subject?

Why do they choose Nakala? Probably because it's free, for one thing. That's a strong argument. It's an important factor. They also choose Nakala because, for many researchers in the HSS community, we appear to be neutral in relation to their university (which may have changed its name, for example). Since the beginning, we have been nakala.fr. And now that we offer DOIs, it's even more stable. So there is this argument that we are neutral with respect to the researcher's local environment. Many researchers also tell us: "I work on subjects that can be sensitive and I don't want my data to be used in another context by my employer. You are neutral, you are not scientists (even though we obviously are). You are a solution that is both public and not linked to the politics of my university, my laboratory or my research organization". And that's very important for a lot of people. This is something that we underestimated a bit at the beginning ourselves. We realized this with the panels. And also, it can be a bit complicated in universities, with information systems departments (ISDs) that regularly change their scope. I remember colleagues who came to see us because their ISD department had decided to stop looking after the databases they had created. They told us: "we don't know where to go, we don't have the money to pay for something at Gandi or OVH"[5]. So this is very important for people.

How do depositors use Nakala? Do some of them use it only for internal file documentation, without intending to publish the data afterwards?

No. Nakala is really made for dissemination in a FAIR framework. For people who simply need to store data, we have other tools that are not publication tools: ShareDocs, in particular, for working within a project. Nakala is reserved for FAIR principles: document your data, publish it, reuse it. Moreover, in the new Nakala, we have a storage system that is progressive in relation to the volume of data that researchers exhibit.

Initially, users are limited to 2 GB of storage space (Figure 6.4). They can store up to 2 GB of data without releasing it. Beyond 2 GB, they are obliged to "free" the data in order to increase their storage quota. It is a model that encourages the publication and dissemination of knowledge. This is central nowadays, including the fight against the improper dissemination of data through the use of the data's timestamps.

How does Nakala comply with the FAIR principles?

It conforms in many ways. In fact, at Huma-Num, we've been doing FAIR for a long time – long before it was called FAIR, in fact. So, we had to have a rethink in that context. Nakala allows us to achieve the first three letters quite easily: F, A and I. The F (findable) because we can search for data on Nakala and more widely in Isidore. We have also developed a complementarity between Isidore and Nakala,

---

5 Gandi.net and OVH are IT companies specialized in web hosting.

which have the same frames of reference and autosuggestions. The A (accessible) is obviously the DOIs, the short URLs and the fact that we deliver data in several types of formats. The I (interoperable) is identifiers, OAI-PMH, the RDF TripleStore and APIs.

Figure 6.4. *Deposit interface on Nakala and display mode of the storage space used*

However, the R (reusable) raises many questions. This is because R is not completely obvious in HSS – at least, there are several ways to understand it. It is true that we are able to develop FAIR metrics (we are currently implementing them on Nakala), but that is not what speaks to researchers. A lot of researchers in HSS don't like FAIR metrics, because they can also be used for evaluation. So, at Huma-Num, we try to rephrase the R by saying that reuse is not necessarily reuse by other people. It also involves reuse by the researchers themselves. We've seen a lot of researchers at Huma-Num who deposit data, forget about it for a while and then reuse it later. So we're trying to promote reuse for its own sake. The idea would be, for example, to have a temporal representation of the datasets that researchers have deposited on Nakala during research projects. This is important for doctoral students, for example, if they want to make a career out of it later.

Why are HSS researchers reluctant to use the R (reusable) aspect of the FAIR principles? Is it because they are skeptical about the possibility of reusing other researchers' data?

That's more or less the official reason. The real reason is: "it's my data". What we're trying to do at Huma-Num is not so much to tell people "You have to publish", but rather "If you don't publish, your data won't survive you. When you die, no one will know how to access your data or do anything with it, because only you designed the documentation. The best way to be known is to publish your data". This is a great catalyst. It's a bit of an "ego-vector". It's something we've been experimenting with in Isidore since 2018 with a feature that allows us to follow authors. We're presenting this feature as a scientific monitoring tool, which incidentally allows us to know what our colleagues are doing. It encourages people by putting them in a situation where they belong to an active community.

Tell us about your communication strategy: how do you encourage researchers to use Nakala? Do you even need to do so anymore, given the number of requests?

It's true that we have a lot of requests and that we are unfortunately not able to satisfy them all. First of all, because we are still a small team. Maybe we're doing it wrong? We can always do better. In any case, we still need to communicate about our services. For a service like Nakala, we need to develop real literacy, and this must be done through the URFIST (*Unité Régionale de Formation à l'Information Scientifique et Technique*) network, university library staff, etc. When I co-created Huma-Num in 2013, I suggested that we mix communication channels, because, to reach researchers, it is also important to reach them directly. This is the role of the Huma-Num Meetings or the Huma-Num Cafés, for example.

One thing that makes researchers in HSS unique is that they generally work alone. From time to time, they set up collective projects, but the individual dimension remains important. They are also researchers who don't tend to frequent university libraries or URFISTs for continuing education (even though this does exist, of course). So we have to reach these people. We have to reach them through other channels. We also have a lot of competition, in France, in the regions, in Europe and internationally. When we started out, we were the only ones, but now there are many other Nakala. It's quite complicated for researchers to find their way around. The proliferation is of great interest, but not necessarily to the researcher, who no longer knows where to deposit their data and doesn't always master the concepts of interoperability. It seems to me that it is important to build a disciplinary dimension in the use and management of data repositories. In terms of IT, there are no longer any real issues, as many tools are available. What counts is training and encouragement by peers and by practice.

In general, how do researchers wishing to deposit on Nakala become aware of this service?

The first source of knowledge is word of mouth in the communities. You'll have a colleague speaking to another at a conference who says something like: "I use Nakala. Don't you know it? I'll show you". The second channel is the *Maisons des Sciences de l'Homme*. In the *Maisons des Sciences de l'Homme*, there are representatives who talk about, present and train Nakala, Isidore and Huma-Num services. The third channel is the data services of university libraries and URFISTs, which are also active. This is perhaps also thanks to the few types of media we have been able to put online and to our Huma-Num Cafés. And then there is one last vector, which I have long underestimated, and that is Twitter. I became aware of this in 2018, when we released the new Isidore and realized that we had over 5,000 Twitter followers just on Isidore. We had more followers on the Twitter account than on the Isidore mailing list, where we only had 400 followers. From there, we stopped the mailing list and redirected everything to Twitter. Today, we have a Twitter account for Huma-Num, one for Isidore and one for Nakala. At first, we used the Isidore and Nakala accounts for support purposes. We answered users' questions such as "I can't connect" or "I can't find a document". With the passage of time, we added a little bit of information to them: we relay information from the Huma-Num account and we also announce new updates from Isidore and Nakala.

Is Nakala interconnected to other infrastructures at the national, European or international level?

There are several levels: there is the European level and the international level. At the European level, we are part of European infrastructures for HSS such as Digital Research Infrastructure for the Arts and Humanities (DARIAH) and Common Language Resources and Technology Infrastructure (CLARIN). Being in these infrastructures allows us to participate in H2020 programs with European partners. Four years ago, we participated in the PARTHENOS program[6], for example. At the moment, we are participating in Social Sciences and Humanities Open Cloud Community (SSHOC), which aims to design the participation of HSS digital services in the European Open Science Cloud (EOSC) for the countries participating in the project. We are also involved in the H2020 EOSC Pillar program or in TRIPLE which will use Isidore, OpenAIRE and other search engines to develop a European discovery tool.

At the international level, we have bilateral collaborations that we contract with grants, such as the Revue2.0 program, in which we participate in Canada. We have about seven collaborations of this type today, mainly in North and South America: in the United States, Canada, Argentina and Chile. We exchange with different structures, contracting various and varied partnerships with them according to specific needs. In Argentina, we are collaborating with the Conicet, which is very close to the CNRS and feeds Isidore with data repositories in the Spanish language used in South America. We have the same thing with Canada, with two or three American universities and with the Redalyc network for the large portal of Spanish-language journals in Latin America.

However, we are limited by the economic model we can create around our services. How do we finance international operations, when European H2020 funding is not really designed for this? There are services, particularly in Europe (Zenodo, OpenAIRE, etc.), which can be correspondents. However, this requires the involvement of research communities (in HSS, our consortia) and isn't solely steered institutionally. It is easy to say: "Take Zenodo". The question is rather: what capacity do we have to be active, within the HSS communities on a country basis, in evolving Zenodo?

What are the current and future challenges for Nakala? What needs will it have to meet?

There are four needs that Nakala will have to meet. The first need is volume: it will have to be able to hold very large volumes of data. Currently, we can accommodate several terabytes on a single account. For example, we have projects in archaeology. I'm thinking of the Karnak mission in Egypt or ArkéoGIS, which represents terabytes of archaeological images. Now, how do we go from 10 to 100 terabytes or 200 terabytes? Especially since, with tools like International Image Interoperability Framework (IIIF) and International Image Interoperability Framework Audio/Visual (IIIF AV), the need to process audiovisual data is developing very quickly. This is the first challenge.

---

6 Pooling Activities, Resources and Tools for Heritage E-research Networking, Optimization and Synergies.

The second challenge, which Nakala will have to meet, will be to integrate (including in a fine-tuned way) the needs of complex structuring of information, meeting the needs of the disciplines. Nakala was designed with a metadata base modeled on the extended Dublin Core. How do we proceed when a community arrives with a specialist vocabulary or a Cidoc-CRM[7] implementation? How do we integrate this type of vocabulary into Nakala? Technically, we know how to do it, that's not the problem. The problem is: how do we make it functional and meet the needs of the communities? How do we manage it scientifically? We are trying to get the consortia to work in this way, the objective being to converge vocabularies that are representative of archaeology or ethnology, for example. And here it is very important to work at the international level, not just at the French level.

There is a third challenge for the future: this is what I would call complementarity within infrastructures. We also call this "seamless". We have just won a joint *"Investissement d'Avenir"* (PIA3) grant with OpenEdition and Métopes for the coming years. We decided that OpenEdition, Métopes and Huma-Num should develop seamless services for researchers. In other words, you log in once and then you go from Isidore to Nakala, to Hypothèses, to Lodel, etc. The data are transferable from one to the other, without the researcher having to pass it through their computer. This is what we are doing today. We are doing it step by step, taking advantage of software rewrites to do so.

Finally, the fourth challenge is internationalization, that is, thinking about opening up our services internationally, or rather, thinking about their use in other countries, in other research systems, different from the one we have in France. There are obviously questions of the economic model, but there are also questions of adaptation to the needs of communities. Some international communities do not function at all like French communities. I'll use Canada as an example. In Canada, what counts is the university. A researcher refers to his university; he does not refer to a national data platform. He would rather have a repository in his university, for example. So, it's very different. You can't just slap on the French Jacobin model and make a nakala.ca like that. It won't work. In Canada, we need a Nakala for each university and different access portals. So, we have to think about how we adapt it internationally. This requires time and dialogue, along with scientific, documentary and IT collaboration. We have just created an agreement between Huma-Num and the CRIHN[8] of the University of Montreal to move forward in this area.

---

7 The CIDOC CRM is a conceptual semantic model specific to the cultural heritage domain.
8 *Centre de Recherche Interuniversitaire sur les Humanités Numériques* (Interuniversity Research Center on Digital Humanities).

The COMMONS project[9]

The *Consortium de moyens mutualisés pour des services et données ouvertes en SHS* (COMMONS), led by OpenEdition, Métopes and Huma-Num, is one of the winning projects resulting from the call for expressions of interest to "Structuring equipment for research: EquipEx+" of the *Programme d'investissements d'avenir* (PIA 3) program.

The aim of the *PIA3's Structuring Equipment for Research* or ESR/EquipEx+ initiative is to provide €224 million in support for new nationwide facilities aimed at scientific research, which promote French scientific leadership. This initiative also contributes to the digital transformation of research and innovation.

The COMMONS project brings together three leading French infrastructures in the field of Human and Social Sciences (HSS): OpenEdition, Métopes and Huma-Num.

The consortium partners have been working for years on the development of open science in HSS. The experience they have acquired enables them to offer the entire French and international HSS community equipment, tools and services that meet the needs of research processes.

The integrated environment of COMMONS covers the whole chain of knowledge production, from the constitution of data to its dissemination in the public sphere. By ensuring both access to publications and data and the linkage between publications and data, COMMONS makes a decisive contribution to improving the conditions of research production in HSS and promotes the discussion and comparison of research results, thus ensuring that scientific integrity is respected in the production and processing of data.

In this perspective, the OpenEdition, Huma-Num and Métopes infrastructures have joined forces to radically advance the dynamics of open science around the following three axes:

– the FAIRization of data;

– opening up publications and data;

– increasing the skills of producers and users.

Box 6.1. *The COMMONS project*

---

9 Extract from: "Equipex + : le projet COMMONS est soutenu par le Programme d'investissements d'avenir (PIA 3) *Blog d'Huma-Num et de ses consortiums*, February 4, 2021. Available at: https://humanum.hypotheses.org/6466.

What do you think Nakala will look like in 5 or 10 years? How will it be used by researchers?

I would say that there are several things. The first is that the same thing is happening today as was about 40 years ago. 40 years ago, it was important for a researcher in geography or history, for example, to pass on their data files to colleagues or when they published a reference book. This took the form of exchanging floppy disks and, later on, burned CD-ROMs. We used to exchange databases with FileMaker, for example. So, 40 years ago, it was already like today. There was already a "research data" problem. That was lost a bit in the 1990s. We became a little more theoretical in certain HSS disciplines. But the invention of the Web, in my opinion, has gradually revived the need for this.

I think that in 10 years it will be important for tools like Nakala to be able to talk to journal platforms. When I say "talk to", I don't just mean making data visible and embedded but allowing data inside the article to be processed and discussed. In this sense, the work conducted by Robert Vergnieux, who trained me in the 1990s, was rather pioneering (Vergnieux and Giligny 2016). That is, researchers will have access to articles, and datasets and processing tools will be integrated within these. They will be able to retrieve these datasets to test the hypotheses of the article or to process the data differently and thus arrive at other results that may be relevant or complementary to the initial results of the article. It is a kind of "GitHubization" of the scientific article. As a reference, I have all the articles that came out about 10 years ago around what was called "liquid information". We are moving from the sum of knowledge at a given moment to something much more fluid; in other words, from scientific information that is a bit fixed to more "liquid" information.

So, in 10 years, I think Nakala will have to respond to these kinds of developments. Why am I talking about this? Because it already exists. In the field of free software, it's called Jupyter Notebook, JupyterLab, etc. In the HN Lab, we are developing a third platform, which is called "Callisto" for the moment. It will be a Jupyter Notebook platform, connected to Nakala and probably to Isidore. It will be possible to write a data article in Callisto. The bibliography will be fed by Isidore and we will have the possibility of creating datasets on Nakala and processing them in Python in Callisto. For the moment, this is a functional proof of concept. If Huma-Num develops it further, it will offer inclusion with GPU and other computing resources in its server infrastructure. Tools such as Stylo[10], developed at the University of Montreal and being co-developed by us today, are also part of this

---

10 See the blog post: Stylo, a text editor for HSS available from Huma-Num (December 1, 2020). *The blog of Huma-Num and its consortia.* Available at: https://humanum.hypotheses. org/6311.

approach. It will be a "new" form of publication, where the data themself will become a publication like any other.

Among the developments, there is a second point, which will be to be able to manage the archiving of data deposited on Nakala in a very operational way, that is, to propose data archiving systems with very large variable geometry and several levels of use. Currently, once we have deposited your data at CINES, which is our operator for the archiving of HSS data, we no longer have control over it, and this is standard. But we know that this can be a problem for researchers. In the physical world of paper archives, this was accepted. But in the digital world, researchers want to be able to access and reuse their data. It's a bit different.

And then there is a third aspect that I think is important: the very high accessibility of our services and their robustness. In the next 10 years, we will have to work on the graphic use, user experience (UX) and user interface (UI) aspects of our platforms. This is essential, because the young researchers of today do not have the time to acquire computer skills as they are on short contracts. This means that we have to think about ergonomic interfaces that are accessible without any particular training. The services we develop must be stable for the end user in a world where technologies are evolving very quickly. This is a very important issue that we have been measuring with Isidore for the past 10 years and that we are seeing today with Nakala.

We are not the only ones to do so. Zenodo and OpenAIRE are doing it. The data visualization platform of the company MyScienceWork[11] also has a foothold in this. And there are others. This is going to become a major issue for the HSS. Tomorrow's data architects will not only have to think about metadata, but also about how metadata is designed to be used. This is an important point because, at the same time, we have a lot of trouble recruiting, because of the low salaries in the public sector (irrespective of status, incidentally). Even if we can increasingly mix with subcontracting, which certainly offers flexibility, this means that we must be able to carry out scientific, documentary and technological integration on short cycles (IT-wise), but with a long-term view to ensure the necessary stability for our users. This requires breaking out of the traditional structures of HSS research. It also requires knowing how to compose project teams, being very up to date in terms of monitoring and knowing how to work on the complementarities between the scientist in the ecosystem, the documentalist, the software engineer and the long-term vision.

---

11 Available at: https://www.mysciencework.com/.

References

Biston-Moulin, S. and Thiers, C. (2019). The Karnak project: A comprehensive edition of the largest ancient Egyptian temple. In *Crossing Experiences in Digital Epigraphy. From Practice to Discipline*, De Santis, A. and Rossi, I. (eds). De Gruyter Open Poland, Warsaw [Online]. Available at: https://doi.org/10.1515/9783110607208-013.

Dillaerts, H., Paganelli, C., Verlaet, L., Catherine, H. (2020). Usages et pratiques en lien avec les données de recherche. Une enquête menée auprès des chercheurs de l'université Paul-Valéry Montpellier 3. Research report, Université Paul-Valéry Montpellier 3 [Online]. Available at: https://halshs.archives-ouvertes.fr/halshs-02902710.

Van de Weghe, T., Bessagnet, M.N., Roose, P. (2018). Des données particulières : les données de la recherche en Sciences Humaines et Sociales. *34ème Conférence sur la Gestion de Données – Principes, Technologies et Applications (BDA 2018)*, October 22–26, Bucharest, Romania [Online]. Available at: https://hal.archives-ouvertes.fr/hal-01928548.

Vergnieux, R. and Giligny, F. (2016). Pour un usage raisonné de la 3D en archéologie. *Les nouvelles de l'archéologie*, 146 [Online]. Available at: https://doi.org/10.4000/nda.3818.

7

The National Repository Option

Louki-Géronimo Richou[1] and Joachim Schöpfel[2]
[1] Sénat, Paris, France
[2] University of Lille, Villeneuve d'Ascq, France

7.1. Introduction

To date (2020/2021), France does not have a research data repository with a national focus. This chapter analyzes the demand for this and describes the functionalities and characteristics of such a system. Some countries have established a repository like this, while others have not. Why have they chosen to do so? And what are the alternatives?

7.2. The concept

The first obvious need of researchers funded by a structure is visibility. This is not just the visibility of their results but also of their underlying data. A complementary need has arisen with the increasing computerization of underlying data: protecting and securing data. Each state is interested in the cultural influence, economic profitability, computer security and digital sovereignty of its research sector. Thus, the challenge of having a centralized state tool for the storage and use of data has arisen in various European countries. This is the whole idea of a "national repository". Research data repositories are online services that allow data sets to be deposited, described and preserved. They can also include analytical tools that open up greater or lesser possibilities for research with the same data, and even

Research Data Sharing and Valorization,
coordinated by Joachim Schöpfel and Violaine Rebouillat. © ISTE Ltd 2022.

tools for publication and dissemination. As of June 2020, there were more than 2,500 different research data repositories, listed in 80 countries[1].

Research data, at the request of national and European funders, but also increasingly at the request of the scientific communities themselves, must be FAIR (*Findable, Accessible, Interoperable* and *Reusable*). In addition, the second axis of the French National Plan for Open Science of July 2018 (MESRI 2018) includes the development of data repositories by theme or by discipline in its objectives.

However, the interests of the state and researchers, funding agencies and publishers, are often only partially convergent. This is why it is interesting to see how these interests combine or overlap in different ways in France, Germany, Italy or the Netherlands, to give rise to projects that are more or less focused on "visibility" and "security", for more or less active uses by scientific communities. These public tools face a challenge: finding an efficient and coordinated way to respond quickly to the needs of researchers when faced with competition from private tools.

The devices studied through the COPIST survey (catalogue of shared STI offerings, with the report of study No. 2: a multidisciplinary shared platform for storing, managing, reporting and sharing research data), carried out by the Ourouk consultancy for the CNRS in 2018 (CNRS 2018), take into account several criteria to sort out the existing repositories:

– national positioning;

– sharing among several institutions and organizations;

– multidisciplinarity;

– independence from specific equipment, procedures or infrastructure;

– interoperability;

– the connection with research projects and scientific publications.

Among the eight systems selected in the CNRS benchmark, several correspond to these criteria, such as *EASY* (DANS) in the Netherlands, *RADAR KIT* (Karlsruhe Institute of Technology) in Germany, *ASEP* (Academy of Sciences) in the Czech Republic and the *Federated Research Data Repository* (Canadian Association of Research Libraries) in Canada. Other systems have a more restricted scope, such as *MédiHAL* of the CNRS, *DIGITAL.CSIC* of the National Research Council in Spain or, more recently, *Edmond* of the Max Planck Gesellschaft in Germany, or, on the

1 According to Datacite's *re3data* directory; available at: https://www.re3data.org/.

contrary, a broader scope, with an international vocation, such as *Zenodo* (CERN), *Mendeley Data* (Elsevier) or even *Figshare* (Digital Science).

Despite all their differences, what these systems have in common is their excellence in terms of acceptance, use and quality of service, and the two-sided nature of a data platform, with services for researchers and producing institutions (including preservation), on the one hand, and services for "consumers" (including presentation and reuse), on the other hand.

A distinction must be made between security and reliability, where the former relates to the container and its completeness, and the latter relates to the content and its quality. "Curators" or collection managers exercise reliability control, while the repository only exercises security control. The responsibility for the content is attached to the researchers, in the same way that online sales platforms are not responsible for the quality of the products sold by the users, but only for the security of the transaction.

The concept of a national research data repository can thus be described, in simple terms, as a platform for depositing and sharing data produced in the course of research by scientific institutions and communities in France. Therefore, the characteristics of such a repository can be better identified by a negative definition – in other words, by determining what it is not.

– **No disciplinary limitation:** in 2014, the TGIR Huma-Num developed a pioneering repository called *NAKALA*. For all that, this repository remains disciplinary: the idea of the national repository is to go beyond any sectoral categorization to be interdisciplinary from the start.

– **No limitation for temporary storage:** the advantage of such a repository would lie in its role as a "backup", an archive of all research data. Indeed, science is built up incrementally, by revisiting everything that has been found. This incremental character justifies the structuring in a repository. We do not know what will be useful to science tomorrow; we must therefore provide ourselves with the means to preserve everything.

– **No storage silo:** however, it should not be seen as an inert archive, a simple library whose shelves are never browsed. On the other hand, the advantage of the national repository also lies in its ability to generate intelligent connections between data, and in the completeness of the accepted formats and extensions. As is often the case in science, new applications can be discovered fortuitously when enough different data and individual curiosities are activated simultaneously; this is serendipity. This serendipity, a concept usually valued in entrepreneurship, is therefore the second assumption on which the idea of the largest possible repository is based.

– **There is no single model or architecture:** the national repository is not a necessity; it is a political choice. Some countries have them, others do not. Italy, for example, does not have a shared, multidisciplinary repository with a national vocation, despite the initiative of the Ministry of the Environment for a "Network Nazionale Biodiversità", which has launched a data repository for its partners. In France, although there has been a broad trend toward decentralization and de-concentration since 2010, the subject of digital technology continues to be dealt with in a relatively Jacobin and centralized manner, as can be seen with the use of data relating to the Covid-19 health crisis.

– **No institutional pre-emption:** the national repository cannot be pre-empted by researchers from a single institution. The two requirements that follow from this at the economic level are that its system and funding must be centralized on the administrator's side, not the user's side. It is therefore a public system, which implies governance but also public investment, as it is not possible to make commercial profits.

7.3. The request

The decision for a major new facility must respond to a clearly expressed and identified request, whether scientific, industrial, technological and/or political. How do we define the request behind a national research data repository project? Here are a few elements.

The 2018 National Plan for Open Science (MESRI 2018) refers to the development of a "generic simple data hosting and dissemination service", where the attribute "generic" arguably describes the multidisciplinary and trans- or non-institutional character. While the term "dissemination" refers to the functionalities of exposure and publication for future reuse, the meaning of the term "hosting" remains unclear: acquisition and collection, deposit, aggregation of data and metadata, storage, or longer-term preservation? Similarly, the limitation to "simple data" remains vague; the Cat-OPIDoR and *re3data* repositories do not know this category of research data. Is it only data associated with journal articles (tables, illustrations)?

The feasibility study for this scheme, launched in February 2020 by the Committee for Open Science (CoSO)[2], specifies that it is indeed a repository

---

2 Feasibility study for a simple data repository service; available at: https://www. ouvrirlascience.fr/etude-de-faisabilite-pour-un-service-dentrepot-de-donnees-simples/.

service, which refers to features described in the first chapter of this book, such as persistent preservation, dissemination and compliance with the FAIR principles. Upstream, this service would explicitly address the institutions that produce research data (and not the researchers who hold the data), guaranteeing them control and management of "their" data, that is, "control of the intellectual property by its holders, licensing, curation, citability, etc.". It would be a public service, not outsourced or delegated, with a non-proprietary system (open source), without specifying the business model.

> The CoSO defines the request as follows (June 10, 2020): this study seeks to meet a need often expressed by researchers in the context of a funded project, namely to have a trusted tool, guaranteeing both the protection of their data and their visibility, to meet the requirements of their funding agency. It is not a question of replacing existing disciplinary repositories, whose quality work has made it possible to federate communities for many years. On the other hand, it seems necessary to offer other disciplines, which do not yet have tools, a suitable space in which to deposit their data.

As for the contents of this national repository, the objective remained vague at the time of the launch of the CoSO study in early 2020, but it has shifted from "simple data" to "long tail data", defined as research data from disciplines that have not been organized for a long time, that do not have repositories adapted to their needs and that must face the new requirements of research funders (European Commission, ANR, etc.) who have made (or will make) "FAIR data" an eligibility criterion for project responses. What about data from a project without specific funding? Also, nothing is said about research data produced on the fringes of, or outside French higher education and research institutions and organizations, by institutes and agencies attached to other ministries, by citizen science, associations, etc.

The results of the CNRS national COPIST survey (2016) demonstrate the need of many institutions – universities in particular – to have a national solution for archiving, reporting and sharing research data, including legal and ethical issues, for their less organized communities in this field. It is a sort of "scientific data cloud" by default, multidisciplinary, independent of the major instruments, and responding to all situations for which there is no specific solution. "It would be urgent to develop an offer for institutions for the storage and conservation [of research data], articulated with the service offer developed locally for dissemination".

In concrete terms, it would be a question of responding at a national level to the needs of (small) research communities that are often transdisciplinary, without any real reflection or practice concerning data management, which do not identify solutions, in France in particular, that correspond to their needs and to the demands made on them to exhibit their data. This response would include the needs of individual researchers. In relation to the identification of demand, three aspects seem important to us:

– **The target content:** what should (or can) be deposited in such a repository? A certain type of ("simple") data? Data from certain institutions or certain types of projects (ANR funding, etc.)? The Australian National Data Service, which had started preparing such a scheme from 2012, defines this target content as "unmanaged, disconnected, invisible and single-use data" (Treloar *et al.* 2012). A working group of the Research Data Alliance (RDA) described the long tail data in a negative way (Horstmann *et al.* 2017):

- no large, structured data sets;

- no unified and standardized formats defined and accepted by the discipline;

- no large equipment with common and well-understood workflows.

Furthermore, this RDA working group highlights the great diversity of this long tail data, "which varies radically in terms of source, discipline, size, subject, source, funding, format, longevity, location and complexity", and which "is less likely to meet common standards". As such, RDA cautions not to underestimate the importance of such data in terms of volume, through the use of attributes such as "small data", "legacy data" or "orphan data".

– **Structuring with the landscape:** given the "negative" definition of part of the request, the establishment of such a national scheme will always be in relation to or dependent on the concrete data services landscape of the country in question, with its specific infrastructures, organizations and disciplinary communities: the so-called research data ecosystem. This means that, on the one hand, a specific needs analysis is required, together with a study of the existing environment, discipline by discipline and organization by organization; on the other hand, there is no single model that can be transposed from one country or landscape (ecosystem) to another.

– **Temporality:** during a meeting in 2017, the CNRS Scientific and Technical Information correspondents (CorIST, 19 October 2017) noted that, for research data, "there are 100 infrastructures in France, but there is no standardized structure that would be an infrastructure by default that would disappear when all of the disciplines were provided for". Is a national system, with a certain development period (the preparation of *RADAR KIT* in Germany took 4 years), and above all, a lifespan of at least 5–10 years not immediately out of step with the dynamics of the research and data landscape? The success of commercial systems which, at an international level, are trying to meet comparable needs (*Mendeley Data*, *Figshare*, *etc.*) seems to show that this is possible, but on one condition: remaining flexible and responsive to changing needs and practices.

7.4. Features and services

Chapter 1 of this book describes the essential features of a research data repository, such as user identification and authentication, curation, data management and retrieval, and persistent archiving. It also lists the main requirements for making a data repository FAIR and trustworthy. It is therefore unnecessary to go into detail here on the functionalities that make up these systems in general; instead, we will focus on a few specific functionalities that are characteristic of a national data repository.

The feasibility study by Ourouk for the CNRS (CNRS 2018) attempted, based on a benchmark of operational platforms and those being set up, to classify the functionalities and services of a national system into three categories according to their degree of priority: must have, should have and could have (Figure 7.1).

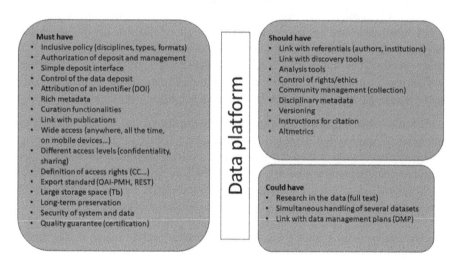

Must have
- Inclusive policy (disciplines, types, formats)
- Authorization of deposit and management
- Simple deposit interface
- Control of the data deposit
- Attribution of an identifier (DOI)
- Rich metadata
- Curation functionalities
- Link with publications
- Wide access (anywhere, all the time, on mobile devices...)
- Different access levels (confidentiality, sharing)
- Definition of access rights (CC...)
- Export standard (OAI-PMH, REST)
- Large storage space (Tb)
- Long-term preservation
- Security of system and data
- Quality guarantee (certification)

Data platform

Should have
- Link with referentials (authors, institutions)
- Link with discovery tools
- Analysis tools
- Control of rights/ethics
- Community management (collection)
- Disciplinary metadata
- Versioning
- Instructions for citation
- Altmetrics

Could have
- Research in the data (full text)
- Simultaneous handling of several datasets
- Link with data management plans (DMP)

Figure 7.1. *Prioritization of functionality for a national repository (CNRS 2018)*

Most of the functionalities – assigning a user ID, managing access levels and rights, long-term archiving, etc. – are essential for any type of repository, whether institutional, thematic, local, national or other. But given its central role in the national ecosystem, five elements seem particularly important for the development of a national repository:

1) Inclusive policy (disciplines, types, formats): insofar as the aim is to offer a "default" repository to all of a country's scientific communities, the operator must implement an open, broad, inclusive acquisition policy that is not very selective with regard to disciplines, data types and file formats. This policy must include other forms of acquisition, in addition to deposits by researchers, engineers and documentalists, in particular via the import of data from journal platforms.

2) Curation: to cope with the diversity of metadata, including a certain poverty due to "simple" repositories and the variety of flows and practices, the system must offer automatic and manual curation functionalities, in order to enrich and standardize the metadata.

3) Link to publications: since one of the reasons for the existence of such a repository is the need to have a place to deposit data related to articles, papers, chapters, etc., the repository must allow, facilitate and enhance this link as much as possible.

4) Quality guarantee (certification): to successfully launch such a new service, it must be made credible (i.e. "trustworthy"), in order to create confidence in French higher education and research communities, and facilitate their acceptance. The best way to do this is through international certification (*CoreTrustSeal*), which implies development according to the criteria of this CTS certificate (see Chapter 1), particularly for the security of the system, and the implementation of the necessary resources for certification, from the outset and over time.

5) Link with repositories (authors, institutions): for authentication and evaluation purposes, the system must be able to reduce or even eliminate any ambiguity concerning authors and institutions. For this purpose, the repository must be able to use international tools (CrossRef, ORCID, ISNI, WoS, etc.), but above all be connected to the various existing national repositories (HAL, SUDOC, RNSR, etc.) and those under development (Conditor, national file of entities, etc.).

Opening up to all higher education and research establishments makes another functionality more than desirable: the community management of data sets and collections deposited in the repository. This implies, on the one hand, the precise identification of the community in question (institution, project team, discipline, etc.) and, on the other hand, the ability to integrate and produce specific metadata profiles, according to the standards and uses of each community. As an example, the *Edmond* National Repository of the Max Planck Gesellschaft highlights the possibility of defining variable metadata profiles for flexible management.

The *Edmond Repository* is a research data publishing service. It is provided by the Max Planck Digital Library (MPDL). Therefore, the terms of use of the digital library are valid for *Edmond*. The *Edmond* service is free of charge for all employees of the Max Planck Gesellschaft and its scientific project partners, with a maximum of 1 GB storage for research project data. The purpose of putting content in *Edmond* is to publish it. However, the submitter can choose whether to publish the content immediately or make it solely available to specific users initially, with an embargo (i.e. a period of time during which the content is reserved for those specific users).

Another desirable feature is the possibility of interconnecting the repository with local research information systems, such as *RADAR* in Germany, for the purposes of monitoring and evaluating scientific production.

7.5. Architecture

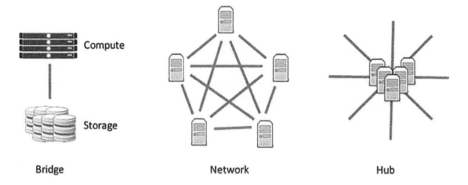

Figure 7.2. *Three types of data services (Xie and Fox 2017)*

There is no single architecture or model for implementing a national data repository. Based on a field study of data services in US universities, Xie and Fox (2017) described three types of arrangements, which are not necessarily mutually exclusive (Figure 7.2):

1) The bridge model: in this configuration, data storage, management and processing are clearly separated in different facilities.

2) The network model: this architecture has a much tighter integration between data storage, management and processing. This model uses many interconnected "nodes", each serving as both a storage and processing unit. These nodes replicate, balance and optimize both the storage and processing of data across interconnections.

3) The hub model: this service model continuously pulls live data from potentially many sources, undertakes the necessary processing and then disseminates the processed information to a potentially large number of data consumers.

The analysis of the devices with a national or international vocation and generic character reveals two main approaches, a centralized solution (*Figshare, Zenodo, EASY*) and a federated or distributed architecture (a "network", according to Goldstein (2017)). In some cases, the centralized solution separates the services of creation, analysis, processing and so on from the function of preservation and archiving ("bridge"), as is the case of the new architecture of the Dutch platform *EASY* with the "layer" *DataverseNL* for data management. However, to date, no national repository appears to have adopted a hub model.

Briefly, let us add other aspects related to the system architecture:

– Interconnection with local systems: a national repository must be able to communicate with local systems, particularly to feed monitoring and evaluation tools. This requires a high degree of interoperability with community standards and other systems (databases, catalogues, research information systems, etc.).

– Integration into European (international) infrastructures: the national repository must also integrate into the international landscape, primarily the European Open Science Cloud[3], and be able to communicate with other research data infrastructures at the international level. This requires compliance with the FAIR principles and again, a high degree of interoperability with international standards (DataCite format, etc.).

– The use of open-source software: the preference for open-source software and the refusal of proprietary software is widely shared by IT specialists in French higher education institutions and organizations. Therefore, the panel of the Ministry's feasibility study, within the framework of the CoSO, included only open-source software solutions, including *Dataverse* (Harvard) and *InvenioRDM* (CERN), which were part of the shortlist for the comparative analysis.

– The focus on security: earlier we mentioned the importance of certification. The analysis of current devices reveals how, for regulatory reasons (personal data, sensitive data, confidential data, etc.), but also to gain the trust of institutions and researchers, operators focus their efforts on guaranteeing the security of the device and the data deposited. This implies detailed communication on the measures taken (daily backups of data and metadata, distributed storage, control and verification of files, etc.).

---

3 EOSC, European Open Science Cloud; available at: https://www.eosc-portal.eu/.

7.6. Alternatives

The analysis of the situation in the major scientific countries confirms that there is no requirement for a national research data repository or a generic, interdisciplinary service with two levels of service, data archiving and data publishing. In some countries such a facility exists or is being developed, while others have not invested in this option. The option of a national repository is clearly a political choice, not a scientific necessity. And like any political choice, such an option must correspond to other criteria, such as timeliness, investment capacity, the mode of financing the operation over time, governance, the scope of public action and the existence of viable alternatives.

However, there is a real demand from French higher education and research bodies to have a service somewhere, where data related to publications, produced by small teams, communities or facilities that have not (yet) developed this kind of tool, can store and disseminate data. What are or would be the alternatives to developing a national repository? In the event that the option of a national repository is not chosen by the public authorities, several scenarios exist.

7.6.1. *Develop disciplinary and local solutions*

The first scenario is the persistence of community, disciplinary, public or private repositories, whose uses are regulated by the free circulation of users. Subsidiarity between certain repository or data providers may then develop.

The development of institutional and disciplinary data services is one of the priorities of the National Plan for Open Science. Public support to improve existing services and develop new services, notably through ANR or CoSO calls for projects, is conditioned by the implementation of a certain number of principles, notably the FAIR principles with their requirements for interoperability and standardization. Similarly, the Research Data Alliance (RDA) has issued recommendations to improve the management of long tail data at the level of institutions and scientific communities, in particular through the strengthening of interoperability, standards and consistency of schemes (Horstmann *et al.* 2017).

Such a strategy will undoubtedly contribute in the long run to a better disciplinary and institutional coverage, thus reducing the demand linked to the "long tail"; it will also reinforce the responsibility of institutions, organizations and infrastructures for the management of research data, and facilitate the integration of French tools in the international ecosystem (EOSC, etc.), provided that the FAIR principles are respected.

7.6.2. *Pooling through aggregation*

The second scenario is the aggregation of data around an associative structure, which functions in all respects like a repository except for funding and governance and therefore audience. It would primarily be an aggregation of metadata.

This scenario of an aggregator system is entirely compatible with the development of institutional, local and disciplinary repositories, among others. The advantage would be twofold: to create a "showcase" for research data in France, a single access portal, and limit the resources to be mobilized for implementation and operation. Such a system will probably also contribute to the implementation of the FAIR principles by the various communities and solutions. On the other hand, it will provide few answers to the issues of dissemination and preservation of research data, insofar as all these problems remain at the level of institutions and disciplines.

The most typical example of a tool that could support this scenario is *Dataverse*. Launched in 2006, the project actually started way back in 1999. Each user downloads the repository, where several virtual archives are then hosted, with data and metadata.

Assisting the archivist and giving credit and audience to the data importer or generator, *Dataverse* fulfills the core functions of the data repository. Beyond that, *Dataverse* is currently seeking to increase its capacity to manage sensitive data, on a large scale and in *streaming*, and increase contributions from the open-source development community. The Institute for Quantitative Social Science (IQSS) and Harvard (University Library and University Information Technology Center) are developing a partnership to form a *Harvard Dataverse*.

7.6.3. *Outsource the system to a service provider*

A number of institutions outsource their data repository to service providers, such as Elsevier (*Mendeley Data* with *Pure*) or Digital Science (*Figshare*). To date, the only example of a public–private partnership on a national scale seems to be the case of Swiss universities, which outsource part of their data management to a private foundation (SWITCH) that offers a cloud-based[4] archiving service. However, the use of a commercial solution seems unrealistic and politically unlikely in France, even if part of the long tail data from French research is already in *Figshare* and *Mendeley Data*.

---

4 SWITCHdrive; available at: https://www.switch.ch/drive/.

One could imagine a partial outsourcing of certain functionalities only. For example, once stored, the data can be enhanced by outsourcing. To do this, several protocols have been developed that could be integrated into the project for a national white label repository. If not, these innovations could at least serve as a source of inspiration.

7.6.4. Develop a partnership with a non-profit actor

A more acceptable scenario than a public–private partnership could be a partnership with a non-profit repository in another country or positioned at the European or international level. Creating a national collection (portal) in such an infrastructure could be a feasible alternative to the national repository. Currently, there would be at least two opportunities: *Zenodo* from CERN (with *InvenioRDM* software) and *RADAR* from FIZ Karlsruhe (with in-house *eSciDoc* software based on *Fedora*). *Zenodo* is an international archive, whose ethos is centered on the premise that such a repository cannot be national.

Another existing non-profitable system is *Dryad*, which also works with a DOI. Authors submit data to *Dryad* when the associated article is under review or has been accepted for publication, depending on the peer review status requested by the journal. They can also add data after an article has been published. *Dryad* emphasizes simplicity and interoperability, supported by a *Dublin Core* metadata application profile – although *Dryad*'s main servers are now located in North Carolina, with a UK mirror. It is not the authors, but the journals directly, that populate the core metadata. This notion of editorial collaboration is essential, and the national repository cannot be achieved without the tactical support of the major publishing groups.

Dryad emerged from a National Evolutionary Synthesis Center (NESCent) workshop in May 2007. Initial funding for *Dryad* was provided by the National Science Foundation (USA). The service began charging submission fees in September 2013, though it did not make a profit. The system is now run by a 12-member board of directors, elected by its members. Members may be independent journals, societies, publishers, research and educational institutions, libraries, funders or other organizations that support the mission. A member of the Data Observation Network for Earth (DataONE), *Dryad* announced a partnership in 2019 with *Zenodo*, aiming to develop best practices in terms of data curation.

A variation on this scenario could be the transformation of an existing platform – *HAL* of the CCSD, for example – into a national facility for the dissemination and curation of long-tail data. With 2,307,328 references and 732,438 scientific documents (June 2020), the multidisciplinary *HAL* open archive also has an international focus, with a strong emphasis on intellectual property and the need to cite authors. Indeed, the opening of data goes hand in hand with a great rigor in the tracing of sources to avoid any plagiarism or weakening of the reference. In other words, the massification of information should neither result in a protectionist reduction of its circulation, nor in a complete loss of its original traceability, but should be accompanied by tools to ensure its dissemination and protection. This observation opens the door to a state tool, the only tool capable of ensuring high levels of performance in these two key areas.

7.7. Perspectives

The reality of a national data repository is neither uniform nor obvious. It is a construction of scientific communities requiring real political will. The feasibility study of the Ministry of Higher Education, Research and Innovation proposes three scenarios for the implementation of a national service (Figure 7.3) and seems to favor a solution similar to the DataverseNO system operated at the Norwegian Arctic University in Trondheim[5], that is, a shared infrastructure with customizable repositories for each requesting institution (CoSO and Datactivist 2021). But independently of these results and the political decision in favor or not of a national research data repository in France, some questions remain.

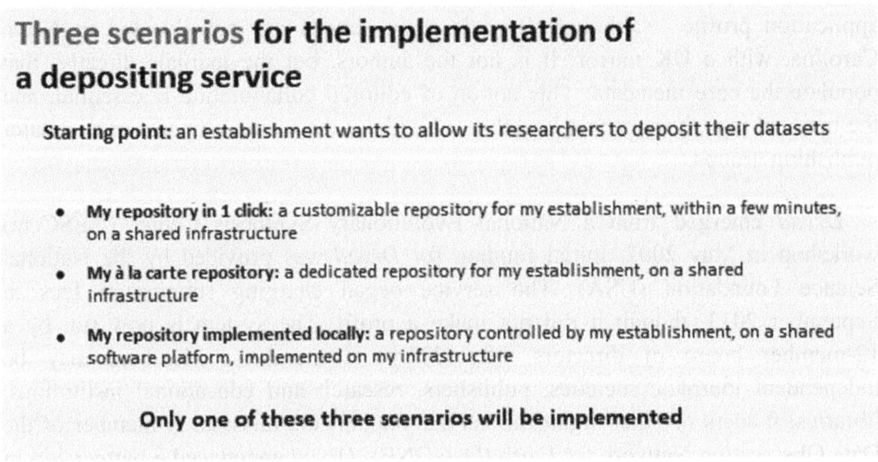

Three scenarios **for the implementation of a depositing service**

Starting point: an establishment wants to allow its researchers to deposit their datasets

- **My repository in 1 click:** a customizable repository for my establishment, within a few minutes, on a shared infrastructure
- **My à la carte repository:** a dedicated repository for my establishment, on a shared infrastructure
- **My repository implemented locally:** a repository controlled by my establishment, on a shared software platform, implemented on my infrastructure

Only one of these three scenarios will be implemented

Figure 7.3. *Different scenarios for a generic simple data hosting and dissemination service (CoSO and Datactivist 2021)*

---

5 DataverseNO, UiT The Arctic University of Norway; available at: https://dataverse.no/.

Governance: how can we find a balance between central steering and management by scientific communities and structures? How can we ensure that public responsibility remains complete and intact and, at the same time, set up, in a spirit of subsidiarity, local bodies with real authority and responsibility for ensuring the visibility and control of access and content and for enriching metadata, etc.? How can we avoid the risk of a new platform that is little known, little used and will quickly become obsolete?

Scalability: how can we avoid the rapid obsolescence of such a system? Information technologies, practices and uses, but also the competitive tools of the research data management sector are evolving rapidly. How can we guarantee a capacity for future investment? And how can we open up the system to the development of other tools and services, particularly in the strategic field of text and data mining, the semantic web and artificial intelligence?

Business model: the Research Data Alliance has published two reports on funding and business models for data repositories and other data services (Benedict *et al.* 2015; Dillo *et al.* 2016), the results of which show that there is no single model that would apply to all situations, and that sustainability requires a diversification of revenue and funding sources. What types of funding would be acceptable for a national repository: government subsidies, consortium funding or funding through agreements with higher education and research institutions and organizations, project funding, fee-based services, a cloud option (software as a service)? It is impossible to answer this question without knowing either the offer and quality of service, or the organization and governance of such a repository.

National sovereignty: the control of personal and health data seems to escape, at least partially, from the French State authorities. How can we ensure national sovereignty over research data? Is it necessary to ensure such sovereignty? What is the role of the state and its administrations, agencies and organizations? What is the function, in this context, of a national repository?

On a European scale, *the European Open Science Cloud* (EOSC), launched in 2018, gives a glimpse of the beginnings of a national repository, which would be the go-to in each member state. This project was proposed in 2016 by the European Commission as part of the Cloud program. Seventy national institutions then approved its convention. The idea is to go beyond the 1.7 million researchers to open up content to the economic intelligence of the 70 million professionals in science, technology, humanities and social sciences, and reduce fixed management costs through economies of scale. A logic of subsidiarity therefore exists, seeking to federate the systems among themselves. This subsidiarity would be even more effective if a centralizing European body could easily ensure that national repositories comply with the applicable Community law (e.g., for the protection of personal data), over and above national variations and regulations.

Common standards of presentation and formulation already existed before the invention of the printing press, to communicate the results of long and successful research. Printing, in order to allow for the uniform dissemination of the same equivalent content and to remove the randomness of individual interpretation, or "misreading", in other words, as much as possible, made it necessary for typographic standards to emerge, such as font, type height, serif impasto or column justification. The same dynamic conflict between particularity (diversity) and universality can be observed in bibliographic referencing standards. There is a wide variety of standards, depending on the country, the school, or even the publishing house, and the formulation of the results does not seem to be universal in the end, because there is competition between the producers of knowledge, who want to see their standard favored.

Standardization, both of the textual content as well as the ancillary content and metadata, is a major issue to enable the algorithms integrated into the repository to find the results of a query formulated by a user. The General Referential of Interoperability goes in the direction of this universalization, formalized by the order of April 20, 2016 (JORF No. 0095 of April 22, 2016). For the moment, it applies mainly to the administration, and there is a need for it; the state itself is not only a funder of research, with notably more than 40% of the 47 billion of the Plans Investissement Avenir financed via the Caisse des Dépôts and the BNP, but also a major customer of data from text and data mining (TDM). Today, the market is calling for specialists capable of deciphering the results of TDM and making them clear to a company director, and yet only three universities in France offer this specialization (Lyon 2, Paris 6 and Nice). The principle of universalism requires that each actor in a given field acts without losing sight of the transferability of the data to other fields, and its need to be clearly formulated to present a durability to the transaction over time.

If a national repository project were to be governed "from above", via an ad hoc agency or administrative directorate, its legitimacy vis-à-vis researchers would be weak. At the same time, having each discipline and institution represented along an "extended table" would not be effective in providing a solution that goes beyond the associative and private solutions that already exist.

Governance is therefore a particularly difficult issue, which coincides with the requirement of national sovereignty. Indeed, both the parentage of the protocols and algorithms used and the physical materiality of the servers supporting them, as well as the data, must be nationally owned. It is therefore necessary that each actor taking part in the decisions respects specific confidentiality and national priority clauses.

We can dream of a universal formulation, which would have the rigor of mathematics and the prospective intelligence of philosophical logic, which would allow us to put all the results in the same software system, thus exponentially increasing the volume and finesse of human knowledge!

The feasibility of a national repository depends ultimately on its social acceptability to the target audience. Researchers must modify their practices to take this interoperability into account, based on the repository and on good practices from their European neighbors. Without this prior adaptation of uses, no IT engineering can maximize the positive externalities of such a platform. In short, data are a question of use before being a technical answer.

7.8. Addendum

In early May 2021, the Ministry of Higher Education, Research and Innovation announced the launch of a national scheme consisting of five modules:

1) a research data repository (Dataverse) to be launched in March 2022;

2) a (meta)catalogue for the retrieval and harvesting of metadata from French research data (launch announced for 2024);

3) the establishment of a network of local data services to support researchers and institutions (2023);

4) the establishment of several thematic reference centers within research organizations and infrastructures;

5) the establishment of several resource centers attached to the national system as support services (allocation of DOIs, creation of research data management plans, etc.).

The creation of the national repository and the data catalogue has been entrusted to INRAE; both tools will initially be hosted by the CEA's Très Grand Centre de Calcul (TGCC). The final structure of this future national data center (joint service unit, foundation, scientific or public interest grouping, etc.) is yet to be determined, as well as its metadata scheme and business model.

7.9. References

Benedict, K., Best, M., Fyfe, S., Habtezion, S., Jacobs, C., Michener, W., Nativi, S., Pearlman, J., Powers, L., Turner, A. (2015). Sustainable business models for brokering middleware to support research interoperability. Report, Research Data Alliance, Harwell, Oxford [Online]. Available at: https://www.rd-alliance.org/group/brokering-ig-brokering-governance-wg/ outcomes/sustainable-business-models-brokering-middleware.

CNRS (2016). Mieux partager l'IST" – Enquête nationale conjointe auprès des universités, organismes et écoles d'ingénieurs sur le partage et la gestion des ressources d'IST. Report, CNRS DIST, Paris [Online]. Available at: https://www.science-ouverte.cnrs.fr/ dist-dossiers/.

CNRS (2018). Une plateforme mutualisée pluridisciplinaire de stockage, de gestion, de signalement et de partage de données de recherche. Etude COPIST 2. Report, CNRS DIST, Paris [Online]. Available at: https://adbu.fr/les-etudes-du-copist-catalogue-doffres-partagees-en-ist/.

CoSO – GT Service générique d'accueil et de diffusion de données simples et Datactivist (2021). Étude de faisabilité d'un service générique d'accueil et de diffusion des données simples. Synthèse de la phase 3 : ambitions du service et scénarios de mise en œuvre. Ministère de l'Enseignement supérieur, de la recherche et de l'innovation, Comité pour la science ouverte, Paris [Online]. Available at: https://www.ouvrirlascience.fr/etude-de-faisabilite-dun-service-generique-daccueil-et-de-diffusion-des-donnees-simples-ambitions-du-service-et-scenarios-de-mise-en-oeuvre/.

Dillo, I., Waard, A., Hodson, S. (2016). Income streams for data repositories. Report, Research Data Alliance, Harwell, Oxford.

Goldstein, S. (2017). The evolving landscape of federated research data infrastructures. Report, Knowledge Exchange, Bristol.

Horstmann, W., Nurnberger, A., Shearer, K., Wolski, M. (2017). Addressing the gaps: Recommendations for supporting the long tail of research data. Report, Research Data Alliance, Harwell Oxford.

MESRI (2018). Plan national pour la science ouverte. Ministère de l'Enseignement supérieur, de la recherche et de l'innovation, Paris [Online]. Available at: https://www.ouvrirlascience.fr/ plan-national-pour-la-science-ouverte/.

Treloar, A., Choudhury, S., Michener, W. (2012). Contrasting national research data strategies: Australia and the USA. In *Managing Research Data*, Pryor, G. (ed.). Facet Publishing, Croydon.

Xie, Z. and Fox, E.A. (2017). Advancing library cyberinfrastructure for big data sharing and reuse. *Information Services & Use*, 37(3), 319–323.

8

Comparative Study of National Research Services

Hugo Catherine

Institut de Recherche pour le Développement, France

8.1. Introduction

Several countries have established national infrastructures for the dissemination and preservation of research data. As part of a working group of the Committee for Open Science, Hugo Catherine has carried out a comparative study of these infrastructures in seven countries. What are the objectives, missions and governance methods of these infrastructures? What are their business models? What are the main features and services? This chapter provides a summary of this study.

8.2. Framework, objectives and scope of the study

In line with one of the development axes of the national plan for open science, which aims to "structure and open research data" (MESRI 2018), the Ministry of Higher Education, Research and Innovation (*Ministère de l'Enseignement Supérieur, de la Recherche et de l'Innovation* – MESRI) attempted to "design a generic service for research data for which existing or future disciplinary repositories are not a suitable solution".

To this end, in 2019 the Committee for Open Science (CoSo – *Comité pour la science ouverte*) entrusted a "feasibility study of a generic data hosting and

For a color version of all the figures in this chapter, see www.iste.co.uk/schopfel/datasharing.zip.

Research Data Sharing and Valorization,
coordinated by Joachim Schöpfel and Violaine Rebouillat. © ISTE Ltd 2022.

dissemination service" to a team of experts led by Jean-Christophe Desconnets (IRD – *Institut de recherche pour le développement*), accompanied by the Datactivist society.

As part of this work, this study aimed to enrich the team's reflection by drawing up an inventory of various national data services. The report of the study (Catherine 2020) was delivered in November 2020. This is in addition to the two other deliverables produced by the working group, which include a section on the collection of user needs (CoSO 2020) and a synthesis of the service ambitions and implementation scenarios (CoSO 2021).

Carried out with the assistance of Jean-Christophe Desconnets and Pascal Aventurier, this work was conducted from January 2020 to October 2020 and focused on the use of data collected from bibliographic research. The selection of devices was oriented toward the following seven service infrastructures:

– Australian Research Data Commons (ARDC), Australia;

– Dataverse Norway (DNO), Norway;

– Dutch Data Archiving & Networked Services (DANS), the Netherlands;

– Federal Research Data Repository (FRDR), Canada;

– JISC Open Research Hub (JORH), United Kingdom;

– Research Data Repository (RADAR), Germany;

– UK Data Service (UKDS), United Kingdom.

Discussions with stakeholders from all the different departments helped to complete and clarify the information gathered from bibliographic research.

8.3. Recent national schemes

With the exception of the UKDS, all of the schemes selected for this study are aimed at developing generic data services on a national scale. The example of the UKDS seemed interesting to analyze because, although the core target of this British infrastructure remains data from the humanities and social sciences, it also aims to support and facilitate multidisciplinary research.

Furthermore, created in 2012, the UKDS offer has been progressively structured around a historical pillar, the United Kingdom Data Archive, which has been building, hosting and preserving a national data collection since 1968. It seemed to be a good example because it contrasts with the very recent nature of the other systems we chose. Indeed, apart from the Dutch DANS network, which was formed between 2005 and 2014, the national services remain initiatives that have developed in recent years: ARDC (2017), DNO (2017), RADAR (2017), JORH (2019) and DFDR (2021). Such initiatives may remain at the project stage, as may be the case for the National Data Services (USA) and the National Institute of Health Data Commons (USA), for which the pilot projects conducted until 2018 did not result in the development of a national service.

8.4. Missions and objectives

The objective of all the services studied is to facilitate access to data. This common purpose pursues, above all, scientific aims: to promote scientific activity and the quality of academic work, which is a strategic axis for the ARDC, the DANS, DNO, RADAR and JORH networks.

The mission of these services may also be to provide an operational framework to meet the contractual requirements of funding agencies for open data (ARDC, DANS, DFDR and JORH).

As the custodian of the UK's largest collection of social, economic and demographic data, the UKDS is committed to ensuring that access to these data is secure and sustainable.

Perhaps one of the most ambitious schemes is the ARDC, which aims to provide access to a national digital infrastructure consisting of platforms, software tools, collections of high strategic value data and a national network of expertise. The Australian infrastructure claims to "transform the national digital infrastructure through its support of leading-edge research and innovation"[1]. The focus is not only on the contribution to research activities but also on the ability of this new ecosystem to generate economic value.

For the ARDC, as for the majority of infrastructures, their role is also to accompany institutions in the implementation of services related to data management. Acculturation to FAIR practices (Wilkinson *et al.* 2016), which aim to make data findable, accessible, interoperable and reusable, is a major focus. More than half of the services surveyed play the role of national coordinator on these issues (ARDC, DANS, DFDR, JORH).

---

1 Available at: https://ardc.edu.au/our-strategy/.

In this context, the proposed service offer is structured around a triple objective shared by all the systems studied:

– to propose one or more technical solutions to deposit and publish research data;

– to offer a sustainable archiving service;

– to support all the actors involved, particularly researchers and research support services.

At the top of the list of audiences targeted by these different services are obviously researchers, lecturers and doctoral students, as well as their institutions, for whom each scheme aims to provide solutions. It should be noted that political actors are clearly identified as target audiences for more than half of the schemes (ARDC, DANS, DFDR, JORH, UKDS), as are students (DANS, DFDR, RADAR, UKDS). To a lesser extent, economic actors are also among the targeted users. Indeed, the ARDC, DANS and UKDS aim to develop tools and services that promote technological innovation activities, carried out by actors in the economic and industrial sector.

8.5. History of the devices

Looking at the genesis of these services, it is interesting to note that there are three different patterns.

First of all, some of the national mechanisms studied were created by building on pre-existing structures. This is the case of the ARDC, born in 2018 from the merger of the following three infrastructures:

– the Australian National Data Service (ANDS), to develop a data management culture;

– National eResearch Collaboration Tools and Resources (NECTAR), which aims to foster the development of collaborative tools and services; and

– Research Data Services (RDS), whose mission is to provide data storage and access services.

Similarly, the DANS network, created in 2005, has gradually structured itself by integrating the Easy archiving service and the Narcis discovery tool in 2011, and then initiated the creation of Dataverse Nederland in 2014.

For its part, UKDS has built its service offering around a historical pillar: the United Kingdom Data Archive, the UK's largest collection of digital humanities and social science data. Established in 1968, UKDA became part of UKDS in the year the national service was launched (2012).

In addition, several devices have emerged from pilot projects. Thus, the scope and functionalities of the Canadian DFDR are the result of several pilot projects conducted since 2014 by the Portage Network, Compute Canada and the Canadian Association of Research Libraries. The same is true for JORH and RADAR, which are, respectively, the result of the "Research Data Shared Service" project conducted between 2015 and 2018, and a project piloted by the Deutsche Forschungsgemeinschaft, the national funding agency.

The creation of a national data service can also be initiated by the successful experience of an institution. This is the case for DNO, the development and hosting of which was entrusted in 2017 to the University of Tromsø, an institution that had already established an institutional Dataverse repository a few years earlier.

8.6. Governance arrangements

It is interesting to note that national funding agencies are behind several national schemes. This is the case for the Commonwealth Scientific and Industrial Research Organisation (CSIRO) for the ARDC, the Nederlandse Organisatie voor Wetenschappelijk (NWO) which initiated the development of the DANS network with the Dutch Academy of Sciences (KNAW), or the Economic and Social Research Council (ESRC) whose contractual agreement with the University of Essex enabled the development of the UKDS. These funding bodies participate in the boards of the various national data services and in the definition and monitoring of strategic objectives within the framework of 5-year plans. They are joined by representatives of the institutional partners (universities, research institutions, etc.), the Dutch Academy of Sciences for DANS, and in the case of the ARDC, by actors from the economic sector.

In the case of both DNO and RADAR, the strategic objectives are defined and planned by the operating institutions, namely the University of Tromsø and FIZ Karlsruhe-Leibniz Institute for Information Infrastructure, respectively.

The direction and development of ex-JORH services is decided by the Joint Information Systems Committee (JISC), which includes representatives from universities, colleges and digital service providers along with JISC representatives.

On the DFDR side, the Steering Committee includes representatives from the Canadian Association of Research Libraries (CARL), the Portage Network, the

Computing Federation of Canada, the DFDR Development Team, the New Digital Research Infrastructure Organization (NDRIO) and the Chair of the User Advisory Committee.

Each of the schemes proposes one or more advisory committees on which all the partner institutions are represented and whose decisive role is recalled in the framework documents.

8.7. Business models

In order to foster their sustainability, the OECD (2017) report "Business Models for Sustainable Research Data Repositories" recommends that data repositories rely on multiple sources of funding. This is the case for all the schemes studied, which rely on at least two separate sources of funding from the following:

– structural funding;

– funding and support from the host institution;

– membership fees for member institutions;

– storage costs;

– data access fees;

– project funding;

– contracts with partners.

Most of them rely on structural funding from a central administration such as the Ministry of Research or the national funding agency, the terms of which are determined in multi-annual contracts. Both DNO and RADAR rely on financial support from their host institutions: the University of Tromsø for DNO, and the *Fachinformationszentrum Karlsruhe* for RADAR.

Apart from the ARDC, which offers all of its services free of charge to Australian academic institutions, the other facilities require a financial contribution from the user institutions. A recurring model contract between the national service and the partner institution requires that the latter pays a fee for annual membership as well as storage fees (DANS, DNO, RADAR).

For its part, the business model of the service offered by JISC (formerly JORH) is essentially based on subscription fees.

In line with the objectives pursued in terms of data openness, none of the schemes charge for access to the data.

8.8. Service offer

When linking the services offered to the different stages of the data lifecycle, it is interesting to note that no single scheme covers the whole cycle. However, the UKDS offers a very wide range of services that cover all stages from data processing to data reuse.

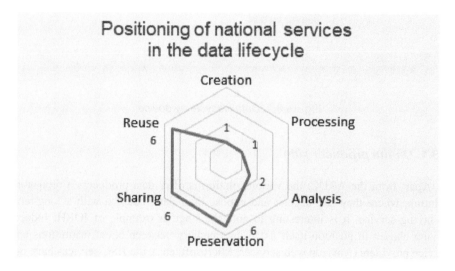

Figure 8.1. *National data and service lifecycle (data aggregation)*

Almost all national services position their service offering on the left side of the cycle (Figure 8.1): preservation, sharing and reuse. Only the ARDC has chosen to provide technical solutions that meet the needs of the first stages of the cycle: creation, processing and analysis (Figure 8.2).

The study has chosen to propose an analysis of the services offered by type of user:

– data producers;

– data users;

– expertise and assistance networks.

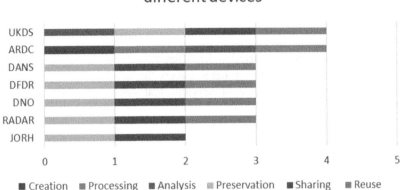

Figure 8.2. *Data lifecycle by device*

8.8.1. *On the producer side*

Apart from the ARDC, the various platforms offer data producers a repository solution, where they can deposit and expose their data, coupled with a long-term archiving service. It is interesting to note the singular example of JORH. Indeed, having chosen to position itself as an intermediary between client institutions and service providers (Amazon web services, Microsoft, etc.), the JISC services have not developed a national repository but direct each institution to external technical solutions.

At the heart of all the platforms' missions, data management assistance takes the form of support services and tools. For example, the DANS network offers a wide range of mediation actions, from tutorials to personalized consultations. The RDM Toolkit developed by JISC is characterized by developing targeted information according to the user category (researchers, research support services) and according to the user's institution (referral to the dedicated pages of the institution concerned).

One of the major objectives of this support is to facilitate the adoption of FAIR principles by data producers. For this purpose, the ARDC offers Australian researchers the FAIR Self Assessment Tool, which enables them to assess the fairness of their data sets. Similarly, as part of the European FAIRsFAIR project, the DANS network has participated in the development of FAIR Aware.

In the same way, all the platforms allow researchers to assign a permanent digital identifier to their data sets. This identifier most often takes the form of a digital object identifier (DOI). The ARDC, which also proposes the attribution of handle identifiers, provides researchers with a decision tree[2].

All of the platforms are committed to ensuring that curation work is carried out on the data sets submitted before they are put online, an activity that is handled by the institutions' support services.

While the "deposit-archiving-support" system is offered by most national infrastructures, some of them are characterized by offering other types of service:

– the ARDC and the German RADAR service provide secure storage solutions for researchers, coupled with computing services in the case of the Australian Nectar Research Cloud;

– RADAR has developed a data access service for scientific reviewers;

– in order to fulfill their mission of supporting and structuring their respective national ecosystems, both the ARDC and the DANS network provide financial support for the development of projects or tools (small data projects, research platforms[3]).

8.8.2. *On the user side*

As seen above, one of the common objectives of these national services is to provide access to an optimum amount of research data produced on a national scale. In this respect, with the exception of JORH, all the services have developed a single access point to data produced by different institutions. This service can take the form of an internal discovery tool (DNO, RADAR) or a federated search engine harvesting external sources (ARDC, DANS, DFDR, UKDS).

For example, the NARCIS search engine, developed by DANS, provides access to a wide range of information: data, publications, institutions, researchers, projects, etc. (Figure 8.3). In order to link researchers and their institutions to all of their productions, DANS participates in the FREYA-PID project, whose objective is to connect the various identifiers, in particular the DOI and ORCID identifiers.

A search engine that federates access to data from more than 100 institutions, Research Data Australia brings together data, software, projects and information

2 ARDC (n/a). Digital Object Identifiers (DOIs): A pathfinder for data managers [Online]. Available at: https://ardc.edu.au/wp-content/uploads/2019/05/DOIs_decision_tree.pdf.
3 Available at: https://ardc.edu.au/services/research-platforms/.

about researchers (Figure 8.4). The extensive editorial work produced around this interface allows users to search by thematic collection, to be directed to suggested data sets on similar topics, or to tools and services related to their research.

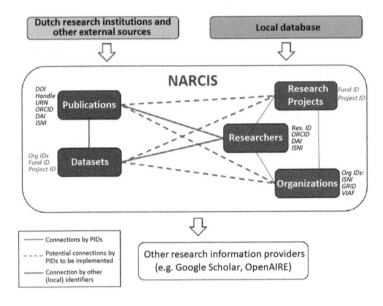

Figure 8.3. *Narcis PID graph*

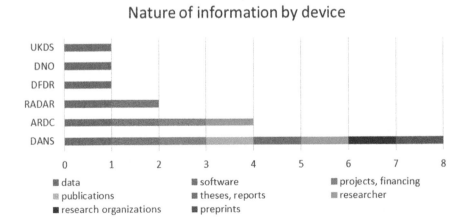

Figure 8.4. *Nature of information by access portal*

While each search engine essentially refers to data from academic actors, it should be noted that some portals harvest resources from other administrative sectors or even private operators (Figure 8.5).

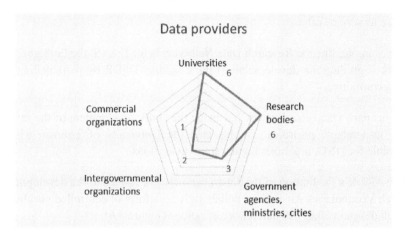

Figure 8.5. *Federated data sources (aggregate data)*

8.8.3. *Computing, analysis and collaboration services*

As mentioned above, the ARDC differentiates itself from other systems because of the Nectar cloud service, which provides access to various computing platforms and 15 virtual laboratories. Each tool is specific to the uses and needs of a defined academic community.

The UKDS also hosts several data access and analysis interfaces, such as Nesstar, which covers key survey data sets, and Qualibank, which covers qualitative data sets.

8.8.4. *Access services for sensitive data*

Supporting users and applicants in managing sensitive data is at the heart of the UKDS's mission. It is the only organization in this study to have developed a service dedicated to this issue: the UK Data Service Secure Lab. This offers users access to this sensitive data via a secure room or allows them to consult it remotely. This second option assumes that the user has received "Five safes" training[4] from the UKDS.

---

4 Available at: https://www.ukdataservice.ac.uk/manage-data/legal-ethical/access-control/five-safes.

8.8.5. *Networks of expertise and support*

In view of the issues related to data curation, each national service is involved in national networks that bring together experts in data management to define and structure its service offer.

For example, like the Research Data Netherlands for DANS, the Portage Canada Network is guiding the development of the Canadian DFDR by participating in its steering committee.

For its part, Dataverse Norway has made the skills development of the referents one of its strategic priorities. To this end, the University of Tromsø, which is responsible for DNO, organizes regular training sessions.

The ARDC's facilitation of the Australian network has led to the development of Research Vocabularies Australia, a collaborative platform of controlled vocabularies that includes more than 150 partner organizations (Figure 8.6).

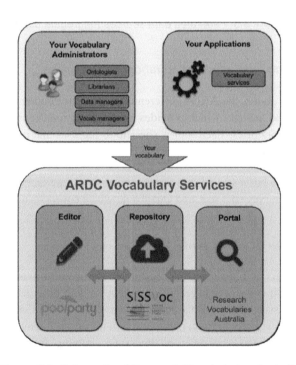

Figure 8.6. *Schematic of Research Vocabularies Australia*

In summary, a pattern emerges from the review of services that the systems are converging toward. Indeed, most of them (UKDS, RADAR, DFDR, DNO, DANS) offer at least the following range of services: data repository and identifier assignment, permanent archiving, data management support and a discovery tool (Figure 8.7).

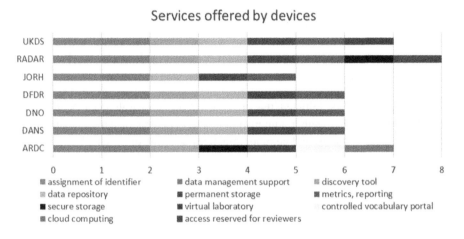

Figure 8.7. *Inventory of services offered by each device*

8.9. Co-constructed services

The first point of interest shared by all the players interviewed is the ability of each platform to fit into the national data ecosystem, to find its place among the pre-existing infrastructures and services. All of the services covered by this study have been built and continue to evolve through ongoing collaboration with all of the partners.

The first stakeholders to be approached were the institutional partners, including universities and research institutions, who were consulted from the beginning of the project. In order to gather information on their needs, more than 70 UK universities were involved in the Research Data Shared Service pilot project that prefigured JORH between 2016 and 2019. Similarly, the DFDR was born out of the synthesis of numerous pilot projects conducted since 2014 by the Portage Network and the Compute Canada infrastructure to assess the feasibility of national services for research data management.

Once the system is in production, the partner institutions are involved in its governance; most often, they are represented on the advisory committees (DNO, RADAR, NARCIS, EASY, Dataverse NL), bodies that play a decisive role in the development of the platforms. This collaboration can also take the form of partnership agreements between the institutions and the national service, as in the case of the DANS network.

In addition to collaborating with institutions, national services also participate in national and international networks. For example, DNO has partnered with the National Library of Norway and the Norwegian Centre for Research Data to form a community of practice and reflection on digital archiving activities.

For its part, DANS initiated the creation of the Research Data Netherlands network, which brings together administrators and managers of data repositories to exchange and converge around common practices in terms of sustainable archiving of data.

Just like the issues related to interoperability between infrastructures, many questions are discussed at the international level. It is, therefore, important for national data services to be part of this process, both to keep up to date with the latest developments and to participate in strategic orientations. For example, the European FAIRsFAIR project is coordinated by DANS and involves UKDS, through UKDA, as a partner, and DNO and DFDR as test repositories. The most active national service on an international scale is undoubtedly the DANS network, which is involved in the governance of numerous organizations: European Open Science Cloud, Council of European Social Sciences Data Archives, Datacite, Dariah-EU, CoreTrustSeal, euroCRIS, Research Data Alliance Europe, etc.

Finally, consultation with the research community is essential for the development of needs-based service offerings. This dialog can take the form of user surveys (DANS) to evaluate existing services. It can also take place upstream of service design, as in the case of the JORH pilot project which mobilized researchers to test and validate the acceptance cycles associated with service development (Fripp 2019). In the case of UKDS, researchers are involved in the development of tools such as the Data Management Costing Tool[5] or QAMyData, both to gather their needs and to participate in the testing phases before the deployment of the services.

---

5 UK Data Service (2013). Data management costing tool. UK Data Archive, University of Essex [Online]. Available at: https://www.ukdataservice.ac.uk/media/622368/costingtool.pdf.

8.10. Key success factors

While the collaborative principle is an essential *modus operandi* for encouraging the commitment of the actors concerned, this bibliographic work has identified other important points that condition the sustainable appropriation of a national data service by users, starting with the reliability of technical solutions.

Indeed, the commitment of institutions and researchers depends on the guarantees provided by the national service in terms of the durability of data access. As a result, most of the systems studied have CoreTrustSeal certification (DANS, DNO, UKDA, and RADAR are in the process of being certified). DANS provides even more guarantees, as it is Data Seal of Approval (DSA) and Nestor Seal DIN 31644 certified. In the case of the UKDS and JORH, this willingness for certification may also relate to information security (ISO 27001). In addition to certifying their own repositories, several departments are involved in organizations that aim to structure the repository landscape around best practices, such as the UKDS (member of the Digital Preservation Coalition, vice-president of CoreTrustSeal), DANS (member of the CoreTrustSeal Board of Directors) and the ARDC (Trusted Data Repositories Community of Practices).

In addition, in order to encourage and maintain the financial commitment of partner institutions, all of the systems place a strong emphasis on the evaluation of services, starting with public access to consultation and download indicators. The DANS network places the use of its services at the heart of its strategy by orienting its roadmap around ambitious objectives: +50% use over the period 2015–2020. For DNO, the evaluation also focuses on the implementation of FAIR principles (Conzett 2020). The reporting service is one of the key arguments of the JORH offer, which provides institutions with access to internal and third-party data.

Finally, like JORH and its motto *"Save institutions time and money as a national, fully managed shared service"*, several national services use the financial argument to convince institutions to subscribe. The research conducted for the study did not provide evidence of economies of scale for the services studied. However, the 2012 report "Economic impact evaluation of the economic and social data service", conducted before the opening of the UKDS, estimated the economic value of the national service to be five times its operational costs, and the returns on investment from hosted data to be 10 times the costs.

In conclusion, given the very dynamic context that characterizes the research data ecosystem, it seems crucial to most of the actors interviewed to opt for technical solutions shared by the international community, so as not to be held captive by "in-house platforms". For the same reasons, developing and running a national service also implies adopting a pragmatic position based on a continuous evaluation of the services or even on an agile approach, as in the case of JORH, in order to adapt its service offer. This is notably the case for the German RADAR service, which was initially designed as a "long tail" data service for institutions, but has been participating in the National Research Data Infrastructure (NFDI) since autumn 2020. The NFDI brings together disciplinary repositories that direct researchers to RADAR's services when there is no suitable solution for their data sets.

In terms of data management, the major issue for institutions is the cost of curation activities. In this context, the role of coordinator and network facilitator played by national services aims to encourage pooling to reduce the "data burden".

Furthermore, in order to respond to competition from private providers, several of the operators interviewed insisted on the need to coordinate national data services, which could be implemented by an actor such as the European Open Science Cloud (EOSC).

8.11. References

Beagrie, N. and Houghton, J. (2012). Economic impact evaluation of the economic and social data service. Charles Beagrie Ltd and CSES [Online]. Available at: https://esrc.ukri.org/files/research/research-and-impact-evaluation/economic-impact-evaluation-of-the-economic-and-social-data-service/.

Catherine, H. (2020). Etude comparative des services nationaux de données de recherche : facteurs de réussite. Ministère de l'enseignement supérieur, de la recherche et de l'innovation, Comité pour la science ouverte [Online]. Available at: https://www.ouvrirlascience.fr/wp-content/uploads/2021/02/Etude-comparative-des-services-nationaux-de-donnees-de-recherche-HC.pdf.

Conzett, P. (2020). DataverseNO: A national, generic repository and its contribution to the increased FAIRness of data from the long tail of research. *Ravnetrykk*, 39, 74–113.

CoSO – GT Service générique d'accueil et de diffusion de données simples et Datactivist (2020). Étude de faisabilité d'un service générique d'accueil et de diffusion des données simples. Livrable de synthèse 1 : Recueil des besoins et des contraintes des usagers. Ministère de l'Enseignement supérieur, de la recherche et de l'innovation, Comité pour la science ouverte, Paris [Online]. Available at: https://www.ouvrirlascience.fr/etude-de-faisabilite-dun-service-generique-daccueil-et-de-diffusion-des-donnees-simples-recueil-des-besoins-et-des-contraintes-des-usagers/.

CoSO – GT Service générique d'accueil et de diffusion de données simples et Datactivist (2021). Étude de faisabilité d'un service générique d'accueil et de diffusion des données simples. Synthèse de la phase 3 : ambitions du service et scénarios de mise en œuvre. Ministère de l'Enseignement supérieur, de la recherche et de l'innovation, Comité pour la science ouverte, Paris [Online]. Available at: https://www.ouvrirlascience.fr/etude-de-faisabilite-dun-service-generique-daccueil-et-de-diffusion-des-donnees-simples-ambitions-du-service-et-scenarios-de-mise-en-oeuvre/.

Fripp, D. (2019). Going off-road. *Research Infrastructure and Data* [Online]. Available at: https://researchdata.jiscinvolve.org/wp/2019/05/22/going-off-road/.

MESRI (2018). Plan national pour la science ouverte. Paris, Ministère de l'Enseignement supérieur, de la recherche et de l'innovation [Online]. Available at: https://www.ouvrirlascience.fr/plan-national-pour-la-science-ouverte/.

OCDE (2017). Business Models for Sustainable Research Data Repositories. OECD Science, Technology and Industry Policy Papers [Online]. Available at: https://doi.org/10.1787/302b12bb-en.

Wilkinson, M.D., Dumontier, M., Aalbersberg, I.J., Appleton, G., Axton, M., Baak, A., Blomberg, N., Boiten, J.-W., da Silva Santos, L.B., Bourne, P.E., Bouwman, J., Brookes, A.J., Clark, T., Crosas, M., Dillo, I., Dumon, O., Edmunds, S., Evelo, C.T., Finkers, R., Gonzalez-Beltran, A., Gray, A.J.G., Groth, P., Goble, C., Grethe, J.S., Heringa, J., 't Hoen, P.A.C., Hooft, R., Kuhn, T., Kok, R., Kok, J., Lusher, S.J., Martone, M.E., Mons, A., Packer, A.L., Persson, B., Rocca-Serra, P., Roos, M., van Schaik, R., Sansone, S.-A., Schultes, E., Sengstag, T., Slater, T., Strawn, G., Swertz, M.A., Thompson, M., van der Lei, J., van Mulligen, E., Velterop, J., Waagmeester, A., Wittenburg, P., Wolstencroft, K., Zhao, J., Mons, B. (2016). The FAIR guiding principles for scientific data management and stewardship. *Scientific Data*, 3, 160018.

8.12. Webography

Australian Research Data Commons (ARDC): https://ardc.edu.au/ [Accessed 30 May 2021].

CoreTrustSeal: https://www.coretrustseal.org/ [Accessed 30 May 2021].

Dataverse Norway (DNO): https://dataverse.no/ [Accessed 30 May 2021].

Dépôt fédéré des données de recherche (DFDR): https://www.frdr-dfdr.ca/repo/ [Accessed 30 May 2021].

Digital Preservation Coalition (DPC): https://www.dpconline.org/ [Accessed 30 May 2021].

Dutch Data Archiving and Networked Services (DANS): https://dans.knaw.nl/ [Accessed 30 May 2021].

European Open Science Cloud (EOSC): https://www.eosc-portal.eu/ [Accessed 30 May 2021].

FAIR Aware, DANS: https://fairaware.dans.knaw.nl/ [Accessed 30 May 2021].

FAIR Self Assessment Tool, ARDC: https://ardc.edu.au/resources/working-with-data/fair-data/fair-self-assessment-tool/ [Accessed 30 May 2021].

FAIRsFAIR: https://www.fairsfair.eu/ [Accessed 21 June 2020].

FREYA Project: https://www.project-freya.eu/ [Accessed 30 May 2021].

JISC Open Research Hub (JORH): https://www.jisc.ac.uk/research-repository [Accessed 30 May 2021].

National Data Service: http://www.nationaldataservice.org/ [Accessed 30 May 2021].

National Institute of Health Data Commons, NIH: https://commonfund.nih.gov/commons [Accessed 30 May 2021].

Nectar Research Cloud, ARDC: https://ardc.edu.au/services/nectar-research-cloud/ [Accessed 30 May 2021].

Nesstar, UK Data Service: http://nesstar.ukdataservice.ac.uk/webview/ [Accessed 30 May 2021].

QAMyData, UK Data Service: https://www.ukdataservice.ac.uk/about-us/our-rd/qamydata.aspx [Accessed 30 May 2021].

QualiBank, UK Data Service: https://discover.ukdataservice.ac.uk/QualiBank [Accessed 30 May 2021].

RDM Toolkit, JISC: https://rdmtoolkit.jisc.ac.uk/ [Accessed 30 May 2021].

Research Data Australia, ARDC: https://researchdata.edu.au/ [Accessed 30 May 2021].

Research Data Netherlands (RDNL): https://researchdata.nl/ [Accessed 30 May 2021].

Research Data Repository (RADAR): https://www.radar-service.eu/ [Accessed 30 May 2021].

Research Vocabularies Australia: https://vocabs.ardc.edu.au/ [Accessed 30 May 2021].

Réseau Portage: https://portagenetwork.ca/fr/ [Accessed 30 May 2021].

UK Data Archive: https://www.data-archive.ac.uk/ [Accessed 30 May 2021].

UK Data Service: https://ukdataservice.ac.uk/ [Accessed 30 May 2021].

UK Data Service Secure Lab: https://www.ukdataservice.ac.uk/use-data/secure-lab/about.aspx [Accessed 30 May 2021].

9

Mendeley Data

Wouter HAAK, Juan GARCÍA MORGADO, Jennifer RUTTER, Alberto ZIGONI and David TUCKER
Elsevier, Amsterdam, The Netherlands

Introduction

Mendeley was launched in 2008 in London by students, as a scientific social network to manage and share publications. After its acquisition by Elsevier in 2013, other services and features were added to Mendeley, including a dedicated research data service. Mendeley Data – the name of this new service – is at the same time a data repository and a search engine to find data in other repositories. We asked Elsevier to tell us about this service, its particularities, positioning, challenge and its perspectives. Here are the responses.

For those readers who do not know about Mendeley Data, please can you describe its main purpose and mission?

Mendeley Data (Figure 9.1) is about storing, sharing, finding and following research data, and this is not restricted to a single repository but encompasses more than 2000 data repositories. At Mendeley Data, we believe when data are openly available, the pace of scientific discovery is increased: researchers can verify findings or reuse data to generate new findings. Funding agencies and publishers are increasingly asking for data to be tracked and shared. Mendeley Data was launched in 2015 to enable researchers to post research data, gain greater exposure and track

For a color version of all the figures in this chapter, see www.iste.co.uk/schopfel/datasharing.zip.

Research Data Sharing and Valorization,
coordinated by Joachim SCHÖPFEL and Violaine REBOUILLAT. © ISTE Ltd 2022.

the usage of their data. When you post your research data to Mendeley Data, it receives a Digital Object Identifier (DOI), so it can be referenced and cited. And we ensure your data will be securely and persistently available. We want data to be useful and reusable, so we encourage dataset authors to indicate the "steps to reproduce" the research that led to their data, to add useful metadata and to publish under an open license. Viewership and download metrics aim to help researchers find data that is more likely to be valuable; we also make sure we track any links to articles for the same purpose. Mendeley Data is developed in-house by a team of dedicated product people, developers and designers, many with a research background. We want to make a product that serves the research community, whether an individual researcher, an academic department or lab group, or an entire institution. In all cases, the data remain owned and controlled by the researchers and institutions.

What are the main functionalities of Mendeley Data?

The main functionalities are the finding, enriching, the storing, the publishing and sharing, and the long-term preservation of datasets, together with a search engine with references from more than 25 million datasets and with specific, value-added tools for institutions and for data management and monitoring.

What has changed since the launch of Mendeley Data?

Changes are happening every month on an ongoing basis. We have published our roadmap as an outline of future plans. It's public, so you can see all the changes over time, and we publish an update every quarter[1]. Some changes are for all users, others are for the institutional customers. Some examples are as follows: in October 2018, we released an update that made it possible for researchers to upload their data to Mendeley Data via Dropbox, Google Drive, Box or Azure, so that all project members can view and download real-time files, and copy them into datasets. At the same time, we facilitated dataset co-editing, that is, every project member can have full editing rights on shared data, while the owner remains the person to publish. In March 2019, we improved the search and discoverability performance of Mendeley Data, with advanced search functionalities, with a push application programming interface (API) that allows third-party repositories to be indexed by Mendeley Data Search, and with optical character recognition (OCR) capabilities to improve discoverability of datasets. In March 2020, we launched the Mendeley Data module to allow librarians and research officers to monitor public research data at their

---

1 Mendeley Data roadmap. Available at: https://www.elsevier.com/solutions/mendeley-data-platform/releases/roadmap.

institution and keep track of compliance with the institutional research data management (RDM) policy and funder mandates. Other improvements have been made for the data repository, such as citation export to reference manager software, collection creation, improved download options, etc. The theme of these improvements is that we listen to the users and customers and quickly act based on their needs. In all cases, the improvements are along the axis to make data more FAIR, that is, more findable, accessible, interoperable, and reusable.

When, in 2016, Mendeley Data came out of beta, you announced an expanded category selection, with over 4,000 categories to choose from. 4,000 data categories, this seems an amazing number. Can you please explain?

Within Mendeley Data, we use the underlying "OmniScience" taxonomy to help researchers annotate the data better. This taxonomy launched with 4,000 terms and branches but has now expanded to more than 40,000 terms and branches. This helps data to become more findable in a standardized way.

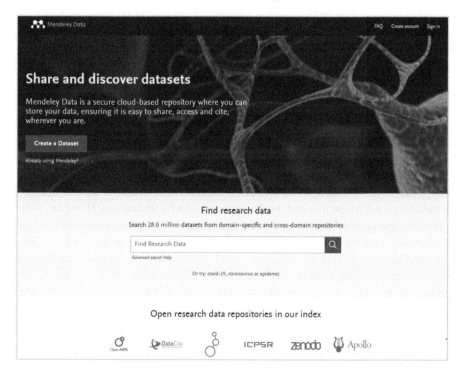

Figure 9.1. *Mendeley Data interface web*

How do scientists use Mendeley Data? Why do they opt for Mendeley Data?

We try to make Mendeley Data a platform where you can actually find and track data because there are many platforms where we can store data but they are not that many platforms where you can actually find data. The distinction is quite different. People normally think if they put data on the Internet, it will automatically be found through the search engines like Google Scholar and PubMed. But this is not true for data, it takes extra effort to make it findable, and our purpose is to make data findable and reusable, in line with the FAIR data principles. A lot of our usage on the platform is for people that go to our platform to find data: they search for data, retrieve it and then download it. The big difference between Mendeley Data and other platforms is that we do not only index data that is stored on the Mendeley Data platform; we index over 2,000 repositories worldwide, and we actually aggregate all that data for the users to be findable[2]. It is particularly important for institutions to track where their research data ends up. Most of their public research data will end up on one of these many repositories, and in order to track, report and potentially showcase these outcomes, they can employ manual efforts like using data management plans (DMPs) or they can use an automated tool like Mendeley Data. We believe the administrative burden on researchers should be reduced; hence an automated method seems to be preferential. On our website, there are interviews with researchers who have used Mendeley Data and who explain its benefits[3].

How do you select these repositories?

Our criteria are that the repository needs to have a permanent identifier, with permanent datasets, and that there are enough metadata to do a qualitative search. We spend a lot of time optimizing our search engine to make sure that only relevant results turn up on top. We also index less relevant results but they are ranked at the bottom, and the user is not confronted with irrelevant results. The relevance is calculated based on metadata, such as the title and the description given by the authors. However, some researchers are great at describing the data and some are less good, and so, to improve the relevance ranking we help them by looking into the data, with what we call deep data indexing. We do this for some but not all repositories. We do not mine binaries but we mine for terms, anything that has a table or figure or a CSV file or a text, raw text or even programs and scripts; and those terms, we add to the metadata. Anything,

2 The list of indexed repositories can be accessed via an API. Available at: https://datasearch. elsevier.com/api/docs#/sources/getSources.

3 See, for instance: https://www.elsevier.com/connect/spotlighting-fair-data-and-the-researchers-behind-it and https://www.elsevier.com/connect/we-dont-want-data-sitting-in-our-desk-says-tropical-cyclone-researcher.

that means, we do mine not only data repositories but also some journal platforms. What we do there is that we extract tables and figures and make them searchable as well. Yet, that is not the main purpose of Mendeley Data. The main purpose is to index data repositories, because we are all about data.

Some numbers: we are indexing roughly 2,000 repositories, in total that results in more than 25 million datasets. Now, roughly 18 million datasets come from data repositories and roughly seven and a half million datasets come from article or journal repositories. This number is expected to increase over time; current numbers are the 2020 snapshot.

Can you please provide some details on the scientists' feedback and usage?

Listening to our customers is critically important as we continue to develop our services. Scientists can post research datas on Mendeley Data just the same way as on other data repositories. Basically, we have two services. We have a free service where researchers can just post their data and share it and store it and make it accessible if the funding body or any institution requires this. We also have a paid version, and there we deliver additional services for institutions. For example, some institutions find it important that their data is stored locally, so we allow for local data storage. Some institutions have specific custom metadata requirements and of course we report on all the datasets that institutions have. Reporting and administration and control and moderation and curation are all things that institutions would like to do. And these are services that we offer.

In terms of metrics, for every dataset that is uploaded on our repository, we see that it is downloaded roughly once per month. An average dataset will be downloaded 10 to 12 times per year. Now of course, numbers of views are much higher. We have hundreds of thousands of unique visitors every month that look at datasets and preview them. But what we really track is of course downloads, because that is a true sign of reuse. Yet, we can only see the download, we cannot track what has been done with a download, unfortunately not. We cannot see if and how the data is reused.

What we can see is that there is a correlation between researchers that share their data and the amount of citations that they get. Papers that have associated datasets generally receive more citations than papers that have not shared their data. Two studies show that that correlation is quite strong: you can actually get lots more citations and impact if you share data than if you do not share data[4]. Another example is shown in Figure 9.2.

---

4 See Piwowar *et al.* (2007) and Colavizza *et al.* (2020).

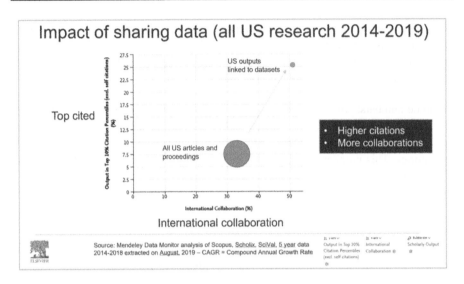

Figure 9.2. *Impact of data sharing*

But this is a correlation, not a causation, and there is no proof yet that there is causality. Another hypothesis could be that good researchers share more data, and then because they are good researchers, they get more citations. We actually believe it's a combination of both because what we see is truly that researchers who share that data, they attract other researchers. We would love to show that there is some kind of immediate "reuse bonus" but we have not seen studies of that yet.

Do you see an impact of the Covid-19 pandemic on the usage?

To be honest, we see a general trend of increased data sharing every year. We see actually a doubling of usage and uploads and downloads every year, with an exponential growth. This year is no different. It's again two times as big as last year. But we see a lot of new datasets being added that have coronavirus or Covid as keywords. Yet, we do not see more data sharing because of Covid, and no more downloads. It is actually the same doubling that we see every year.

Do French scientists use Mendeley Data?

If you search on Mendeley Data and you look for the CNRS organization, there are 15,000 datasets that pop up. Of course, not all of them are from Mendeley Data. Figure 9.3 shows the geographical distribution of the usage of Mendeley Data in France.

Figure 9.3. *Geographical distribution of unique visitor counts from France*

Figure 9.4 shows the evolution of usage from France from January 2018 to today. It shows that the monthly unique visitor counts have more than doubled from April to May 2020.

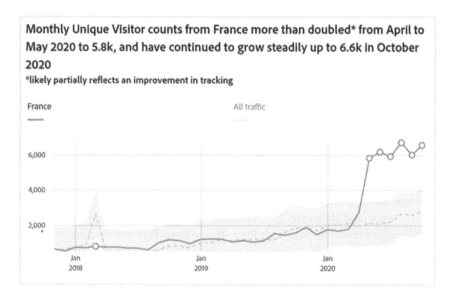

Figure 9.4. *Monthly unique visitor counts from France 2018–2020*

Recently a scientist, Narendra Kumar Bhoi from the Indian Statistical Institute, considered Mendeley Data as a "platform for research data management"[5]. Is this more than sharing and archiving?

Mendeley Data allows you to do more than store, publish and share the data. Researchers can organize their dataset files in folders and sub-folders, and they can edit, share and remove (and delete) draft datasets, with versioning functionalities, and work on the metadata. Institutions have additional value-added services, in particular the Mendeley Data Monitor, to identify, attribute and track datasets from their researchers, and the Mendeley Data Manager, an active research data collaboration tool, which enables research groups to gather, organize, annotate and share data all in one place. If they want, institutions can moderate and review posted datasets, they can set a custom metadata template with fields for all datasets, they can create their own research data collections, and they can integrate Mendeley Data with their local storage servers, so that all data file uploads and downloads go to and from their storage.

A product review mentioned in 2016[6] the potential of Mendeley Data for the creation of a "seamless, unified workflow", in particular through integration with Elsevier's products Pure[7]. What has been done?

We have actually focused on the integration with Pure and with other CRIS systems. Take a step back. If you are an institution, researchers will share data, but do you, as an institution, know where those data are shared? Because the data might be in repositories worldwide, and you have no idea where these data end up. So, we have done a lot of work to make sure that those datasets are attributed to institutions and to researchers, and we are counting where those datasets end up and who published it and to which institution they belong. The biggest integration we have made is to help institutions follow where their data ends up. That is an integration between Mendeley Data and the institution.

We can do that directly to an institution, but a lot of institutions use CRIS systems to track and showcase their output. Pure is one of those systems, and we have integrated Mendeley Data with Pure. If you have Pure and you would like to know where your data ends up, you can just go to the Pure team and the tracking of the data will be switched on. But we are also working with a couple of other

---

5 See Bhoi (2018).

6 See Swab (2016).

7 Pure. Available at: https://www.elsevier.com/fr-fr/solutions/pure.

research information management systems from other vendors to deliver these data. That is the integration we are focusing on.

We share the metadata with Pure directly through the Pure APIs, without the CERIF[8] standard format. But we are currently looking to implement with another vendor and there we will probably use the CERIF format to do that integration because it is the common standard for CRIS integrations now. This integration with research information management is new; it is something that we launched since this year. And for the moment there are quite a few universities interested in this because they have no clue where the data end up, and we help them to track this.

Beyond Elsevier's products, the published dataset metadata is aggregated to DataCite's metadata index (a comprehensive research datasets metadata index) and to the OpenAIRE portal, the European Union's research portal which aims to make as much European-funded research output as possible available to all.

In the same product review[9], the potential of Mendeley Data was discussed with ELNs (electronic lab notebooks), particularly with Hivebench. What has been done?

Hivebench is Elsevier's very simple to use and easy lab notebook solution, and we thought that if we integrate it with Mendeley Data, it would change the landscape. But in fact, researchers use thousands of different electronic lab notebooks. Now we make sure we are open to any electronic lab notebook, we have open APIs. Go and integrate if you want to. But we have stopped specific integrations with specific ELNs, because there is too much diversity.

A product presentation mentions "data monitoring" as a service provided by Mendeley Data[10]. What does it mean? How does it work?

If you think on a high level, what we deliver as Mendeley Data is three services – we help users find data because data are everywhere; second, we help researchers store and share their data; and third, we help institutions follow their data and where it ends up. This is data monitoring. The Mendeley Data Monitor is available for

---

8 Current European Research Information Format. Available at: https://www.eurocris.org/services/main-features-cerif.

9 See Swab (2016).

10 See García Morgado (2019).

institutions in several ways: as a standalone module, or alongside the other Mendeley Data modules as part of the Mendeley Data platform, as an integration with Elsevier's CRIS solution, Pure.

The monitor helps librarians and research officers tracking public institutional research data held in about 2,000 open data repositories and to stay up to date with research data sharing habits of the institution's researchers from your institution. For instance, they can view the list of shared public datasets, they can also view metadata of the individual datasets one by one and access actual public datasets and linked publications. In order to support research data archival needs or for further analysis, the monitor can export the list of all or selected datasets in different file formats, and it can provide information on how the actual datasets can be modified or retracted at the source.

I read on the Mendeley Data website that the researchers remain the owner of their data. What does this mean?

In our terms and conditions, we state that the data are owned and controlled by the researchers. The data are theirs. It is stated, too, that we don't share the private or publicly posted data. These terms and conditions for us are binding. When they publish their data with our service, they choose a license to publish it under, from a range of Creative Commons and open software and hardware licenses. Elsevier doesn't own the uploaded data. Researchers and institutions retain complete control and copyright over the data, and choose the terms under which others may consume and reuse it. They may delete draft datasets within the web interface or API, even published datasets. The accepted terms grant Mendeley Data permission to "publish, extract, reformat, adapt, build upon, index, re-distribute, link to and otherwise use [published data]". At least currently and as far as we can foresee, we only seek to carry out these activities to the extent needed to provide services on our website and in our API for end users, such as enabling discovering and accessing public datasets.

With universities, we of course have all kinds of additional terms, where we agree that in case that Elsevier ceases to exist or in case Elsevier stops the service, there are provisions in place that we hand the data back to the university in a standard format, or we put it in a place where they can access it. We put all the terms and conditions and provisions in place for high security and privacy.

How do you handle classified, confidential data, such as health data?

In terms of dataset uploads, we roughly have a hundred thousand datasets hosted on Mendeley Data, out of which roughly 35,000 are publicly visible. Not all datasets are public because researchers do not always want to share their data publicly. We do not accept datasets that contain copyrighted content (audio, video, image, etc.) to which the researchers do not own the copyright, and we do not accept datasets that contain sensitive information, for example, patient details, dates of birth, and so on.

As for health data, simply put, we think our platform is not the right platform to store patient data records from medical data. There are platforms where you can do that. Having said that, we do allow for confidential or "restricted" data. There are processes to make data confidential so that they are never published, and then there is a process where you can then share those data in a sensible way, using specific permission workflows. We work a lot with researchers that have some form of confidential data where they need to choose and control who these are shared with, and that is possible on this platform. We have restricted data, and we have different access levels.

Researchers working in a sensitive domain, if they need to store their data but do not want to show that they are working on these data, can do it on Mendeley Data. Many researchers are still working on active data or they are still processing them, and at that stage, usually they do not want to share with anybody, or at least they want to be very in control of who they share that data with. In fact, for two-thirds of our data, the metadata is not visible, the data are not indexed or referenced. The researchers can later decide to publish that metadata if they want to, or even the data, but they don't have to.

Why is a leading academic publisher interested in research data? What is the specific value of Mendeley Data for Elsevier?

We actually believe that Elsevier is more than just a publisher. We are a content and data analytics company. What we are trying to do is to make the world of research better. Our aim is to make the whole world of health and research better. So, in a way, articles are ways to communicate science but data are also ways to communicate about science and findings, and we believe that we can help in all aspects of data and content because we are good at cleaning it up, enriching it, editing it, putting it through a review process... We do that with data and we do that with content. Somebody has to do that work, and we think we are good at doing the "plumbing".

What is the link between Mendeley Data and the ScienceDirect platform?

With regard to ScienceDirect, we help researchers store and share their data[11]. Research has already shared their data somewhere else. We make sure that that link is visible on the journal article in what we call a data availability statement (DAS)[12]. We do this for all journals, with five standards journal guidelines A, B, C, D, and E, which are increasingly strict about data sharing[13]. For example, in policy A it is very loose. We just encourage researchers to share their data. But, for example in policy B we ask the researchers a data availability statement, which means that we ask them to tell us where the data are or if not, why they cannot share the data. We are not forcing them to share the data, but at least we are pushing them to be transparent. The majority of our journals are currently in policy B where we encourage data sharing and we ask them why if they don't share.

Now we want to make it as easy as possible for researchers to share their data. So, if they haven't already shared their data, we give them a very easy flow in Mendeley Data to share their data on Mendeley Data if they have not done that yet. And then, of course, that link is there as well. The nice thing about sharing it on Mendeley Data is that from the article, you can see the files that have been shared, as well as the metadata. It is not just a link; you actually can see the files themselves.

We do this also for other research materials, the codes of data analysis and so on, for example, if the data or codes are shared on GitHub. Then we make sure that that link to GitHub is also available and that the codes and the scripts of GitHub or GitLab are put next to the data.

How do you work with academic publishers? How do you link documents and data?

Yes, what we see is that many researchers who publish their articles with other publishers also publish their data on Mendeley Data and then of course that is completely okay and the link is there. At this stage, we have no formal agreements

---

11 Available at: https://www.elsevier.com/authors/author-resources/research-data.

12 Available at: https://www.elsevier.com/authors/author-resources/research-data/data-statement.

13 Available at: https://www.elsevier.com/authors/author-resources/research-data/data-guidelines.

with other publishers but potentially that can come in the future. At the moment, this is not a commercial service for publishers but it is mostly a service for institutions that we offer.

Do you partner with research institutions, universities, etc., or do you primarily target the individual scientists?

No, it is equal. We get, actually, many thousands of individual scientists that publish their data on Mendeley Data. But we do not sell to scientists. For them, it is a free service. The value-added service for us is toward institutions and countries. For scientists, we help them with a basic need to store, share and find data. Institutions have higher level needs. So, for example, as an institution, what happens with the data after the researcher leaves? Do you still understand what is left? So, one of the services we deliver is that we help institutions understand what the data were that are left over after a researcher leaves. For example, we help institutions track the data that are out there because it is impossible for them to track where that data end up. Now, these are all value-added services that we can deliver to institutions. Many institutions build their own solution and that is okay; but we are kind of an easy "Plug and Play" solution, if you may call it. So, institutions that want to focus on doing research, and doing research well, again, we can provide the "plumbing", the support that their research will get higher impact and be found and have more effect. We provide local solutions.

How do you assure long-term preservation?

Data are stored on Amazon S3, a storage and hosting service, servers in Ireland, which assures the integrity and security of data. Our service has been extensively penetration tested and received certification. In addition, published datasets are archived with Data Archiving and Networked Services (DANS)[14], the Netherlands institute for permanent access to digital research resources where at least the public datasets, the ones that are public, are also put in a dark archive that is not owned by Elsevier. This really shows to the world that they are deep archived and available for eternity. DANS is a long-term archiving provider, which is an institute of the Dutch Academy KNAW, and NWO, the Netherlands' national research council. We have a contract with DANS to archive all valid, published datasets in perpetuity. The agreement ensures that the DOIs we provide for datasets will always resolve to a

---

14 Data Archiving and Networked Services. Available at: https://dans.knaw.nl/en.

web page, where the dataset metadata and files will be available. Data archived at DANS are backed up and stored in three locations for redundancy (Figure 9.5).

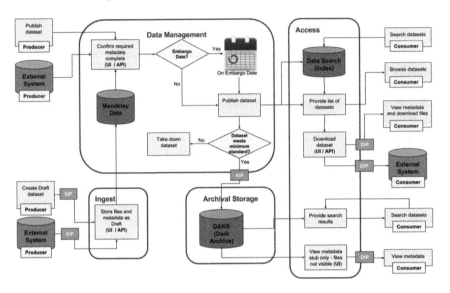

Figure 9.5. *Data workflow in Mendeley Data (source: Mendeley Data)*

Mendeley Data has been recognized with the CoreTrustSeal certification? Why is this important? What does this imply for Elsevier?

Yes, Mendeley Data has received the industry-recognized CoreTrustSeal certification, which means that your data will be safe and accessible for the long term. Mendeley Data acquired the CoreTrustSeal on June 22, 2017. The CoreTrustSeal board confirmed then that the "trusted digital repository" Mendeley Data complies with the guidelines, version 2017–2019, set by the CoreTrustSeal Board. To receive the certification, repositories are evaluated against 18 guidelines, covering security, preservation, long-term availability and other factors. The complete audit report is available on the CoreTrustSeal website[15].

The CoreTrustSeal organization is a group of research data repositories that do these certifications based on an independent peer-review process.

---

15 CoreTrustSeal. Available at: https://www.coretrustseal.org/wp-content/uploads/2017/12/ MendeleyData.pdf.

Mendeley Data and the FAIR guiding principles for research data management

FINDABLE	
F1. (Meta)data are assigned a global, unique and persistent identifier	All Mendeley Data datasets are assigned a Persistent IDentifier (PID) in the form of a Digital Object Identifier (DOI).
	Folders and files in a dataset have a PID as well, derived from the DOI. Different versions of datasets get different DOIs, but the main DOI always resolves to the latest version.
	Dataset authors and their affiliations are also enriched with PIDs (Mendeley Profile ID, ORCID, Scopus Author ID, Scopus Affiliation ID, Mendeley Institution ID, SciVal ID).
F2. Data are described with rich metadata (defined by R1 below)	The MD default metadata schema is very rich, for example it includes steps to reproduce, description fields at the level of each folder and file, semantic links with other research outputs, categories from controlled vocabulary (Omniscience).
	Furthermore, MD enables institutions to enrich the default metadata schema with additional metadata templates, including a flexible choice of field types, with guided data entry (e.g. date fields, drop-down, auto-complete, check boxes) and validation rules. Fields can be chosen to be shared upon publication or can remain available only to selected users.
F3. Metadata clearly and explicitly include the identifier of the data they describe	The DOI is a mandatory field for the dataset and it is automatically generated. It can also be personalized with the institutional prefix, if the institution is a DataCite member.
F4. (Meta)data are registered or indexed in a searchable resource	MD dataset metadata are available via several searchable resources:
	– Mendeley Data Search, which indexes over 1700 repositories. The MD datasets are among those where deep-indexing is provided, meaning that not only metadata, but the files themselves are indexed.
	– Google Dataset Search: MD exposes metadata via schema.org.
	– DataCite Search: MD uses DataCite to mint DOIs and sends metadata to DataCite for indexing.
	– OpenAIRE: MD can be harvested via OAI-PMH.
	– Google: MD exposes dataset metadata in the web page using the Dublin Core schema and each dataset page is added to Google's sitemap.
	– Share from Open Science Framework.
ACCESSIBLE	
A1. (Meta)data are retrievable by their identifier using a standardized communications protocol	Published datasets can be accessed via the HTTPS protocol with the most popular web browsers. Dataset URLs are constructed easily from the DOI: if the standard DOI is 10.<DOI prefix>/<dataset id>.<version>, the URL is https://data.mendeley.com/<dataset id>/<version>
	Furthermore, access is available through a simple REST API at the URL: https://api.mendeley.com/datasets/<dataset id>
	Other access options are available through URL:
	https://dev.mendeley.com/code/datasets_quick_start_guides.html

A1.1 The protocol is open, free, and universally implementable	Mendeley Data uses HTTPS as its main protocol. All product features are available via HTTPS, whether as a user interface or an API.
A1.2 The protocol allows for an authentication and authorization procedure, where necessary	Mendeley Data does not require access to openly shared datasets, but it does require authentication and authorization to access any other resource. To do so, it provides a broad range of authentication options: – The user can register for free and obtain login credentials to access their own resources. – Users from an institution that is subscribing to the commercial version can authenticate using the institutional credentials, including multi-factor authentication, if supported. – Any institution that wishes to subscribe to MD can integrate their institutional authentication, provided that it is compatible with the industry standard SAML 2.0 protocol (for example using Shibboleth). – Authorization is managed by Mendeley Data. Users of the free version are assigned the default role, which allows them to create and publish datasets. Users of the commercial version can be assigned multiple roles: - administrator; - moderator; - project owner; - default user.
A2. Metadata are accessible, even when the data are no longer available	MD supports "tombstoned" DOIs, meaning that, if a dataset is removed from the system, the DOI will still resolve to the dataset page, where a message that the dataset is not available anymore will be displayed. Furthermore, MD supports long term archiving with DANS, the Netherlands'. Institute for permanent access to digital research resources. Every dataset published in MD is sent to DANS for dark archiving. Should MD cease its operations for any reason, the dataset DOIs will resolve to the copy of the dataset (including metadata) stored at DANS, where the dataset and metadata will remain available in perpetuity.
INTEROPERABLE	
I1. (Meta)data use a formal, accessible, shared and broadly applicable language for knowledge representation	MD uses the JSON format to represent metadata and applies controlled vocabularies and identifiers on fields such as: – authors and their affiliations; – categories; – licenses. Besides, custom metadata fields can be added with values taken from controlled lists, and relationships to other research objects are semantic, enabling datasets to be linked to other datasets, research articles and software in a way that fully describes the existing relation. Finally, metadata are exposed via standard, interoperable formats such as Schema.org and Dublin Core, besides the JSON format, using interoperable protocols (HTTPS/REST).
I2. (Meta)data use vocabularies that follow FAIR principles	The data vocabularies used in custom metadata fields for controlled values can be inspected via the REST API. Metadata fields and allowed values can be accurately described both individually and as a group (template) for documentation purposes.

I3. (Meta)data include qualified references to other (meta)data	In MD, the references to other research objects are fully qualified. We support references to articles, datasets and software, with the following relationships: – is related to this dataset; – cites this dataset; – cited by this dataset; – compiles this dataset; – compiled by this dataset; – data derived from this dataset.
REUSABLE	
R1. Meta(data) are richly described with a plurality of accurate and relevant attributes	The datasets in the MD repository are annotated in ways that enhance reuse and not just discovery. For example: – Methods can be described in the "Steps to reproduce" field. – Support for folders in datasets makes grouping and classification of the data immediate. – The ability to annotate individual files and folders with text provides maximum accuracy and completeness in describing the data. – Custom metadata templates can be applied to further enrich the metadata.
R1.1. (Meta)data are released with a clear and accessible data usage license	MD supports 16 different licenses out of the box, including the most common and relevant CC variants, software licenses like GPL, MIT, BSD and Apache, as well as hardware licenses. Metadata sent to DataCite are licensed with the most liberal CC0 license.
R1.2. (Meta)data are associated with detailed provenance	MD supports detailed provenance by providing standard fields such as contributors, links to source or derived data or software, steps to reproduce. Furthermore, custom metadata fields can be added to document other aspects that support provenance, based on the specific nature of the data. Furthermore, versioning capabilities enable one to track data changes over time. Finally, our Data Search engine indexes the geographical location and temporal coverage of the data, when available. All the data in the MD platform are accessible in a machine-readable format via the APIs.
R1.3. (Meta)data meet domain-relevant community standards	MD supports standard metadata schema such as Dublin Core and Schema.org, besides it supports the use of controlled vocabularies, both in standard fields (e.g. Omniscience taxonomy for categories) as well as custom metadata files, which can be configured to use values from existing taxonomies).

Which metadata standards does Mendeley Data support?

We use the common basic metadata standards. Of course, we follow the DataCite standard; we follow also Dublin Core data format, using OAI-PMH exchange method and the Schema.org metadata standards. These are all the common standards we follow, but on top of that, there are usually some standards that are domain-specific or university-specific and we cannot predict those. So, for those we work with universities to help them define their own custom standards that they want to define on top of the common standard that is already available.

What about disciplinary metadata formats?

We support local metadata formats; this is part of the value-added services that we provide to institutions.

How does Mendeley Data handle localization of data and metadata?

We actually decouple the application from the metadata from the data in a physical way. The application sits in the cloud, serviced from Elsevier while all the data and the metadata and the custom metadata can stay local so that the institution is fully in control of their own data and house store. Because the application is operated by us, there is no downtime, guaranteeing up time, off after hour service – all the things you would expect of a modern solution. But still, your data has a local life.

Many people say that research data repositories should be disciplinary and community-driven. Isn't this a threat for Mendeley Data?

No, we don't think of data sharing as a threat. Data sharing in disciplinary and community-specific repositories is very important, and we actually index most of these already as part of the Mendeley Data Search and Monitor functions. Not all data can be shared this way. Data sharing is actually something that is happening at large scale and it is happening in many different ways. Some researchers still use email and cloud solutions to just share data directly. But what we would like as the world of research is to make sure that these solutions start talking to each other. For this reason, we actually index over 2,000 repositories that are already there. If I were a researcher, I would make sure that at least I am sharing a data on one of the repositories that is being indexed. So at least the data are findable. Because there are some repositories that are so niche that nobody finds the data.

We don't think it is a threat that there are a lot of local repositories. But it is very important that when you have a repository, it is up to the top-level standards, and the problem that we see is that there are many small repositories that are being started, that are not really good and they're there for, let's say, 10 or 20 years and then at some point that will go out and nobody looks at that again and then the data that are there are becoming obsolete, and that is a waste of resources.

What do you think about the concept of "thematic generalist repositories"?

Mendeley Data is a generalist open research data repository, applicable to all areas of science. We do believe it makes sense to add value to specific themes by applying specific metadata. And we support this. In a way, the division between generalist repositories and subject-specific repositories are starting to become more "blurred", which is a natural trend given the more interdisciplinary collaboration between researchers from various domains.

What is your vision of the future for Mendeley Data?

If you compare the research data management with the IT infrastructure of bigger companies in the market, you can see that there is a mandatory infrastructure to be used along with some personal infrastructure for personal uses because they don't rely on the basic infrastructure or they feel more comfortable. The same thing is happening with research data management. In big institutions, there is a specific repository that everyone should use but there are also the departments or research groups and they don't always rely on the official infrastructure. What Mendeley Data does very well is to connect to and to index such infrastructure, not only to the institutions, but also outside institutions to other researchers. This helps institutions manage their data better. Our data monitor module does that very well. So, one of the most important features that most of our customers are looking at is such an engine, because although they are setting up even a big infrastructure, they don't rely on this infrastructure storing everything, and they want to measure what kinds of datasets are stored in other institutions as part of joined experiments.

How will the research communities need Mendeley Data in the future?

We see the data sharing doubling every year, and this is a trend that we believe will continue for several years. It is a commonly held belief that research communication will happen more around the data itself, and Mendeley Data will be there to support researchers and institutions in this transition.

Do you assess the quality of the Mendeley Data content? Can you detect fake data?

If you just put your data to Mendeley Data, we only do a superficial check. All posted datasets are currently manually checked to ensure the content constitutes research data (raw or processed experimental or observational data), is scientific in nature and doesn't solely contain a previously published research article. Datasets that meet the requirements will become publicly visible on the dataset index, and will be archived with DANS. Datasets that don't meet the requirements will not become publicly visible. We do not accept spam or non-research data. But we don't currently validate or curate the contents of valid research datasets.

Then, there are two types of datasets where we do a deeper check. First, for some journals, for example, like *Cell Press*, the peer review process includes looking at the data. If you publish an article in *Cell Press*, the associated data are then also asked for, and the editors and reviewers do look at the data and they check – "Does this make sense?" The second way data are being checked is that we have a journal called *Data in Brief* which is a specific journal where you can publish your data, and the data themselves are peer reviewed. Frequently, Mendeley Data and *Data in Brief* go hand in hand, when the data are published in Mendeley Data. The data are then described in the *Data in Brief* journal. And then, of course, as part of the peer review process both items are assessed.

At the moment we are looking into automated machine learning detection of fraud and statistical fraud and that kind of thing. This is one of the future challenges. Together with Humboldt University in Germany, we work on mechanisms to check the integrity of the articles, the images and the data. But that is still a research project, and it is not yet operational in our systems.

What are the main challenges for Mendeley Data?

The main challenge is that people believe it's really easy to build their own repository. What is really hard is then to maintain it and to keep it updated and to keep it at the top level for, let's say, the standards in 10 years' time. The biggest challenge is that people underestimate the maintenance and the keeping up to date of the future.

The ever-growing volume and complexity of research data is not a challenge but an opportunity because as long as you put those data into modern infrastructure and you keep on track on par with modern standards, you can probably then reuse that data. You can also monitor the reuse. Thus, it will be more quickly evidence which parts of the data are not so valuable, and then it is easier to decide what data to delete. It is never easy to decide what data to delete, but then if you are truly tracking and following it, if you have the metrics on downloads and reuse, at least then you have better tools to make those decisions. If the data on your servers just have names, but you don't even know which projects they were created in or what they were used for, it will be very hard to make those decisions.

How do you see Mendeley Data in five years?

We would hope that lots of universities start to understand and to use the data, and to track the data where it ends up. It is such a basic thing to track and reward your researchers for sharing data, that is where it starts. And then we will also hope that many universities start either to invest to build their own repository and spend a lot of money there or come to Mendeley Data and get it out of the box. We tend to believe that we are a simple and good solution. Perhaps universities in France will also see that. So, our view for in five years' time, we would hope that we see a more connected world where data are connected, findable, shareable and visible, and we think we can play a role there.

References

Bhoi, N. (2018). Mendeley Data repository as a platform for research data management. In *Marching Beyond Libraries: Managerial Skills and Technological Competencies*, Rautaray, B., Swain, D.K., Swain, C. (eds). Overseas Press India Pvt. Ltd, New Delhi.

Colavizza, G., Hrynaszkiewicz, I., Staden, I., Whitaker, K., McGillivray, B. (2020). The citation advantage of linking publications to research data. *PLoS ONE*, 15(4), e0230416.

Garcia Morgado, J. (2019). Open data – How to make the data available with Mendeley Data. *XVIII Workshop REBIUN de Proyectos Digitales/VIII Jornadas OS Repositorios*, September 25–27, 2019, León [Online]. Available at: https://buleria.unileon.es/handle/10612/11221.

Piwowar, H.A., Day, R.S., Fridsma, D.B. (2007). Sharing detailed research data is associated with increased citation rate. *PLoS ONE*, 2(3), e308.

Swab, M. (2016). Mendeley Data. *Journal of the Canadian Health Libraries Association*, 37(3), 121–123.

10

Figshare – A Place Where Open Academic Research Outputs Live

Mark Hahnel

Figshare, London, UK

Introduction

Launched in 2012, Figshare is today one of the major international research data repositories. What is its status? What are its objectives, functions and strengths? Most repositories are disciplinary. What is the place for a generalist or generic repository? What are the challenges and prospects? We asked all of these questions to Figshare founder and director Mark Hahnel.

For those readers who do not know Figshare, please can you describe its main purpose and mission?

Figshare[1] is a repository where users can make all of their research outputs available in a citable, shareable and discoverable manner. Figshare's aim is to be the place where all academics make their research openly available. We provide a

---

For a color version of all the figures in this chapter, see www.iste.co.uk/schopfel/datasharing.zip.

Interview conducted by Joachim SCHÖPFEL, May 15 and 18, 2020.

1 Available at: https://figshare.com/.

Research Data Sharing and Valorization,
coordinated by Joachim SCHÖPFEL and Violaine REBOUILLAT. © ISTE Ltd 2022.

secure cloud-based storage space for research outputs and encourage our users to manage their research in a more organized manner, so that it can be easily made open to comply with funder mandates. Openly available research outputs mean that academia can truly reproduce and build on top of the research of others.

As Thelwall and Kousha (2016) wrote, Figshare "does not target a specific discipline, but allows multiple types of resources to be uploaded, and seems to be the main current example of this type of universal scientific repository" (see Figure 10.1).

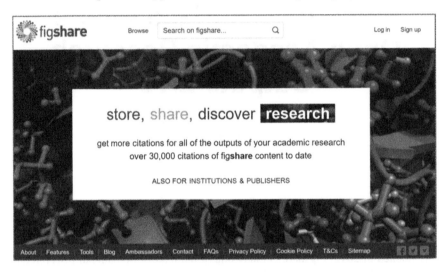

Figure 10.1. *Web interface: Figshare*

Which are the main functionalities of the Figshare platform?

Figshare allows individual researchers to publish all of their research outputs in seconds in an easily citable, sharable and discoverable manner. All file formats can be published, including videos and datasets that are often demoted to the supplemental materials section in current publishing models. Also, researchers remain the owners of their data. Our website mentions the main features for free accounts, in particular:

– upload files up to 5 GB;

– 20 GB of free private space;

– unlimited public space;

– minting of DOI for datasets (including reservation before publishing);

– acceptance of any file format;

– global accessibility;

– desktop uploader;

– open APIs;

– collaborative spaces;

– private link sharing;

– creation of collections.

In April 2020, we updated our search functionalities. The new faceted search page offers dynamical filters that update themselves upon every interaction; they include the content type, various dates (published, accepted, etc.), source, license, category (subject) and item type.

Other features have been developed for our partners, that is, publishers, universities and funders. These include datastore and portal functionalities, research data management, curation workflows, and reporting and statistics options.

Have they changed since the launch of Figshare in 2012?

Yes, there are different parts of Figshare. At the beginning, we focused purely on the free service that everybody can use and benefit from. But then, how do we make sure that this is sustainable in the long run? We see a lot of infrastructure projects that come and go or have a fantastic amount of research done and tools built and then just go away. We wanted to focus on making sure Figshare was sustainable. And by doing so, we now have clients that we provide infrastructure for, and so a lot of our roadmap is focused on developing functionality for clients.

In particular, we are building policy-compliant infrastructure for institutional clients in the cloud. For instance, when the US Department of Homeland Security asks for a repository on *AWS govcloud*, compliant with ISO standards, we do it for them and adapt the platform to their specific requirements.

We focus much more on that today than at the beginning, when we focused solely on end-users. The end-users still get a lot of functionality, for instance we just added a faceted search, which is immediately available for all end-users, for free. But today we spend more time working on metrics recording at the institutional or funder level that can be exported in different dashboards in interoperability, rather than on individual author metrics.

Another change is that while Figshare has been mainly launched as a data repository, today it offers a comprehensive repository solution for all kinds of scientific outputs, like preprints and journal articles, dissertations, books, software, educational resources, reports, posters and presentations.

Do you partner with research institutions, universities, etc., or do you primarily target individual scientists?

As I said above, today we focus much more on the customers and clients, that is, universities, funders and other institutions, than at the beginning when we focused on individual end-users. This is important for our sustainable business model. Yet, we do not forget the end-user and our initial mission.

This relates to my own personal experience as a scientist. At the beginning, when I set up Figshare, I was looking for a free generalist repository for my own data in genetics, and today I try to make sure that that is the role that Figshare still serves, to give people the opportunity to use it for free.

Actually, we have partnerships with over 100 universities and other research institutions (including University College of London, Brunel, Carnegie Mellon, Amsterdam, Stockholm[2], Cape Town, Stellenbosch and Sydney universities), research funders (National Science Foundation, Wellcome Trust, National Institutes of Health, etc.), preprint servers (*ChemRxiv*, *Advance* from SAGE, *TechRxiv* powered by IEEE), and many academic publishers.

Our value proposal for institutions: Figshare offers a web-based platform to help academic organizations manage, disseminate and measure the public impact of their research outputs, and to meet the key funder requirements around open research data. We focus on four key areas: research data management, reporting and statistics, research data dissemination and user group administration. The addition of datasets will allow institutions to discover and analyze trends in publicly available data at the institutional level and makes even more linked data available in one platform, rather than disconnected databases.

For instance, in September 2019, Loughborough University launched their new combined open access institutional and data repository, *Loughborough University Research Repository*, powered by Figshare. All institutional research outputs – from papers and theses to datasets and media – are hosted in one place, providing a single location for all research outputs. Researchers can upload any file type to the

2 See, for instance, Wennström *et al.* (2016).

repository and over 1,200 file types are displayed directly in the browser for maximum engagement and impact.

We also created two portals to specific Figshare content types: theses.ai with more than 40,000 theses, and preprints.ai with about 6,000 items. Both portals are free for every end-user.

How do scientists use Figshare? And why do they opt for Figshare?

With the growth in popularity of data sharing among academics and the increase in funder mandates, it's clear that all researchers are going to need data sharing solutions. Subject specific and institutional repositories form an overlapping and occasionally incomplete patchwork of coverage for authors looking to place content, particularly data that doesn't fit into the predefined data formats that structured repositories support. Figshare is one option for them.

There has been very little research into the volume of data produced by academics. The true scale and nature of research data is unknown as much of it sits on institutional and departmental servers or on the hard drives of computers under researchers' desks. Anecdotally, researchers generally have large personal collections of data in a diverse range of formats.

As part of Figshare's partnership with Nature Publishing group and their journal *Scientific Data*, we were able to analyze user behavior and preferences a couple of years ago. *Scientific Data* asks researchers to place data in structured data repositories, institutional repositories, or both when suitable ones exists. In fact, over 30% of data submissions were made to Figshare, making it the most used repository. From this we know that the majority of researchers require an unstructured, generalist repository for their data. The extent to which this will change over time as codification and structuring efforts proceed is arguable. It is our opinion that there will always be a need for unstructured repositories because it is the nature of research that many experiments and techniques are novel and unique.

So why Figshare? We offer a user-friendly, easy-to-use interface, for all subjects and all kinds of data. There are no fees, as it is free service for individual scientists. Content is not locked in. Another reason is that we cooperate with publishers, institutions and funders, and because of their recommendations and incentives, scientists opt for us and use Figshare.

Can you please provide some details on the scientists' feedback and usage?

Similarly to other platforms, Figshare has altmetric scores, that is, views and downloads. But a functionality, which makes the difference with some other repositories, is Figshare's citation count. Altmetrics can be an early indicator but I think the true metric in academia is citations. So, the first problem we have is that seven out of eight datasets we looked at were not cited in the reference lists; they were cited in the methods or the data availability statements. Fortunately, we have a sister company, *Dimensions* (from Digital Science), which has the full text of many types of resources, other than articles, and we can use their database to see how many times a dataset DOI is mentioned in the literature anywhere.

With the *Dimensions* database, we get eight times the amount of citations. This is useful because you can start to see patterns of usage. For instance, there is not a lot of software on the platform, relatively, less than 20,000 codes out of five million outputs. However, four of the top 10 most cited items on Figshare are software. Software is written to be reused, and it is described to be reused, there is a "read-me", whereas a lot of the other types of content are less used. Among the 100 most cited items, for example, I can only see one presentation and two posters. People don't really cite posters or presentations. But they do cite codes and datasets.

And then the question comes, if there is one citation of a dataset, it is usually from the author of the paper, saying where the data are available. That is not a citation, that is a link. But when there is more than one citation, then you can start to investigate if it is reuse, if there are different authors. This is interesting, and we are working on filtering citations in order to provide reliable citation counts, along with the other metric scores.

An interesting point is that there is no real link between metadata and citations. Some data with many citations have poor metadata. We thought that there would be a strong correlation between high amounts of metadata and the number of citations but we can't find that.

However, there are other results. Recently, we created a repository for the National Institute of Health, the biggest Life Sciences funder. They have a new policy coming out which says that from January 2021, if they fund you, you need to make your data available when you publish your paper. And if you don't have a subject-specific repository, they want you to put it in a generalist repository, but they want somebody to be checking the files to try and make sure that they are findable and accessible. We did this for the NIH. We created a repository for them with the possibility for a librarian to check the files. The early results with a small number of deposits on the NIH platform show that the data uploaded there with the curation workflow have four times more views and downloads than similar NIH files on the generalist free version of the Figshare.com platform. This means that curated metadata may increase usage but again, these are early results from a small sample.

A recent study said that an average of over 30 views per dataset is substantial, given that they are presumably only of interest to people wishing for detailed knowledge of any associated paper or wanting to investigate the data for reuse (Thelwall and Kousha 2016). The authors of the study also said that their results give no suggestion that any particular resource type is ignored in Figshare, and they concluded that it seems reasonable for funders and journals to continue to encourage dataset sharing and for academics to consider sharing wider types of outputs.

Do you see an impact of the Covid-19 pandemic on the usage?

Yes, there is an impact. We were quite happy with the annual growth of usage year by year. In terms of traffic to the content, between January 2019 and January 2020, the amount of usage doubled, and the number of visits to the site doubled. And then between January 2020 and March 2020, it tripled again. Today, I think people are starting to understand what we do, and why we do it.

Do French scientists use Figshare?

Yes, they do. With the *Dimensions* database, we can assess how many published papers link back to DOI data strings on Figshare.com, and then we can analyze where these papers come from. We conducted an analysis of 80,000 papers; United States has the most datasets, followed by the UK and Germany. France is in fourth position, followed by Australia and China.

For example, a research team from the Grenoble Institute of Technology, CNRS, published their paper on Down syndrome in the *Journal of Speech, Language, and Hearing Research* and deposited the related dataset on the Figshare platform (Figure 10.2). They were funded by the European Research Council (FP7). Their dataset was cited twice (including by their own paper) and received 69 downloads. And this is not a single case, there are many other examples.

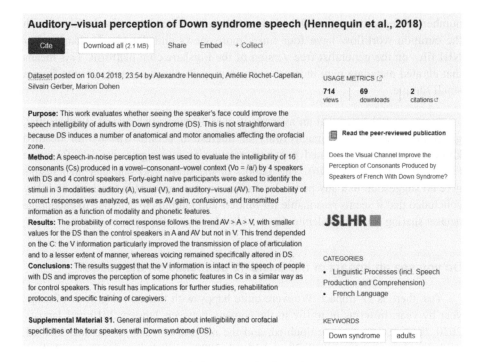

Figure 10.2. *Example of a French dataset*

For the moment, we have no partnership with French publishers, platforms or institutions. We are present in the European Open Science cloud, and we do have somebody starting in August 2020 who will focus on Europe. We already work with 10 or 15 universities in mainland Europe, but nobody in France, so far. But I envision that will change.

How do you work with academic publishers? How do you link documents and data?

When funders started requiring that data be made available at the point of article publication, academic publishers took steps to help researchers comply with these requirements. Partnerships with repositories such as Figshare allow journals to preview the digital files embedded within the HTML version of the article (viewer). The long-term preservation of the data is contractually maintained and each object is individually citable.

Our very first agreement was immediately after launch in 2012, with F1000 Research. Actually, we have agreements with more than 30 publishers, including Springer Nature, Wiley, Taylor & Francis, Frontiers, PLoS and SciELO. With Figshare, their authors can publish any file, without impact on their system, each supplemental data object is assigned a unique DOI, and their discoverability is enhanced because each file on Figshare is indexed by Google.

Data can be linked to papers on other platforms but also, of course, on Figshare. You can link data to papers in two ways: you can add the paper's DOI to the metadata set and say, this is the paper the data is associated with; or you can just list out references of papers, Wikipedia and any other resources related to the data.

As for data papers, for the moment we don't consider them as relevant for scientists' credits. We can't see a real demand for them, and Figshare doesn't allow the automatic creation of data papers based on the metadata.

How do you ensure long-term preservation?

We first had an agreement with CLOCKSS[3], a collaboration of the world's leading academic publishers and research libraries that provides a secure distributed infrastructure for long-term preservation and access. But then they cancelled the contract because they hadn't expected so much data.

Then we used the Digital Preservation Network (DPN) in the United States, but they disbanded, in 2018. Now we use the Chronopolis digital preservation network service from the University of California San Diego (UCSD)[4]. Chronopolis guarantees long-term preservation and access.

We have other integration programs with some institutions, such as DANS in The Netherlands and The British Museum, and with universities that backup Figshare items in their own system.

What about standards?

We have a partnership with DataCite and we attribute DOIs for research data. This is a free service for the generalistic Figshare.com platform and for all other,

---

3 Available at: https://clockss.org/.
4 Available at: http://libraries.ucsd.edu/chronopolis/.

customized Figshare repositories. We are a DataCite node and I am on the board of DataCite. We support three scenarios:

– You deposit one file, with its own, single set of metadata, and we mint one DOI for the file.

– You deposit 2–20,000 files belonging to the same dataset, with one set of metadata, and we mint one DOI for all of the files.

– You deposit many files, all with their own metadata and with their own DOIs, and then all files are grouped together in a collection.

When we work with universities and funders, we can also support minting identifiers for other items, like CrossRef DOIs, as we do with the *ChemRxiv* preprint server, or handles.

We adhere to DataCite standard metadata requirements, which means that we can ensure all records are consistent, while creating a single non-traditional academic output metadata catalogue.

We support the ORCID initiative for a unique author identifier. Regarding interoperability, Figshare aims to integrate with existing workflows and offer a seamless user-experience for researchers and administrators. We work together with the European ODIN project, which is based on the ORCID and DataCite initiatives to uniquely identify scientists and data sets and connect this information across multiple services and infrastructures for scholarly communication, in order to reference a data object, track use and reuse and link data objects, subsets, articles, rights statements and every person involved in its lifecycle.

Our metadata formats are customizable. We can adjust the metadata fields to specific requirements from institutions and communities. When customers want a repository compliant with ISO standards, we do this for them. Standards are important for customization and for interoperability.

We have a couple of things we do with metadata.

– First, there is the ability to export metadata from any of our systems, where we support the DataCite standard, Resource Description Framework (RDF), Metadata Encoding and Transmission Standard (METS), qualified Dublin Core and other formats.

– Second, we allow paying customers to customize their metadata by adding extra fields by extra groups.

You can have customized, subject-specific Figshare repositories with specific formats. But Figshare will not integrate all kind of metadata formats because it is too difficult; for instance, metadata standards and schemas of humanities are too different from those of neurosciences…

The thing we are working on now, that we don't have yet, is the ability to create or upload any schema and then crosswalk it into the different metadata schemas, so that you can export everything in a particular format.

Is Figshare compliant with the FAIR guiding principles for research data management?

There is a lot of content to make available. The FAIR principles, on the top level, make all people point in the same direction. Yet, the definition of FAIR has some ambiguity. FAIR is different for different people. Findability and accessibility require descriptive titles, but there is no check for this, and people just name their datasets "datasets" and so they are not findable.

In 2017, we published a set of guiding principles that can be adopted by publishers, funders and institutions as we work toward a FAIR-er future, such as openness of academic research outputs by default (as open as possible, as closed as necessary), no paywall, identifiers for everything and interoperability of infrastructures (Hahnel *et al.* 2017). Our conviction is also that academic research outputs should be human and machine readable/query-able and that researchers should never have to put the same information into multiple systems at the same institution.

Yes, Figshare is compliant with the FAIR principles (see Figure 10.3). Our intention is to make it as simple as possible to make research findable, accessible, interoperable and reusable. We publish research data in any file format and assign an institutionally branded DOI. We have had an agreement with DataCite since 2012. Figshare can also mint DOIs on behalf of the institutions, and if an institution moves away from the Figshare platform, the DOIs will be passed over to the institutional administrators in a pre-agreed format.

Our content is discoverable across major search engines and academic frameworks. All files are indexed by Google. In February 2020, Digital Science's *Dimensions* database integrated more than 1.4m datasets as a new content type. The datasets are available to all users – including those using the free version of *Dimensions*. Data are sourced from Figshare and include datasets uploaded on Figshare, as well as from other repositories such as *Dryad, Zenodo, Pangea* and

Figshare-hosted repositories, including ACS and NIH. Such cooperation requires interoperability and accessibility, and improves the findability of the Figshare data.

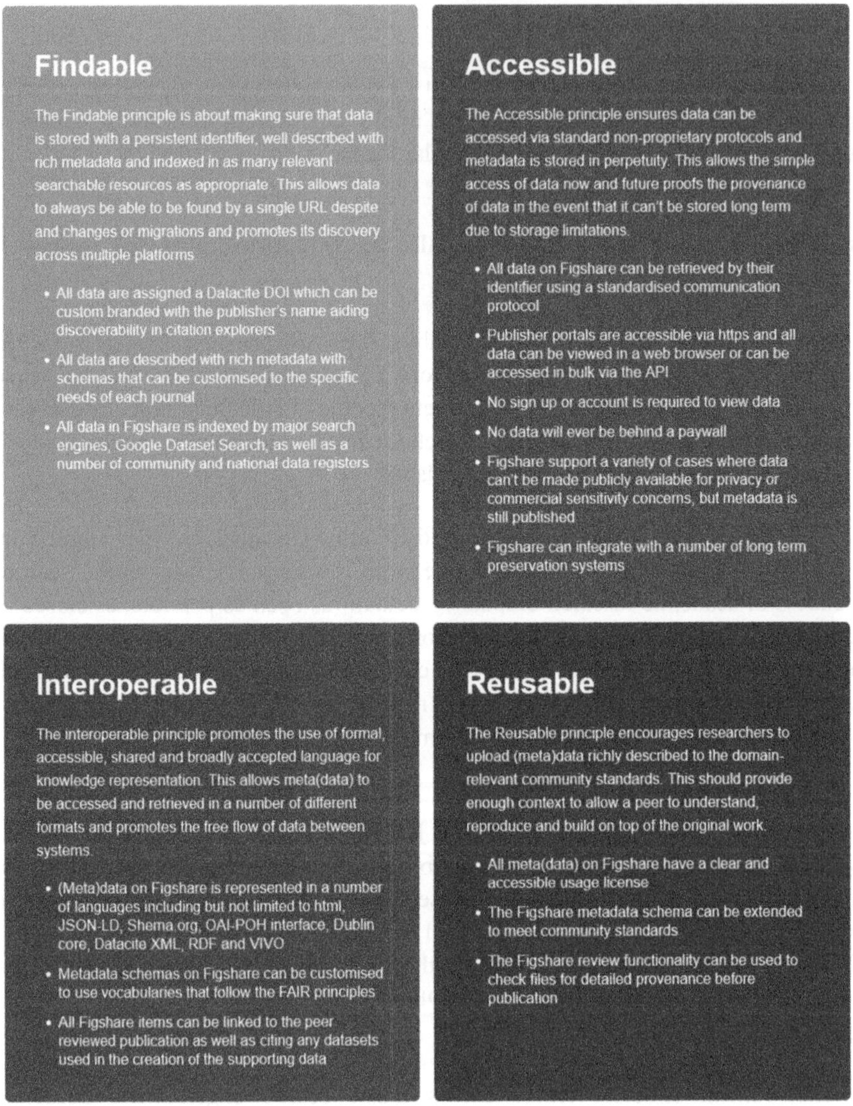

Findable

The Findable principle is about making sure that data is stored with a persistent identifier, well described with rich metadata and indexed in as many relevant searchable resources as appropriate. This allows data to always be able to be found by a single URL despite and changes or migrations and promotes its discovery across multiple platforms

- All data are assigned a Datacite DOI which can be custom branded with the publisher's name aiding discoverability in citation explorers
- All data are described with rich metadata with schemas that can be customised to the specific needs of each journal
- All data in Figshare is indexed by major search engines, Google Dataset Search, as well as a number of community and national data registers

Accessible

The Accessible principle ensures data can be accessed via standard non-proprietary protocols and metadata is stored in perpetuity. This allows the simple access of data now and future proofs the provenance of data in the event that it can't be stored long term due to storage limitations.

- All data on Figshare can be retrieved by their identifier using a standardised communication protocol
- Publisher portals are accessible via https and all data can be viewed in a web browser or can be accessed in bulk via the API
- No sign up or account is required to view data
- No data will ever be behind a paywall
- Figshare support a variety of cases where data can't be made publicly available for privacy or commercial sensitivity concerns, but metadata is still published
- Figshare can integrate with a number of long term preservation systems

Interoperable

The interoperable principle promotes the use of formal, accessible, shared and broadly accepted language for knowledge representation. This allows meta(data) to be accessed and retrieved in a number of different formats and promotes the free flow of data between systems.

- (Meta)data on Figshare is represented in a number of languages including but not limited to html, JSON-LD, Shema.org, OAI-POH interface, Dublin core, Datacite XML, RDF and VIVO
- Metadata schemas on Figshare can be customised to use vocabularies that follow the FAIR principles
- All Figshare items can be linked to the peer reviewed publication as well as citing any datasets used in the creation of the supporting data

Reusable

The Reusable principle encourages researchers to upload (meta)data richly described to the domain-relevant community standards. This should provide enough context to allow a peer to understand, reproduce and build on top of the original work.

- All meta(data) on Figshare have a clear and accessible usage license
- The Figshare metadata schema can be extended to meet community standards
- The Figshare review functionality can be used to check files for detailed provenance before publication

Figure 10.3. *Implementation of FAIR principles by Figshare*

As for reusability, we have adopted a CC0 license as the default tool for researchers to share their datasets. We understand that it is difficult for researchers to know whether research data are subject to copyright law and so, all datasets (by default) are published under CC0. This therefore removes any legal doubt about whether researchers can use the data in their projects. But we realize that publishing under a CC0 license is not always ideal and in order to ensure that scientists get credit for their research data, we have also enabled the option to publish under a CC-BY law.

However, there is some work to be done. Last year we surveyed five subject-specific data repositories and five generalist data repositories in an attempt to not only assess the levels of FAIR-ness, but provide a number of simple recommendations to help standardize the academy's data repository infrastructure and bolster interoperability. Our results highlighted high levels of existing commonalities with regard to core FAIR principles. Even so, there are areas for improvement, for example, APIs and accessibility for all (Hahnel and Valen 2020). Also, I think we should start to cooperate with other repository providers in order to create a framework for all repositories to adhere to, should they wish to be FAIR, including the establishment of standards for interoperability between different research data repository platforms (generalist API, import/export formats, etc.).

On your website, I read that "Figshare proved to be a good idea". Why? What are Figshare's key success factors?

Figshare is a success story. Since 2012, Figshare represents more than five million outputs, with more than 100 million views and 50 million downloads. Many items are from life sciences and medicine, but we cover the whole range of scientific research, including mathematics, social science and humanities, engineering, information and computer sciences, business and management.

What are our key success factors? Figshare started with a user-centered approach, user-friendly, free, easy and intuitive. We tried to provide a useful service for the specific needs of the individual scientist. And we still do so. But in the meantime, we developed institutional and corporate partnerships, as we wanted to make sure Figshare was sustainable. And I think we have managed to put ourselves in a good position, diversifying ourselves has always been the aim.

On our website, we share our mission statement and core beliefs[5]. You can read there that we have "a vision to change the face of academic publishing with the

---

5 Available at: https://knowledge.*Figshare*.com/articles/item/mission-statement-and-core-beliefs.

improved dissemination and discoverability of all scholarly research and content". Openness, accessibility and interoperability are key factors for our success: "Born out of frustrations within the academic system, the Figshare team are firm believers in the power of open access to knowledge".

Another key factor is innovation: "Since day one, we have always focused on making use of new technologies such as cloud hosting and new browser functionality to better aid researchers, publishers and institutions in their attempts to better manage and disseminate academic research".

Many people say that research data repositories should be disciplinary and community-driven. Isn't this a threat for Figshare?

In an ideal world, every subject would have a subject repository, and if we move to that world, generalist repositories will go away. When I did research, it was in genomics and genetics, and when I did genomic sequences, they went to *GenBank*. But I didn't just create genomic sequences, but all kind of other digital files. How would I share them? They couldn't go to *GenBank*.

We see Springer Nature say through their scientific data publications, if there is a subject-specific repository, put the data in there, and if there is no subject repository, put it in a generalist repository; in fact, 70% of their files are in generalist repositories, like Figshare.

There is a slight contradiction. When speaking of research data, people usually think that there are certain areas that already take care of their data. For instance, you think that neurosciences and genetics already have a lot of specific repositories, and you should expect that all of the data is in there; and yet, this is not so because the most uploaded category on Figshare is neurosciences. So, people in this area are already familiar with sharing data, and when their data doesn't fit with the specific repositories, they don't know where to put it and they put it in a generalist repository like Figshare. So, even in this area, specific repositories do not solve all problems with data sharing.

Interestingly, Thelwall and Kousha (2016) observed that "successful use of Figshare is not limited to any particular discipline, resource type or audience. Although there are differences between subject areas in the average popularity of their uploaded resources (…) it seems that people from many different subject areas have found effective uses for the repository".

I can understand politics from the landscape quite well, and I think this is a problem many people have with data repositories, idealism versus realism. In an ideal world, every specific subject would have its subject-specific repository, as every specific subject would have its subject-specific journal. But it doesn't mean that all of these would be sustainable. If academic publishing had been invented today, it would be quite different; but it has not been invented today, it has been around for hundreds of years. For this reason, I think that there must be a balance between sustainable repositories and those which have been funded with a lot of money, but which have little content and a small amount of usage, and which will go away. You need to play the game and think about how to make it sustainable and build on top of the platform.

There are some big success stories but it is hard to get there. People from a national public repository asked us about sustainability, and what will happen if all of our customers stop funding us. But we have more than a hundred customers and they will not all decide to stop funding at the same moment. And then I asked them, "who funds you?" And they answered, "our government, and they just cut our funding". This is not sustainability.

To come back to your question, no, I don't think there is opposition with disciplinary repositories. In fact, Figshare.com is designed as a multidisciplinary repository, but our metadata format is customizable, datasets can be documented with discipline-specific metadata, if required, and the Figshare platform can be customized as a subject-specific, structured repository.

Which is your vision of the future of Figshare?

When we launched Figshare in 2012, one major reason was that falling online storage costs and increasing global internet access allowed new and alternative business models for scholarly publishing. Our conviction was that "basing the publication process online allows users to take advantage of new features that did not exist in the 17th century, such as version control, making the content dynamic – just as the research process itself is" (Hahnel 2012). In simpler terms, the first decade of Figshare has been about files and data on the Internet. I feel that the next decade will be all about checking and stamping those files, and filtering content based on quality, that is, the quality of metadata and reproducibility.

Since 2015, we have really seen the funding policies and mandates come on strong and I think funders want to offer their researchers a place to research. The goal of the funders is to improve the speed of research, to make it go further and faster. And the first step is to make data available. We want the published papers to be defendable. If there are no data behind the papers, papers are just advertising. Context is very important. If the funders want to move further faster, we need more: not only the file we ask for, but all other files like this one, so that we can amalgamate them, to find trends within the data, or new areas of research, or new answers in the research, based on querying large amounts of data. The first step is to make research more reproducible by making the data available. This is possible. But for the next level, I need data to be FAIR so that I can build on top of it. The availability of data is important for innovation and to accelerate research. Today, as I have already said, because of Covid-19, people are starting to understand what we do, and the need to make content available.

We live in a world of fake news, and we need some level of curation. I do believe in preprints and I do believe that peer review is important, but I don't think that the model that we have for peer review for journals is going to scale to data. There are five million outputs of data on the Figshare infrastructure already, who is going to check all of those? I think there have to be new models for checking files, and maybe they will mostly be subject specific, but that is the only way to get FAIR data standards, and that will be the next 10 years.

When you have a Figshare repository at the institutional level, you can implement a curation workflow. The librarian can check the files before they go live. That is a module in the repository. And because we have this off-the-shelf software that you can use to upload a file and add some metadata, somebody can check the file and then make it public without peer review. It works well with data but it also works with preprints. We provide the infrastructure for *ChemRxiv* (Figure 10.4) or *TechRxiv* and they have really seen a huge growth in usage. We had to update the platforms for them to say that these files are not peer reviewed, on every landing page. I think the balance between publishing fast and understanding the quality has been highlighted by the funders, and now it is getting highlighted by Covid-19. The quality is a big challenge.

TechRxiv (Figure 10.5) is a good example of another point, that is, further integration. Figshare is not a stand-alone product, but is increasingly integrated in institutions and infrastructures. The growth of preprints to share knowledge has been one of the biggest improvements to academic publishing in the last few years. In 2019, IEEE, the leading technical professional organization advancing technology for humanity, launched *TechRxiv*, a new preprint server for electrical engineering, computer science and related technologies. Figshare is the platform of the *TechRxiv* preprints, and the Figshare interface enables authors to efficiently upload unpublished research in a monitored environment, allowing members of the technical community to provide feedback on the draft.

Figure 10.4. *Web interface of ChemRxiv*

Figure 10.5. *Web interface of TechRxiv*

How will the research communities need Figshare in the future?

A recent report on open data identified three trends in non-traditional research outputs (Hahnel *et al.* 2017):

1) The growth in the incentivization of researchers through credit. The number of funder policies grows, along with suggestions about how to enforce compliance – yet the majority of researchers still don't think they have a publisher, funder or institutional mandate to share data.

2) The lack of researcher knowledge is the second trend. Institutions continue to hire research data librarians, big publishers are employing data curators, and yet the majority of researchers are still unclear about licensing requirements.

3) The third big trend in the space has been the buzz around preprints. With physics, chemistry and biology all having strong community-driven solutions, the concept of open access to all research outputs looks ever more likely. A rebrand of the institutional repository to an institutional preprint server may encourage compliance with open access mandates in a way that incentivizes the researchers. This all then becomes an infrastructure issue, one that is at least technically resolvable.

This was the case three years ago. The situation has changed since then, but not much. Academic scientists and institutions will need Figshare as a unique platform for all academic output, and they will use it, too, as a valid data source for research information systems, that is, for evaluation and management. For instance, at Loughborough, with their new repository, researchers are able to showcase their papers alongside their data, giving citable, persistent, branded DOIs and handles to each individual item in the repository. The university has integrated their research information management system, *Symplectic Elements*, with this research repository to allow for seamless depositing of publications from *Elements* to Figshare. Data are deposited directly into the research repository and theses are deposited through a submission system directly into the research repository, to be reviewed by members of the library team before publication. This is but one example of how research will use Figshare.

Another example is our partnership with GitHub and Mozilla since 2014, to sync GitHub releases to Figshare accounts and thus to improve academic credit of code, software and scripts. When people upload their datasets, we back it up for them with Chronopolis. But if somebody wants their software be archived in their own archive then they can do it via the open API and pull the files from Figshare. We push metadata via the harvesting protocol, but we don't push content.

Which are the main challenges for Figshare?

Our main challenge is being able to continue to create policy-compliant infrastructures. We must listen to academic institutions and funders, and reach out to them. The University of Amsterdam, for instance, said that their data cannot be in American owned software, Amazon or Google cloud, but has to be in a European owned cloud, and so their Figshare data repository is hosted by a German company[6] (see Figure 10.6).

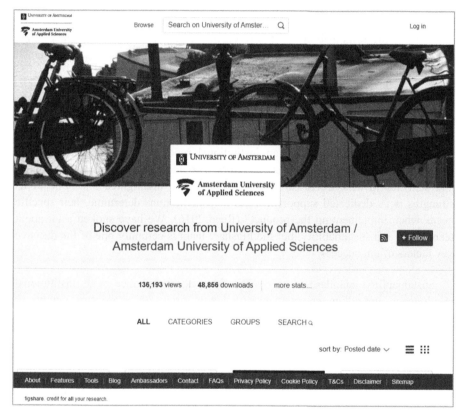

Figure 10.6. *Web interface of the data repository of the University of Amsterdam*

The major risk with data repositories is lack of sustainability – what is the sustainable model? I think we are in a good position, with many customers and strong partnerships, but we must continue diversifying ourselves. Figshare seems

---

6 Available at: https://uvaauas.figshare.com/.

relatively well prepared. In 2017, the University of Cape Town (UCT) eResearch team conducted an extensive evaluation process of data repository platforms, aimed at provisioning an effective research data service based on emerging standards and best practice (Hahnel *et al.* 2017). In comparing open source and licensed options, and taking into consideration the cost of infrastructure support staff, Figshare was identified as the most appropriate solution: "The concurrent development of an institutional research data management policy, together with an extensive advocacy programme gave substance to the evaluation, in the valuable feedback from the research community". In particular, they observed that "the functionality provided by Figshare to separate data upload from data publication has found wide appeal", recognizing the responsibility of the researcher to determine the necessary limits on openness, particularly relating to personal information and commercial considerations.

A review of our product Figshare for institutions assessed that it is "up to date on current technologies and funder requirements and continues to add functionality to assist with researcher needs" and concluded that it can be "a valuable tool for universities looking to employ an institutional repository for data management compliance or enhance an existing repository with additional administrative control and statistics to measure research impact", and then highlighted that "one of its strengths is its dedicated support team to help institutions determine their specific needs when implementing the product" (Reed 2016). We have spoken a lot about technology and sustainability, but the Figshare team is certainly one of the decisive key factors of our success.

Sustainability, standards, appropriate features, compliance with institutional requirements and policy, engagement with data librarians, these are some conditions for our future development.

What will Figshare be in 5 or 10 years?

There are a few things we are looking at in the short term, such as curating the content, open-sourcing the platform and making it machine-queryable. For the moment, we can't look into the files, so we are working on file-specific APIs, to allow querying inside the files.

We just act as a publication layer, and then the models around curation and file-checking will be built on top of that. We have the repositories, and the model is, who checks the files and who pays for it? We are not so far away from academic publishing in general when we have preprints and then peer review. However, I don't think the old model of peer review is going to scale to this level. So, perhaps there will be pay-peer-review? We need immediate publication of academic content, and we need technology to better handle it. In fact, in the longer term, Figshare just becomes a place where open academic research outputs live.

There will be a lot of tools, such as data mining applications on the top of the platform, and we are investigating how to bring computing power to the actual files. We are an infrastructure provider, allowing people to query the content in any way that they want, through apps, command lines, etc. But we must pay attention to subject-specific issues in relation to subject metadata.

I already mentioned our guiding principles, our mission statement and core beliefs about openness, interoperability and so on. Academic infrastructures should be interchangeable. So, we work with any institutions. We have integration with university systems, with Digital Science products, such as *Symplectic*, *Dimensions* or *Altmetric*, and even with Elsevier products like *Pure*. But there will be no kind of lock-in with any vendor or product. This is part of our core beliefs.

Open APIs reduce the risk of lock-in. You can pull the files out of Figshare and make a backup. I can't see lock-in becoming a problem for us. We provide infrastructure, which I see in the future as being open source, and then there is a service level on top of it, whether it comes from Digital Science Consulting or from academic libraries. We try to make it sustainable and provide the data, and that moves a lot of the lock-in problem away.

Four years ago, together with a colleague, we said that:

> the publishing industry has made strides over the last decade or so to integrate with institutional, funder and community-based repositories. Together with groups interested in the standardization of data formats, a lot of progress has been made to codify formats in many fields. There remains, however a large quantity of data on researchers' hard drives and servers that don't fit into easily standardized formats because the techniques are either new or unique (Jones and Hahnel 2016).

I think this is still true, and there are still many open questions in data publishing, from how to deal with embargoes or sensitive data, to how best to assess the quality of the diverse range of digital research outputs. Progress is being made, surely, but the field of data publishing is still in its formative stages, and represents an opportunity for both publishers and libraries to help academics adapt to new requirements. I think this will remain a challenge for the next decade.

References

Hahnel, M. (2012). Exclusive: Figshare a new open data project that wants to change the future of scholarly publishing. Impact of Social Sciences Blog [Online]. Available at: http://eprints.lse.ac.uk/51893/.

Hahnel, M. and Valen, D. (2020). How to (easily) extend the FAIRness of existing repositories. *Data Intelligence*, 2(1–2), 192–198.

Hahnel, M., Treadway, J., Fane, B., Kiley, R., Peters, D., Baynes, G. (2017). The State of Open Data Report 2017. Digital Science [Online]. Available at: https://digitalscience.Figshare. com/articles/The_State_of_Open_Data_Report_2017/5481187/1.

Jones, P. and Hahnel, M. (2016). How and why data repositories are changing academia. *Against the Grain*, 28(1), 11.

Kraker, P., Lex, E., Gorraiz, J., Gumpenberger, C., Peters, I. (2015). Research data explored II: The anatomy and reception of figshare. arXiv preprint, arXiv:1503.01298 [Online]. Available at: https://arxiv.org/ftp/arxiv/papers/1503/1503.01298.pdf.

Reed, R.B. (2016). Figshare for institutions. *Journal of the Medical Library Association: JMLA*, 104(4), 376.

Singh, J. (2011). FigShare. *Journal of Pharmacology and Pharmacotherapeutics*, 2(2), 138–139.

Thelwall, M. and Kousha, K. (2016). Figshare: A universal repository for academic resource sharing? *Online Information Review*, 40(3), 333–346.

Wennström, S., Edqvist, K., Anderberg, S., Wincent, M. (2016). Stockholm University & Figshare – Doing it "right" or doing it at all? *Figshare Fest*, London.

11

Community-Driven Open Reference for Research Data Repositories (COREF) – A Project for Further Development of *re3data*

Nina WEISWEILER[1] and Gabriele KLOSKA[2]

[1] *Helmholtz Open Science Office am Deutschen GeoForschungsZentrum GFZ, Potsdam, Germany*
[2] *Karlsruhe Institute of Technology (KIT), Germany*

Before speaking about the COREF project, please could you describe the main purpose and mission of *re3data*?

re3data is a global registry for research data repositories and covers research data repositories from all different academic disciplines. It includes repositories that enable permanent storage of and access to data, for researchers and funding bodies, for publishers and also for scholarly institutions. The *re3data* mission is to promote a culture of sharing and increased access and visibility of research data.

Interview conducted by Joachim SCHÖPFEL, May 21 2021.

Research Data Sharing and Valorization,
coordinated by Joachim SCHÖPFEL and Violaine REBOUILLAT. © ISTE Ltd 2022.

What are the main functionalities of the *re3data* platform?

The first, which is pretty obvious, is the search and discovery of research data repositories. That's the main purpose of *re3data*: helping people to find appropriate repositories to search research data or to deposit research datasets. This is very relevant for our end users, for the researchers themselves but also for data curators or data librarians.

Then we have a second area, which is also quite important, especially within the COREF project, which is the reuse, administrating and referencing of *re3data* metadata. Our metadata is being used by discovery systems and other infrastructures to enrich their own metadata or to monitor the landscape. It's possible to administer the metadata in *re3data* via a suggested form: users can suggest changes for existing entries, which is a feature that we would like to automate further in the future.

Could you provide some more details on the content of *re3data*?

The *re3data* registry provides information on more than 2,600 research data repositories, as of May 2021. The service uses an extensive metadata schema to describe the repositories, containing 41 main properties that cover general information, responsibilities, policies, legal aspects, technical standards and quality standards regarding the repositories.

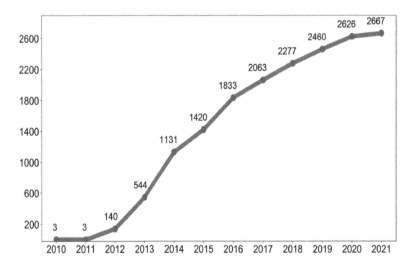

Figure 11.1. *Number of repositories indexed in* re3data *per year*

During the schema development, we consider all kinds of input from relevant research communities and also from repository and infrastructure operators. We are currently working on new versions of the schema, which will be implemented in several iterations as part of the COREF project. At the moment, we have published the first request for comments for the upcoming schema update to incorporate user feedback, which is also gathered by attending and organizing workshops or conferences and talks. Our goal is to reach out to the community, for example, through the Research Data Alliance (RDA), to collect more feedback.

We encourage repository owners to add their repository descriptions and keep them up to date in *re3data*. In return, the *re3data* service provides badges for the repositories that they can download. They indicate whether the repository has a certificate, what its legal status is, what kind of access restrictions may apply, etc. We offer several types of badges that can be integrated as a widget.

How does *re3data* select the data repositories? Do the providers themselves declare their repository on the platform and make the indexing, referencing and so on?

Yes, that can be the case, but our own editors also submit new entries. We have a selection and curation process which is performed by our international editorial board, together with editors at the Karlsruhe Institute of Technology (KIT).

The review process usually works as follows: we receive a new suggestion – coming from the repository itself, or from a user thinking "oh, that repository is not in *re3data*, I want it to be in there", or from our own editors who discover a new repository, which is then ingested. Normally, the first editor to take care of this would contact the repository or submitter to clarify any potential issues. Then we have a double check process: another review by a second editor. If everything looks good to them, the entry will go live. In cases of doubt, there might be even a second review where a third editor is consulted to find out whether the proposed repository is actually suitable for *re3data* or not.

So, there is some kind of quality control, a real review process?

Definitely, yes. This is one of the big strengths of the service. It's also a challenge, especially in terms of scalability, because the repository landscape is continuously growing. In general, we take great care to ensure that the metadata and content data are of high quality.

Only a small number of research data repositories has been certified so far (CoreTrustSeal, etc.). Does this mean that many data repositories are not really trustworthy?

Of course not! I would say that the *CoreTrustSeal* (CTS) is something like a gold standard: it's one of the highest levels that can be achieved in terms of certification. But it is also sometimes difficult to achieve, especially for small or very specialized repositories. It can be costly and time-consuming, and it may not be worth the effort for all repositories, for example, because they serve a small community that already knows where to go to find the right data – so why would you get any certificate?

On the other hand, it provides very valuable orientation, not only for users who are new in a certain area and not familiar with the repository landscape. For *re3data*, we have a lower threshold for repository registration. Besides that, *re3data* also captures other certificates in its metadata that can provide guidance to users.

In addition, in this context it is important to look at the relationship between concrete certificates and overarching principles – for example, the FAIR principles for data or the TRUST principles for repositories – and how these are related to certification. It might also be useful for a repository to figure out how it can work according to the TRUST principles without already aiming for a full certificate.

Does the inclusion in *re3data* become a kind of quality label for research data repositories, similar to the Directory of Open Access Journals (DOAJ) for academic open access journals?

Yes, you could compare it in a way, although I would like to emphasize that we are not in a position to judge the quality of repositories or the data they contain. We apply some basic criteria for the inclusion into a repository, which are that, first, it must be operated by a legal entity, a sustainable institution. It must also clarify the access conditions to the data and repository as well as the terms of use. Third, it must have a focus on research data, which may be matter of discussion among our editors (see below).

In addition to this openness, we are looking for solutions for a recommendation function that is desired by several user groups. To this end, we have introduced our badge system. And as part of the COREF project, we are developing a new community profile feature that will allow users to select subsets of repositories for display.

In fact, what are research data? How do you make the distinction between a repository that contains research data and repositories that have some content but not research data?

We could probably have a philosophical discussion about that for the rest of the day (laughs). Well, I can explain our own definition or perspective, which is very broad. For us, research data is what researchers consider as such. That includes software – we have also an entry for GitHub, for example – it includes images and publications like digitized literature, bio samples and so on. There are a lot of different repositories for all kinds of research materials. When you deal with this term, you need to look at your purpose: what implications does it have, where do you implement it and so on. In our case, it makes sense to be very open with the definition.

Who is your primary target: the individual scientists? Research institutions, universities etc.? Academic libraries and information centers?

In fact, all of them are important to us – we do have a lot of different users and user stories. We have collected these for our service model update. Yet our main users, the end users, are the researchers, the data curators and data librarians. Other important stakeholders are funding bodies and publishers, also scholarly institutions that are interested in their research output, repository operators, of course, as well as other research or federal infrastructures. We provide data to the European Open Science Monitor, for example, a pretty broad field.

Could you please tell us a little bit more about the uptake and usage of *re3data*?

Besides the typical search and discovery function, the *re3data* metadata is often used to monitor research infrastructures, for example in the European Open Science Monitor[1]. For the same purpose, it is utilized by infrastructures and communities like OpenAIRE[2] or COPDESS[3] and, on a smaller scale, by the Helmholtz Open

---

1 Open science monitor of the European Commission; available at: https://ec.europa.eu/info/research-and-innovation/strategy/strategy-2020-2024/our-digital-future/open-science/open-science-monitor_en.

2 OpenAIRE; available at: https://www.openaire.eu/.

3 *Coalition for Publishing Data in the Earth and Space Sciences* (COPDESS); available at: https://copdess.org/.

Science Office to regularly create a list of research data repositories with association to Helmholtz Centers[4].

Another common use of *re3data* is for repository recommendation: the DARIAH-EU Humanities at Scale project[5], for example, developed an easy-to-use data repository recommender[6] that relies on *re3data* as its data source.

Do French scientists and institutions use *re3data*?

We currently have 113 French data repositories indexed in *re3data*, mainly in the field of natural sciences. *re3data* is an international service, as science itself is international. Thus, we do not provide any particular service specifically for French researchers. Nevertheless, *re3data* has obtained a list of ISSN numbers for French repositories from the French National Library and has integrated them, for a certain number of repositories.

In our reference collection (Zotero group), 55 French-language publications related to *re3data* could be identified (plus nine publications by Joachim Schöpfel published in English).

We also had discussions with French institutions about repository proposals and received requests for info material about *re3data* from research data communities in France who wanted to use it for their purposes.

In 2020, *re3data* announced the launch of a new project called COREF. Please could you tell us the motivation for this new project?

COREF and *re3data* are very closely linked to each other. The goal of the project is to further develop the *re3data* service and its functionalities, in line with the latest developments in the field of research data management (RDM). In addition, we seek to connect with the community and other infrastructures to provide the right services for their needs – the right metadata, the right widgets, etc.

---

4 List of research data repositories and portals with Helmholtz participation; available at: https://os.helmholtz.de/open-science-in-der-helmholtz-gemeinschaft/offener-zugang-zu-forschungsdaten/forschungsdatenrepositorien-und-portale-in-der-helmholtz-gemeinschaft/.

5 DARIAH-EU Humanities at Scale; available at: http://has.dariah.eu/.

6 Data Deposit Recommendation Service for humanities researchers; available at: https://ddrs-dev.dariah.eu/ddrs/.

We plan several steps to reach our project goals.

We are currently updating and expanding the metadata schema and there will be several more versions, which will be reviewed in an open, public process. We also intend to develop a model of trust for the metadata to enable authorized editing and adding and automate the curation process further. This includes the implementation of authority files or persistent identifiers like ROR and ORCID that can be used to identify institutes, users or editors. In this way, we know where the data are coming from and ensure a trust-based process.

More options for machine-to-machine communication will reduce the manual work that editors have to do. We also work on the technical infrastructure, building additional widgets and tools, and improve the API. We would like to provide more sophisticated functions for monitoring and recommendation, especially regarding FAIR-enabling repositories. To this end, efforts in COREF are aligned with the project activities and developments in FAIRsFAIR.

We are also conducting a study on the status quo of quality assurance measures at research data repositories. In this survey, we ask the repositories themselves how they do quality assurance, and the results will then be incorporated into our metadata schema.

As all these activities are quite complex, we are therefore building a new service model that provides guidance to pull all the threads together. It is currently being written and edited and will be published soon.

Who are your partners?

Our partners are DataCite[7], the Helmholtz Open Science Office[8], the Berlin School of Library Information Science[9] at the Humboldt-Universität Berlin and the KIT Library[10] at the Karlsruhe Institute of Technology (KIT). We also work closely together with Purdue University[11], in particular, Michael Witt, who initiated *Databib*, a service that merged with *re3data* in 2013.

---

7 DataCite e.V.; available at: https://datacite.org/.

8 Helmholtz Open Science Office; available at: https://os.helmholtz.de/.

9 Berlin School of Library Information Science; available at: http://www.ibi.hu-berlin.de/.

10 KIT Library; available at: http://www.bibliothek.kit.edu/.

11 Purdue Libraries; available at: https://www.lib.purdue.edu/.

Who provides the funding?

re3data COREF is funded by German Research Foundation (DFG) for 36 months. The project officially started on January 1, 2020.

Please could you give some details about the planning? Where are you now, what are the next steps?

Our survey for repository operators on data quality management at research data repositories will run until June 2021, after which it will be analyzed. As I mentioned, the results will support our schema development.

The request for comments period for the new schema version 3.1 was closed in May 2021 and now we discuss and implement the comments and changes in the XML structure and technical architecture. Furthermore, we intend to move the schema from XML to RDF format in the long run.

As for the community management and outreach, there will be presentations on upcoming conferences, namely the Open Repositories Conference 2021 and the 109th German Librarian's Day.

For our service model, we conducted a stakeholder survey with three supplementary workshop sessions in 2020. Based on the outcome, we now create the service model and a workshop report.

Could you please give one or two examples of new service development?

A larger project for this year, in collaboration with DataCite, is the implementation of a repository search function in DataCite Commons[12], which I already discussed earlier; the idea is to create a separate repository search tab in Commons, in addition to the entities of organizations, works and people. This will enable users to find repositories which are connected in the DataCite research graph.

We also want to integrate our system with CTS[13] so that we can show the up-to-date certification status of repositories.

---

12 DataCite Commons; available at: https://commons.datacite.org/.

13 CoreTrustSeal; available at: https://www.coretrustseal.org/.

Will *re3data* be connected to other directories, like Cat OPIDoR?

We haven't talked to them so far, but it sounds like we should. We are very open to networking and figuring out how to connect and share information. There are multiple registries of different types for repositories and they all serve a specific purpose and have their own focus, so, it makes a lot of sense to collaborate and to figure out where we can connect the dots.

How could this new project be interesting for the French Higher education and research communities?

re3data increases visibility for French repositories when they provide their metadata and keep their records up to date, which will become easier with more automated processes. *re3data* can support French researchers and data stewards in research data discovery. In addition, we are happy to assist French RDM activities directly with our know-how and experience in the field.

At a higher level, *re3data* has worked with the Swiss National Science Foundation (SNF)[14] to monitor the Swiss research and infrastructure landscape (von der Heyde *et al.* 2019a, 2019b). French institutions could also benefit from using *re3data* for this purpose.

re3data launched in 2012 – How has the landscape of research data and data repositories changed since then?

We are seeing strong growth and diversification in the repository landscape. The overall complexity and the number of stakeholders in the research data landscape have significantly increased. There is a greater awareness regarding the value of research data; this dynamic is reflected in the current uptake and discussions around the FAIR data principles. We observe a higher impact and perceived value of research data in academia and also the professionalization and standardization of infrastructures.

In the last about five to seven years, we have also noticed the trend of publication repositories opening up for research data. This is perhaps the greatest change. Furthermore, there are far more advanced certification processes in place today, beginning with the Data Seal of Approval (DSA) and the World Data System (WDS) certification, which have evolved into the CTS.

---

14 Schweizer Nationalfonds; available at: http://www.snf.ch/de/Seiten/default.aspx.

Are there national repositories in the *re3data* directory?

Well, I have to ask in response: what does "national" mean? It really depends on what angle you're looking at it from, or what your actual goal or use case is. Various aspects may be involved, such as operations, hosting, funding, legal requirements, users, who is allowed to deposit and so on.

I think for certain purposes a national repository might be quite helpful, for example, to monitor the output. You could create something comparable to a National Library that collects all the output from one country. But then again, research usually takes place on an international level: if you have a research group that consists of 20 people from different countries, is their output then supposed to go into a national repository or not?

There are a few national repositories indexed in *re3data*. But it's important to keep in mind that research and academic communities don't necessarily restrict themselves to national borders, as I mentioned. *re3data* resembles that international landscape.

In Germany, the National Research Data Infrastructure (NFDI)[15] is currently being established. It follows a different approach, trying to link individual communities and initiatives together to create an interdisciplinary infrastructure.

Could you please describe the connection and integration of *re3data* into the European Open Science Cloud (EOSC)?

re3data is currently going through the onboarding process of the EOSC portal marketplace[16], and will be listed there shortly.

The *re3data* team participates in and works closely with large European projects and infrastructures like FAIRsFAIR[17] and OpenAIRE[18], which foster, integrate and complement the EOSC services. Together with DataCite and FAIRsFAIR, we have been working on the latest update of the *re3data* metadata schema. We are also collaborating with OpenAIRE: if a repository wants to be registered for the OpenAIRE graph they need to be registered with *re3data*, the *re3data* metadata is

---

15 NFDI; available at: https://www.nfdi.de/en-gb/.
16 EOSC marketplace; available at: https://marketplace.eosc-portal.eu/.
17 FAIRsFAIR; available at: https://www.fairsfair.eu/the-project.
18 OpenAIRE; available at: https://www.openaire.eu/.

used for the validation process. We also have collaboration with B2Find to align and refine our subject classification together with the European RDM communities.

How do you work with the Research Data Alliance?

Members of *re3data* participate in RDA Interest and Working Groups to connect with the community and listen to their needs. We also participate in the plenaries. Last April at the 17th Virtual RDA Plenary, we won the poster contest, which was quite a pleasant surprise[19].

The *re3data* COREF partners are also individually committed to RDA. For example, the Helmholtz Open Science Office is involved in organizing the annual meetings of the German RDA chapter. In addition, the GFZ, where the Open Science Office is located, hosted the 11th Plenary Session 2018 in Berlin. Furthermore, the KIT and Michael Witt from Purdue University are very involved in RDA. We make sure that we take into account the input from there.

In the future, do you think *re3data* will allow direct access to research data?

No, at least, that's not planned at the moment. *re3data* provides API descriptions and directs researchers to the repositories for further search of research data. Also, there are other providers like DataCite[20] or B2FIND[21] that refer directly to the datasets. We keep having ideas and discussion on this topic, but it's not in our scope right now.

What are the main challenges for *re3data*?

A central challenge is language and community barriers. As an international registry, we are faced with the issue of how to deal with resources that are not available in English. We have started to register some of these with the help of our international editorial board.

Another challenge that all infrastructures comparable to ours face is keeping pace with the latest technological and social developments. Scalability is an important topic too: earlier, I described our editorial process. Communicating with

---

19 *re3data* poster from the 17th RDA Plenary; available at: http://doi.org/10.5281/zenodo.4705209.

20 DataCite search; available at: https://search.datacite.org/.

21 B2FIND; available at: http://b2find.eudat.eu/.

repositories and users and the careful data curation take a lot of time, so we are looking for solutions to automate that process to a certain degree.

Another endeavor is the constant adjustment of our service model. Looking at the different users and stakeholders and their individual needs, *re3data* could be compared to a Swiss Army knife. But creating a true "all-in-one device" is impossible. Getting the focus right, in concert with the communities we serve – that's the main challenge, I think.

What will *re3data* be in 5 or 10 years?

We think big, imagining *re3data* as a truly international resource with representation and engagement in all countries of the world and with globalization of features and functionality that engages deeply with scientific communities and stakeholders in research, including researchers, repository operators and other research infrastructure providers, funders, publishers, librarians and so on.

It means that we aim to achieve robust and agile metadata about data repositories that is expressed in functionality as well as interfaces that are trusted by and meet the needs of the research community. Our goal is for the service to continue to be sustainable and to be developed as an open and effective substrate upon which other applications and services can be integrated and built by others.

To achieve these goals, we continue to focus on the user and stakeholder community and ensure that we listen to them and take their needs into account.

References

Gohain, R.R. (2021). Status of global research data repository: An exploratory study. *Library Philosophy and Practice*, 2021, 1–13.

Kim, S. and Choi, M.-S. (2017). Registry metadata quality assessment by the example of re3data.org schema. *International Journal of Knowledge Content Development & Technology*, 7(2), 41–51.

Kindling, M., Pampel, H., van de Sandt, S., Rücknagel, J., Vierkant, P., Kloska, G., Witt, M., Schirmbacher, P., Bertelmann, R., Scholze, F. (2017). The landscape of research data repositories in 2015: A re3data analysis. *D-Lib Magazine*, 23(3–4) [Online]. Available at: doi:10.1045/march2017-kindling.

Pampel, H. and Vierkant, P. (2015). Current status and future plans of re3data.org – Registry of research data repositories. In *GeoBerlin2015: Dynamic Earth from Alfred Wegener to Today and Beyond; Abstracts, Annual Meeting of DGGV and DMG*, Wagner, J. and Elger, K. (eds). GFZ German Research Centre for Geosciences, Potsdam [Online]. Available at: https://gfzpublic.gfz-potsdam.de/pubman/faces/ViewItemFullPage.jsp?itemId=item_1369620_13.

Pampel, H., Vierkant, P., Scholze, F., Bertelmann, R., Kindling, M., Klump, J., Goebelbecker, H.-J., Gundlach, J., Schirmbacher, P., Dierolf, U. (2013). Making research data repositories visible: The re3data.org registry. *PLoS ONE*, 8(11) [Online]. Available at: https://doi.org/10.1371/journal.pone.0078080.

von der Heyde, M., Ulrich, R., Kloska, G. (2019a). Open Research Data (ORD): Landscape and cost analysis of data repositories currently used by the Swiss research community, and requirements for the future. Report [Online]. Available at: https://doi.org/10.5281/zenodo.2643460.

von der Heyde, M., Ulrich, R., Kloska, G. (2019b). International open data repository survey: Description of collection, collected data, and analysis methods. Report [Online]. Available at: https://doi.org/10.5281/zenodo.2643450.

Witt, M., Stall, S., Duerr, R., Plante, R., Fenner, M., Dasler, R., Cruse, P., Hou, S., Ulrich, R., Kinkade, D. (2019). Connecting researchers to data repositories in the earth, space, and environmental sciences. In *Digital Libraries: Supporting Open Science. IRCDL 2019. Communications in Computer and Information Science*, Manghi, P., Candela, L., Silvello, G. (eds). Springer, Cham [Online]. Available at: https://doi.org/10.1007/978-3-030-11226-4_7.

12

Issues and Prospects for Research Data Repositories

Joachim SCHÖPFEL

University of Lille, Villeneuve d'Ascq, France

12.1. Introduction

Repositories play a key role in the management of research data. This chapter summarizes the main challenges facing these systems, which include not only data volume and complexity, integration into the ecosystem of research infrastructures and openness to the world, but also data quality and acceptance by researchers. What are the prospects? The future of data repositories will be affected by scientific and technological developments, along with political and economic choices. It will also be affected by the search for a balance between the specific needs of communities, the trend toward standardization and, last but not least, the consideration of the human factor.

12.2. The central role of repositories and diversity in the field

In his foreword to this book, Renaud Fabre underlines the essential function of research data repositories in the process of building data sharing: "the repository is the current canonical form, global or local, of any constructed data policy process". As a vehicle for a new scientific practice, the data repository is "the very place for researchers to learn collectively in favor of sharing". Renaud Fabre agrees with Jeffery *et al.* (2021) who place data repositories at the heart of the data-driven science process (Figure 12.1).

Research Data Sharing and Valorization,
coordinated by Joachim SCHÖPFEL and Violaine REBOUILLAT. © ISTE Ltd 2022.

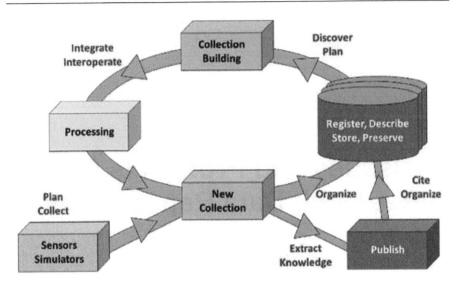

Figure 12.1. *The research data cycle (source: RDA Data Fabric IG; Jeffery* et al. *2021). For a color version of this figure, see www.iste.co.uk/schopfel/datasharing.zip*

In this process, the digital devices of data repositories play a central role for recording, describing, curating, searching (discovering) and disseminating data sets (Cocaud and Aventurier 2017). These are essential functionalities for the efficiency of the whole process, from data collection, organization and analysis to knowledge extraction and production via the publication of scientific results. Jeffery *et al.* (2021) emphasize three key needs that trusted data repositories must fulfill:

1) data must be stored, managed and made accessible for long periods of time;

2) the data must be identified by universally unique, persistent and resolvable identifiers;

3) the data must be associated with appropriate and complete metadata.

As for sustainable research data infrastructures that guarantee long-term preservation and accessibility, this is also the concept of the international *re3data* repository. However, when we compare the different approaches and definitions and, most importantly, when we look at the different projects and achievements in the field, it is clear that:

– the lowest common denominator of these devices is the combination of one form of content (research data), two key functionalities (preservation and dissemination) and the essential features of a two-sided platform (repository, access);

– diversity is the rule: diversity in data typology, scope, services offered and commitment, governance, business model, commitment to sustainability, openness and inclusiveness, quality assurance and credibility.

Above all, two approaches coexist and sometimes clash: the community approach and the generalist approach. Many repositories are the result of a research community, built around a facility, a theme or discipline or an institution. Some sites follow another approach, in that they are *top-down* achievements, without any organic link with a community or an institution, proposing a service offer that meets other needs more or less successfully.

Our book aims to contribute to an enlightened vision of the research data landscape in France, and, more specifically, of the supply of research data repositories for researchers. This landscape is dynamic and changing rapidly. While the June 2020 snapshot of the French data repository landscape is still valid in terms of its main characteristics (see Chapter 2), the number of data repositories in France is still growing, with a gradual diversification of their scope and functionalities and with more tools and services, including at the level of calculation and expertise, following the example of TELMA (*Traitement électronique des manuscrits et des archives*)[1]: this CNRS service and dissemination platform for the electronic publishing of primary source corpora and the research tools needed to use them has established itself as a research data repository[2] but in fact covers a large part of the data lifecycle, including upstream, for the production of data (corpora).

So, diversification, not convergence. Is this a problem or an opportunity? Probably both at the same time. Recent studies show that a lot of data is managed in devices where established practices are maintained and where a wide variety of files, clouds and databases are used, which does not facilitate integration and interoperability with other infrastructures (Jeffery *et al.* 2021). Yet, on the other hand, this reflects the diversity of situations and the close link between data management, epistemology and scientific instrumentation; it also reflects the ability of researchers to create data communities in the field, in perfect adaptation with their practices and needs. This is a paradox that we will return to a little later.

In the following, we will summarize the challenges that research data repositories are facing today, and we will present some potential avenues and prospects for their development in the years to come.

---

1 Available at: TELMA http://www.cn-telma.fr/.
2 See referencing on Cat-OPIDoR; available at: https://cat.opidor.fr/index.php/Telma.

12.3. The issues

For each case study in this book, we have probed the issues facing the data repository in question. The answers reflect both the point of view of our intermediaries and the particular situation of each device, its technology and environment, its development strategy and its community with its practices, expectations and needs. At the same time, these same responses reveal a number of shared challenges which all these data infrastructures face, in one way or another and to some degree.

Scientific evolution: as Françoise Genova and Mark G. Allen of the CDS point out, all sciences are constantly evolving, and data repositories must be able to take into account the new fields that are opening up to research, both in terms of content (support for new types of data, definition of new metadata, etc.) and technical capabilities. New equipment produces other data, on other subjects, with other purposes.

Data volume: these changes generally have an impact on data volume. The CDS thus anticipates new research projects that will generate streams of data that will have to be filtered to extract the events and subjects to be studied. Data are becoming increasingly massive, both in terms of volume and number of subject matters. For Stéphane Pouyllau, this is the first challenge that Nakala must address: "Currently, we know how to accommodate several terabytes on a single account. [...] Now, how do we go from 10 to 100 terabytes, 200 terabytes?" The challenge for CDS is as follows: "The Rubin Observatory will produce 20 TB of data each night and accumulate 60 PB of data over the 10 years planned for its operations [...]. The Square Kilometre Array [...] will produce 5 TB per second. The catalog of observations of the second version of the Gaia satellite [...], published in 2018, amounts to 1.7 billion objects". Astronomy is already in the era of Big Data...

Data complexity: however, being able to handle very large volumes of data is not everything. You also have to deal with the increasing complexity of data, new formats, combinations of data from several sources (devices), and the increasingly complex hierarchization and structuring. But, as Wouter Haak and his colleagues at Elsevier point out, the volume and complexity of data is not only a challenge; above all, it is an opportunity to develop new services.

Data quality: the debate around coronavirus research confirmed that one of the major challenges of data management is its quality, reliability and credibility. Are the data and the services that disseminate the data trustworthy? Access to the data is necessary to verify the quality and integrity of the published results, but how do you verify the integrity of the data itself? How do we know we can (re)use the data with confidence? In fact, it is a double challenge because it is a question, in the words of Françoise Genova and Mark G. Allen, of maintaining "the content of the databases and the tools made available to users at the highest level of quality". The content (data and metadata) and the container (the repository) not only maintain the quality of the service but enhance it, adds Esther Dzalé Yeumo of INRAE, despite the constant increase in the number of deposits.

Integration into the ecosystem: a data repository is not a stand-alone system but must be integrated into an ecosystem of research infrastructures (journal or book platforms, open archives, large scientific facilities, etc.), an issue that Stéphane Pouyllau described as "complementarity within infrastructures" or "seamlessness". For Nakala this involves, for example, a connection with the OpenEdition platform and the Métopes project to facilitate the exchange and transfer of data and metadata related to scientific articles. For the CDS, it is a question of linking the repository to other tools and other sources of information. For Data INRAE, the challenge is to bring the data closer to the calculation, that is, "to have adequate infrastructures to be able to analyze the data from the cloud, without having to download them first", and more generally to achieve an "integrated repository, which is part of national or European infrastructures relevant to our fields". Another aspect of integration is sharing with other institutions and establishments so as to reduce investment and operating costs and also to contribute to a convergence of practices, formats, etc. An example of successful sharing is the international 4TU.ResearchData repository of a consortium of three Dutch universities of technology (Delft, Eindhoven, Twente), developed and implemented with Figshare[3].

Opening up to the international scene: integration into an ecosystem of research infrastructures is closely linked to another issue, opening up to the international scene. This is primarily a question of integration into the emerging *European Open Science Cloud* (EOSC). The CDS, for example, should be a thematic data center in the EOSC. Participating in the EOSC implies demanding quality criteria for the repository and its content (FAIR principles, certification, etc.). However, the international challenge is broader. For Stéphane Pouyllau, thinking about opening up internationally means thinking about the use of the service "in other countries, in other research systems, different from the one we have in France", with other needs, another way of working, and sometimes another economic model as well, so "we have to think about adapted internationalization", which requires long-term investment, time, dialogue, collaborations, etc. For SEANOE, internationalization also means reaching a critical mass of deposits and "sufficient visibility at the international level so that this visibility leads to new deposits".

---

3 4TU.ResearchData; available at: https://data.4tu.nl/.

Acceptance by researchers: another major issue is the development of the actual use of the device. How can we make the repositories known (see Rebouillat 2017)? For the SEANOE team, the main challenge is to attract more deposits in order to reach a "critical mass of deposits", which is difficult to estimate but likely to increase visibility, which would itself lead to new deposits. All repositories are asking themselves the question: how can we propose an attractive service offer? How can we develop interfaces appropriate to researchers' practices and tools? Moreover, there is an empirical link between the acceptance of a digital device, the perception of its usefulness, its usability and the quality of the data (Figure 12.2).

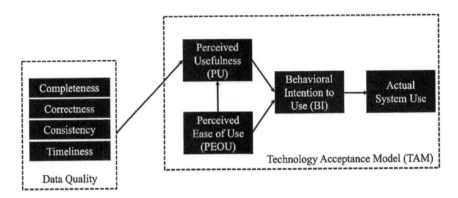

Figure 12.2. *A model of technology acceptance (source: Azeroual et al. 2020)*

According to this model, the acceptance of a research data repository by researchers therefore implies work at several levels, both to develop the usefulness of the service offer and to facilitate its use (deposit, description, search, reuse, etc.) and guarantee the quality of the data and metadata. It is a real challenge.

A word on usefulness: the two chapters on Figshare and Mendeley Data reveal two other issues directly related to the perceived usefulness of a repository by and for researchers. On the one hand, repositories must meet the criteria of funding agencies, notably those of the European Commission and its EOSC initiative (FAIRization of devices, links with publications and projects, etc.). On the other hand, they must integrate the dimension of research evaluation, allowing the monitoring not only of the repositories but also (and increasingly) of the reuse of the datasets (tracking): who uses which data and for what purpose?

12.4. The dynamics of technology

Another major challenge for the development of research data repositories is the rapid evolution of technologies. On the one hand, this involves the evolution of repository systems and functionalities, and on the other, the evolution of their technological environment.

Adapting to technological changes means developing the internal architecture and the organization of services and interfaces (CDS), redesigning the system (back office), deposit forms and interfaces with other systems (SEANOE), integrating and converging several vocabularies, and developing dialogue (bridges) with other infrastructures (Nakala, INRAE Data). The question of interfacing and gateways is all the more relevant when it comes to potentially having a national repository in the future, whose overall architecture is not yet known – a central infrastructure with institutional or thematic collections; a central platform with "personalized" institutional or thematic repositories; or a software base with local institutional or thematic implementations?

At a completely different level, how do repositories meet the challenge of sustainable archiving and ensure long-term access to data? The solution is outsourcing: Nakala has a partnership with the CINES which is its operator for the archiving of HSS data; Mendeley Data works with two service providers, one of private status in Ireland (Amazon S3, a file hosting site offered by Amazon Web Services), the other of public status in the Netherlands (Data Archiving and Networked Services (DANS), the national center of expertise and archiving of research data), while Figshare, having worked with the CLOCKSS consortium and the Digital Preservation Network (DPN) in the United States, now uses the Chronopolis network service of the University of California San Diego and has concluded several contracts with institutional partners in several countries, such as DANS and the British Museum.

Gradually, some repositories are also beginning to make use of the new possibilities offered by artificial intelligence. CDS in particular uses the hierarchical data structure, a new tool developed for a more detailed and more efficient data ingestion and for the implementation of more links between items and data. Mendeley Data is interested in the detection of data quality problems (such as fraud) by machine learning, but this remains, for the moment, marginal.

More generally, it can be observed that research data repositories are broadly following the technological trends described by companies such as Gartner[4],

4 Gartner, Inc.; available at: https://www.gartner.com/en.

Forrester[5] and Forbes[6], both in terms of increasing automation (ingestion, transfer, indexing, controls, etc.)[7] and the "platformization" of devices, and in terms of outsourcing, whether through pooling, outsourcing of certain functions or by offering a service "in the cloud".

On the other hand, another aspect seems to be missing so far, or at least no one has mentioned it: even though the security of research data is a concern, none of the operators have mentioned Blockchain technology, which, according to Gartner and others, is one of the emerging technologies and which could offer, in the next five to ten years, interesting solutions to secure the storage and use of research data.

Meeting the challenge of new technologies, practices and user expectations does not necessarily require a great deal of investment – that's what Mark Hahnel seems to mean when he envisages opening up the system for Figshare. Offering the repository code would allow scientific communities and/or other operators to develop new services from Figshare's data and functionalities, much like other platforms such as PubMed Central. Such an open infrastructure would also, according to Mark Hahnel, reduce the risk of "locking in" or "locking out" the repository.

12.5. The "new generation" data repository

Adapting to technological and scientific change – what might the research data repository of the future, or the second-generation repository, look like in this environment? The question is perhaps poorly posed. The diversity of data, equipment and technologies is such that the very idea of a single type or model of repository seems absurd. Precisely, as a Knowledge Exchange report found, the complexity and fragmented nature of the research data landscape is a major challenge for data infrastructure development (Goldstein 2017). At best one could imagine a range of products, a family of systems that share a number of technical features and functionalities. But there is another reason: the future of data repositories will not only depend on the evolution of technologies for producing, processing, storing, publishing and using data. The appropriation of these technologies will be shaped by the scientific communities themselves, by the

---

5 Forrester Research, Inc.; available at: https://go.forrester.com/.

6 Forbes Media LLC; available at: https://www.forbes.com/.

7 Speaking of automation: some of the work of the Research Data Alliance explicitly addresses the automation of procedures (e.g. recommendations for "machine-actionable policy templates" or "machine-actionable procedures" for data collection), as do the FAIR principles (see Wilkinson *et al.* 2016).

practices and needs of researchers and engineers, and by public policy (transparency), scientific (efficiency) and economic (value creation) choices. It is a device rather than merely a system or a tool.

So, let's start with the principle of diversity. This raises the question of the development framework, that is, the guiding principles for the design of a data repository. In a similar approach, a working group of the Confederation of Open Access Repositories (COAR) has proposed a catalogue of criteria for the development of a new generation of open archives (COAR 2017)[8], some of which appear to be quite relevant and even essential for the future development of research data repositories:

1) shared governance of these infrastructures to ensure public and transparent control by institutions, organizations and communities, to avoid over-centralization and also to reduce the risk of a monopoly or oligopoly in research data;

2) a balance between the necessary diversity of devices, in unique and particular contexts, and their integration around certain compulsory standards. This also concerns the implementation of a minimum level of common functionalities and standards ensuring interoperability between institutions and with other services;

3) the guarantee of a certain durability, that is, a promise of service in the medium and long term.

COAR describes two other criteria: the accessibility of deposited resources and the use of standard and open technologies, architectures and protocols. These criteria have their relevance, but in comparison to the others and in this specific context they seem less important. Furthermore, COAR advocates a pragmatic (preference for simple, proven solutions) and evolutionary rather than disruptive approach, one that focuses on users in their working environment and on the data, not just the metadata.

Beyond these rather generic criteria, both COAR and the Research Data Alliance (RDA) have recommended a number of features and characteristics for a quality, reliable, trustworthy research data repository. The COAR report, for example, describes 11 new features for "next generation" archives, while acknowledging that these features will evolve as technologies evolve and that the COAR study did not consider all technologies on the market (COAR 2017).

Some of these features are similar to the quality criteria for research data repositories described in the first chapter (TRUST principles, CTS certification, FAIR principles, etc.), such as the use of identifiers, licensed dissemination,

8 Available at: https://www.coar-repositories.org/files/NGR-Final-Formatted-Report-cc.pdf.

findability and long-term preservation. Others, on the other hand, seem to go further and could represent interesting avenues for the future development of data repositories, in particular, everything related to the monitoring of uses and practices, interaction with content, exploitation of data related to the use of content, identification and authentication of users and the production and dissemination of usage statistics. The repository as a producer of data and generator of knowledge is an idea that remains to be explored.

In addition, an RDA working group[9] has developed, based on an analysis of 11 repositories, a matrix with 44 functional specifications for a "best repository", the most important of which can be described as follows:

– metadata: support for different metadata formats and schemas, taking into account domain specificity and interoperability;

– persistent identifiers: assigning a persistent identifier (DOI) to data and the collections it belongs to;

– authentication: authentication and authorization at a relatively granular level to be able to manage different access rights for groups and individuals on collections, especially in case of confidential or proprietary data;

– data access: allow data providers to choose the level of data access.

Other specifications concern efficient and functional access interfaces, (automated) use of data policies, dissemination of data access statistics, or the provision of interfaces (APIs) for automated execution of standard repository tasks and for interoperability with external tools useful to stakeholders. Together, these specifications form the basis of a "next-generation" data repository specification – provided that they are regularly evaluated and, if necessary, updated.

12.6. Toward a "new normal"?

How can we sum up? Research data repositories play an essential role in the management of research data and, more generally, in the scientific process. However, even if they are not a particularly new type of device, they still seem to be quite far from being stable or mature, in such a dynamic and rapidly evolving technological and scientific environment, driven by a paradoxical dialectic between the development of ever greater diversity and specificity and a strong orientation toward ever greater technological and organizational integration and

---

9 RDA Repository Platforms for Research Data IG; available at: https://www.rd-alliance.org/groups/repository-platforms-research-data.html.

interoperability. As a result, it seems difficult to speak of a "model" or an exemplary type of research data repository. One size doesn't fit all, as the expression goes. On the other hand, there are solutions that are more or less appropriate to the needs and practices of scientific communities (bottom-up) and to political, financial and technological constraints and expectations (top-down).

According to several observers, the technological development of research data infrastructures lies somewhere between the "peak of inflated expectations", with political and scientific hype leading to exaggerated and unrealistic expectations, and the "trough of disillusionment", characterized by the realization that projects and achievements fail to meet all expectations, partly due to the fact that community peculiarities and traditions have not been sufficiently taken into account (Koureas 2021; Strawn 2021).

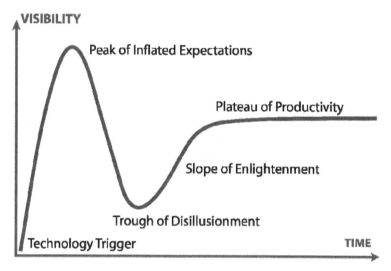

Figure 12.3. *The Gartner hype cycle (source: by JeremyKemp on Wikipedia, CC BY-SA 3.0, https://commons.wikimedia.org/w/index.php?curid=10547051). For a color version of this figure, see www.iste.co.uk/schopfel/datasharing.zip*

While waiting for these infrastructures to go back up the "slope of enlightenment" of the hype cycle (Figure 12.3), with next-generation repositories (see above) and with a consolidation of the landscape and the market, and before perhaps one day reaching the famous "plateau of productivity" where these devices would become a "new normal" of the scientific process, we will limit ourselves to formulating five questions that seem essential for the future orientation of this evolution.

12.6.1. *The policy dimension*

National policies and regulations increasingly require access, management and preservation of digital data (Cerin *et al.* 2017). Clearly, the policy of open data is gradually being applied to open research data. The stated objectives are similar: modernization of public research, greater efficiency, transparency and integrity of scientific activity, opening up research to society, stimulation of economic activity and creation of economic value from scientific results.

In relation to research data repositories, this policy raises several questions. Who owns the data[10]? Who owns the usage rights and who controls the data? Is it common property? In comparison with personal data, especially public health data in France, we could add the question of national sovereignty in the field of research data (see also Chapter 7). Is there some kind of research data heritage? And, as research data need infrastructures to "live", the question of governance also arises at the level of these infrastructures: who owns these infrastructures? Who has control over them? With what governance? Is there a national sovereignty, and should there be?

We can also phrase the political question differently: the European Research Infrastructure Cloud (EOSC) project is presented in the form of a "marketplace", with a multitude of public and private service providers, whether part of a community or not[11]. In the field of data warehousing, there is a high-quality, high-performance and attractive commercial offer, with a complete range of dynamic, customizable cloud or local solutions, and with a strong capacity for investment and innovation. In other areas, the state does not hesitate to outsource, or at least to develop, public–private partnerships; why not in the area of research infrastructures and, more specifically, in that of research data repositories?

Another issue related to the policy dimension is that of monitoring. Many research infrastructures have put in place impact assessment processes, either by measuring use in a quantifiable way or through formal review mechanisms overseen by governance bodies. However, a Knowledge Exchange report found that impact assessment often remains limited or sketchy and is a challenge for infrastructure (Goldstein 2017)[12]. How, in these conditions, to evaluate the policy in favor of open research data and, more specifically, the support for the development of data repositories? How can the link be made, for example, with research information

10 For the legal perspective, see Stérin and Noûs (2019).

11 EOSC marketplace; available at: https://marketplace.eosc-portal.eu/.

12 Also see the recent report by Egret and Fabre (2019) on the scientometric evaluation of large research infrastructures.

systems? To date (2021), monitoring tools are lacking, and the Ministry's open science barometer has no indicator in this area[13].

12.6.2. *The business model*

The economic dimension is closely linked to policy choices. The aforementioned study by Knowledge Exchange observed that the sustainability of such infrastructures was often a problem and that their business model (too) often corresponded to short-term, project-based funding (Goldstein 2017). Several works of the Research Data Alliance[14] point in the same direction, in that they show that (public) core grants are no longer sufficient and that data services are increasingly resorting to other sources of funding, such as federated funding, a consortium model or even a Software as a Service (SaaS) cloud service offer. These RDA studies point to some emerging, hybrid, scalable business models, but do not say whether these models are able to guarantee accessibility and archiving in the longer term.

The lack of a longer term funding strategy and weak business models calls into question the policy of opening up research data and developing data infrastructures. Private providers are positioning themselves exactly within this niche; Figshare and Mendeley Data offer cloud solutions to reduce maintenance and development costs, with the promise of longer term service.

The fragmentation of data infrastructures generates too many maintenance and development costs. In fact, the diagnosis of a recent study from an RDA working group (Jeffery *et al.* 2021) concurs with Mendeley Data's analysis, and like Mendeley Data, it advocates the mutualization of the development and maintenance of common components. However, Mendeley Data proposes an outsourced solution, a commercial cloud solution, while Jeffery and colleagues suggest a mutualization of public infrastructures.

Nevertheless, one should probably avoid generalizing. Here again, one size does not fit all, and we must never forget the major operational, organizational and financial differences between research institutions, organizations and structures. The model for financing a data repository on the campus of a major research university

---

13 See   https://data.enseignementsup-recherche.gouv.fr/explore/dataset/open-access-monitor-france. For further discussion, see Schöpfel *et al.* (2017), Rebouillat (2020) and Fabre *et al.* (2021).

14 These include *IG Publishing Data Cost Recovery for Data Centers* and *WG Brokering Governance*.

such as Paris-Saclay (a member of the Udice association[15]) is probably not transposable elsewhere.

Let's ask a final question: can we imagine that the use of data could one day finance the free use of the system, like the business model of certain large platforms (Facebook etc.)? In other words, what is the value of the usage data from these repositories, and in what form (services, indicators, intelligence) can these data be used?

12.6.3. *The content*

A third question concerns the content of research data repositories. We will not restate here the question of the definition of research data (see Chapter 1); more pragmatically, the question concerns the selection of data to be deposited and stored:

– What is the quality control at the time of the deposit, and what criteria is this based on? Who carries out this control?

– What kind of data? For example, is it "simple" data (see Chapter 7)? What about sensitive data, for example from medical research, or personal data?

– Which approach to apply: an *open data* or *big data* strategy, that is, to deposit and keep by default everything that can be stored? Or rather an "archive" approach, with strict selection and rules?

The Committee on Open Science has published recommendations that tend to support a selective strategy, reaffirming the role of archivists in managing research data: "It is not possible – and probably not useful – to keep everything. It is therefore necessary to select the data to be retained" (CoSO 2019). The same report suggests a number of good practices, including:

– a programmed destruction of part of the data;

– the definition of a lifetime per data type in a data management plan;

– sample retention (either random or not) in the case of very massive data.

In a sense, it is applying the rules of administrative archives to research data repositories. In part, this is consistent with the recommendations of the White Paper on Contemporary Approaches to Data Hosting and Management:

---

15 Udice is an association of French research universities formed on October 1, 2020, which today includes 10 major French research universities; available at: https://www.aefinfo.fr/depeche/636897-udice-une-nouvelle-association-pour-porter-la-voix-des-universites-de-recherche-aupres-des-decideurs-et-de-la-societe.

The appraisal of records to be retained refers to the process of identifying files and other documents to be retained by determining their value. Many factors are typically considered in making this decision. It is a difficult and critical process because the records selected will shape that organization's researchers' understanding of the records, or collections (Cérin *et al.* 2017).

Then, other questions arise. On the one hand, who determines and applies the archiving rules and, on the other hand, what value is involved? The value of the data for the research from which it originates? The potential value for other research? Value for whom: for a research community, for an institution, for a particular person, more generally for society, or economic value for a company? All this ties in with another analysis, that of the risks of loss or destruction of research data, and the estimated costs in the event of loss. Data protection and the security of data repositories are closely linked to the question of content (what type of data) and its "fate" (how long it should be kept).

The white paper by Cérin *et al.* (2017) insists that the preservation of research data cannot be the responsibility of scientific projects alone and suggests "a structured and permanent approach within each scientific project and program", a structuring within research communities and organizations, but above all a close connection between the research world and specialized structures (dedicated and specialized data center, virtual observatories, etc.), following policies defined at the national and, especially, international level.

12.6.4. *Diversity versus standard*

Whether relating to policy, business models and content, the questions illustrate the reality of an (eco)system where all these elements are closely linked. We systematically return to the notion of a scientific community with its particularities, methods, tools, practices and values (not to mention data), to the need for (or interest in) an interdisciplinary, standard, national or international level approach, and to the tension between these "two states" that Jeffery *et al.* (2021) summarize as five main paradoxes:

– narrow disciplinary efforts versus broad interdisciplinary efforts;

– start of scientific process (data collection) versus end of scientific process (publication);

– conservative behavior (staying with what you know) versus radical behavior (changing the way you work);

– funding for conservative behaviors versus difficulty in obtaining funding for radical behaviors (conservative reviewers/funders);

– independent activity of individual researchers versus various regulations and conditions.

The diversity and heterogeneity of the field versus the adoption of new methods and tools, within a global software framework, is to be constructed: of course, such an opposition is a simplification of reality. But the tension is real: between, on the one hand, the practices and expectations of researchers, with their methods, tools and data, and, on the other hand, the more generic, more standardized, more, in a way, "universal" constraints imposed by the development of the technological environment and the open science framework. This tension is expressed at every moment when it comes to the management and infrastructure of research data.

For Nakala, for example, there is the issue of integrating the needs for complex structuring of information, responding to the needs of disciplines (with a business vocabulary), in a metadata base based on the extended Dublin Core; does the "cohabitation" of several metadata formats and/or terminologies necessarily require a convergence of the vocabularies representative of the different disciplines? Does the concept of a generalist thematic repository advocated by Figshare[16] offer a solution for the diversity of curation practices?

Within the framework of the National Plan for Open Science (MESRI 2018), France supports the development of institutional and disciplinary repositories as a priority, in line with a mutualization approach, without duplicating projects. However, this tension, or paradox, becomes tangible when it comes to the integration of these infrastructures in the European framework (EOSC) and the links with "data mesocentres" in different regions, or in the reflections around a national device, be it a national repository with institutional collections, an aggregation platform, a software base for local facilities or a search engine. There is no simple and unique solution, just the need to work together to obtain appropriate and acceptable achievements.

12.6.5. *The human factor*

The objective of appropriate and acceptable achievements raises the question of the human factor. What are the conditions for a data repository to be accepted by

---

16 See, for example, the COVID-19 Open Research Data repository; available at: https://covid19.figshare.com/.

users, including by the researchers themselves, first and foremost? We have already mentioned the quality of the data, their perceived usefulness and their ease of use (see Figure 12.2); we have also mentioned the quality of the repository as a device – content, container and use – and the interest in having appropriate and recognized certification. We should add that even upstream of the service offer, the involvement of data producers and future users of the device seems crucial for its development and for the success of its implementation (Goldstein 2017).

Other questions arise: Who should be in charge of curating and depositing the data? Is it a scientific job or not? Which jobs, profiles and skills should they have? How can we encourage the various actors to invest in data management? How can we convince them to deposit data in one system or another (see Schöpfel and Azeroual 2021)? Here again, we should probably avoid overly simplistic answers and look for solutions according to disciplines, institutions, infrastructures, etc., knowing that, to date, there is no shared nomenclature for research data management.

Finally, a last question: since citizen science is one of the objectives of the open science policy, how can interested citizens be involved in the co-construction of research data, its management, curation and deposit, and the reuse of published data? The question of the "citizen" human factor is probably not the same in all disciplines and for all data repositories; nevertheless, if the idea of citizen science is to be taken seriously, this question will increasingly be posed to the operators of research data repositories, with a definite impact on choices in terms of curation, usability and functionality.

12.7. References

Azeroual, O., Saake, G., Abuosba, M., Schöpfel, J. (2020). Data quality as a critical success factor for user acceptance of research information systems. *Data*, 5(2), 35.

Cérin, C., Tanghe, H., Ait Daoud, S., Gibert, P.-O., Sahri, S., Benbernou, S., Totel, J., Bertin, L., Diaconu, C., Ghorbel, I. *et al.* (2017). Livre blanc : approches contemporaines en hébergement et gestion de données. Villetaneuse, LIPN Université de Paris 13 [Online]. Available at: http://lipn.univ-paris13.fr/~cerin/Livre_blanc_data_hosting.pdf%0D.

COAR (2017). Next generation repositories. behaviours and technical recommendations of the COAR next generation repositories working group. Confederation of Open Access Repositories, Göttingen [Online]. Available at: https://doi.org/10.5281/zenodo.1215013.

Cocaud, S. and Aventurier, P. (2017). Participer à l'organisation du management des données de la recherche, gestion de contenu et documentation des données. *Action Nationale de Formation organisée par les réseaux Renatis et Médici*, Centre National de La Recherche Scientifique (CNRS), 3–6 July, Vandœuvre-lès-Nancy, France.

CoSO (2019). Usage et gouvernance des données. Comité pour la science ouverte (CoSO), Groupe de travail du Collège "Données de la recherche", Paris [Online]. Available at: https://www.ouvrirlascience.fr/usage-et-gouvernance-des-donnees/.

Egret, D. and Fabre, R. (2019). Mission "Publimétriques". Apprécier l'impact scientifique des TGIR/OI "Comment mieux tracer les dynamiques du travail scientifique". Report, Ministère de l'Enseignement supérieur, de la recherche et de l'innovation, Paris [Online]. Available at: http://perso.obspm.fr/daniel.egret/Publimetriques.pdf.

Fabre, R., Egret, D., Schöpfel, J., Azeroual, O. (2021). Evaluating scientific impact of research infrastructures: The role of current research information systems. *Quantitative Science Studies*, 1–25 [Online]. Available at: https://doi.org/10.1162/qss_a_00111.

Goldstein, S. (2017). *The Evolving Landscape of Federated Research Data Infrastructures*. Knowledge Exchange (KE), Bristol.

Jeffery, K., Wittenburg, P., Lannom, L., Strawn, G., Biniossek, C., Betz, D., Blanchi, C. (2021). Not ready for convergence in data infrastructures. *Data Intelligence*, 3(1), 116–135.

Koureas, D. (2021). Comments to Jean-Claude Burgelman's article "Politics and Open Science: How the European Open Science Cloud Became Reality (the Untold Story)". *Data Intelligence*, 3(1), 26–28.

MESRI (2018). Plan national pour la science ouverte. National plan, Ministère de l'Enseignement supérieur, de la recherche et de l'innovation, Paris [Online]. Available at: https://www.ouvrirlascience.fr/plan-national-pour-la-science-ouverte/.

Rebouillat, V. (2017). Inventory of research data management services in France. In *Expanding Perspectives on Open Science: Communities, Cultures and Diversity in Concepts and Practices*, Chan, L. and Loizides, F. (eds). IOS Press, Amsterdam.

Rebouillat, V. (2020). Entrepôts de données de recherche : mesurer l'impact de l'Open Science à l'aune de la consultation des jeux de données. *7ème Conférence Document Numérique & Société – Humains et Données : Création, Médiation, Décision, Narration*, 23–28 September, Nancy, France [Online]. Available at: https://hal.archives-ouvertes.fr/hal-02928817.

Schöpfel, J. and Azeroual, O. (2021). Rewarding research data management. *Sci-K 2021: 1st International Workshop on Scientific Knowledge Representation, Discovery, and Assessment*, 19–23 April, Ljubljana, Slovenia.

Schöpfel, J., Prost, H., Rebouillat, V. (2017). Research data in current research information systems. *Procedia Computer Science*, 106, 305–320.

Stérin, A.-L. and Noûs, C. (2019). Ouverture des données de la recherche : les mutations juridiques récentes. *Tracés*, (19), 37–50.

Strawn, G. (2021). Open science and the hype cycle. *Data Intelligence*, 3(1), 88–94.

Wilkinson, M.D., Dumontier, M., Aalbersberg, I.J., Appleton, G., Axton, M., Baak, A., Blomberg, N., Boiten, J.-W., da Silva Santos, L.B., Bourne, P.E. *et al.* (2016). The FAIR guiding principles for scientific data management and stewardship. *Scientific Data*, 3(1), 160018.

Appendices

Appendix A

Websites

DoraNum

https://doranum.fr/

DoRANum offers a coordinated access distance learning system, integrating various self-training resources on the theme of research data management and sharing. Existing or created within the framework of the project, these resources offer several learning pathways and formats. The diversity of the resources and the complementarity of the modes and paths make it possible to meet the expectations and uses of the target audiences: researchers, scholars, doctoral students and information professionals from higher education and research institutions.

This service brings together the Urfist network (regional training units for scientific and technical information) and the Inist-CNRS, as well as representatives of the higher education and research community.

OPIDoR

https://opidor.fr/

The OPIDoR portal provides the higher education and research community with a set of tools and services facilitating the application of the FAIR principles, to make data Findable, Accessible, Interoperable and Reusable. This portal is implemented by Inist-CNRS and is part of the French National Plan for Open Science, and hosted by the Committee for Open Science (CoSO). OPIDoR offers three services:

– DMP OPIDoR: a tool to help develop data management plans;

– Cat OPIDoR: a wiki of services dedicated to research data;

– PID OPIDoR: a DOI persistent identifier assignment service.

Research Data Sharing and Valorization,
coordinated by Joachim SCHÖPFEL and Violaine REBOUILLAT. © ISTE Ltd 2022.

re3data

https://www.re3data.org/

re3data is a global directory of research data repositories in all scientific fields. The registry went live in autumn 2012 and was funded by the German Research Foundation (DFG). Project partners include Humboldt University Berlin, Helmholtz Gemeinschaft, Karlsruhe Institute of Technology (KIT), Purdue University and DataCite; the *re3data* repository is supported by the European Commission. In the future, *re3data* will be connected with other services and infrastructures as a reference for research data repositories.

RDA France

https://www.rd-alliance.org/groups/rda-france

This space – the RDA France National Node – is dedicated to *Research Data Alliance* activities carried out in France and/or by the French community. Within the framework of the European project RDA Europe 4.0, which was launched on March 1, 2018, the CNRS is in charge of developing the RDA National Node. The Ministry of Higher Education, Research and Innovation (MESRI) supports the operation of the National Node, as part of the National Plan for Open Science. The National Node carries out the following activities:

1) creation, organization and hosting of a national GDR community;

2) interactions with national research structures (ministry, organizations, universities, thematic groups, funders, etc.) and GDR governance;

3) organization of events (meetings, workshops, training, etc.) to disseminate information on RDA activities and results, with a view to encouraging the French community to participate and promote the use of the recommendations, especially those classified by the European Commission as ICT Technical Specifications;

4) more generally, the dissemination of information on the activities of the RDA, taking advantage of the knowledge of the local fabric, with the same objectives as #3;

5) promotion of events organized by the RDA and the RDA Europe project, and stimulation of French participation in these events (plenary meetings, support programmes, "ambassadors", early career programmes, etc.);

6) identification of strategic themes and areas for the RDA Europe 4.0 project calls;

7) participation and representation of the French national node in the RDA Europe steering committee.

One of its priorities is to advance the certification of data repositories and services in France.

DataCite

https://datacite.org/

DataCite is a leading global non-profit organization that provides persistent identifiers (DOIs) for research data and other research outputs. Organizations in the research community join DataCite as members so that they can assign DOIs to all of their research outputs. In this way, their results are accessible and the associated metadata is made available to the community. DataCite then develops additional services to enhance the DOI management experience, making it easier for its members to connect and share their DOIs with the broader research ecosystem and evaluate the use of their DOIs within that ecosystem. DataCite actively participates in the research community and encourages data sharing and citation through efforts to strengthen the community and outreach activities.

Open Science CNRS

https://www.science-ouverte.cnrs.fr/

Scientific and technical information includes all of the information produced by research. It is a precious and necessary asset for researchers. The provision of quality scientific resources that meet the needs of research units is therefore at the heart of the CNRS's concerns. Open science consists of making research results, most of which come from public funds, "as accessible as possible and closed as necessary". The CNRS has been very involved in the development of open science for many years. This portal contains reference documents, news, background information and other files related to open science. It is maintained by the CNRS STI Department.

Open Science Committee

https://www.ouvrirlascience.fr/

The Open Science Committee is part of the political will and the National Plan for Open Science presented by Frédérique Vidal, Minister of Higher Education,

Research and Innovation, on July 4, 2018, during her speech at the annual conference of the League of European Research Libraries (LIBER).

This plan proposes three axes:

– generalizing open access to publications;

– structuring and opening up research data;

– being part of a sustainable, European and international dynamic.

The ouvrirlascience.fr website, managed by the committee for open science, accompanies and supports the measures of the national plan. It is intended for all actors who play a role in open science and all interested citizens. Its objectives are as follows:

– to raise awareness of open science;

– to explain the challenges to its implementation;

– to raise awareness of scientific, societal and financial issues.

It contains news, resources – founding texts, reports, studies, sites and databases – and a calendar of events, all related to the three axes of the plan and covering all scientific disciplines.

It also reports on the activities of the colleges and the various groups set up by the Open Science Committee.

Appendix B

Reference Documents

MESRI 2018 National Open Science Plan

July 2018

Source: Ouvrir la Science – National plan for Open Science | 4th July 2018

Released under a Creative Commons Attribution 4.0 International (CC BY 4.0) license

Secondary aim: Structuring and opening up research data

Our ambition is to ensure that data produced by government-funded research in France are gradually structured to comply with the FAIR Data Principles (Findable, Accessible, Interoperable, Reusable) and that they are preserved and, whenever possible, open to all. During the announcement of the "Artificial Intelligence" plan at the Collège de France on March 29, 2018, the President of the French Republic announced plans to implement a compulsory Open Access dissemination mandate for all data published through government-funded projects. Certain exceptions to this obligation will be admitted as set out in law, such as when the data in question involve professional secrecy, industrial and trade secrets, personal data or content protected by copyright. The mandate will also include the best practices determined by each scientific community, such as setting the lengths of embargo periods.

Furthermore, the Ministry of Higher Education, Research and Innovation will create the position of Chief Data Officer (CDO) for research data. The CDO will work with the French government's Chief Data Officers and oversee a network of research data officers in the relevant institutions. An ANR FLASH call will accelerate the structuring of the scientific community to promote the FAIR Data

Principles and open up data. Generally speaking, the inclusion of data processing costs will be allowed in calls for projects.

Researchers will be asked to file data in certified data repositories, whose governance and intellectual property rules must comply with best practices. Accordingly, national and European research infrastructures will be given priority, especially subject-based and discipline-specific repositories. Data management plans (DMPs), a key tool in defining rules for structuring, preserving and disseminating data, will be generalized. A research data award will be created to showcase and reward teams that have performed exemplary work in this area.

France will support the Research Data Alliance (RDA), an international network that establishes the best practices concerning research data. It will also support the development and preservation of software, an inseparable part of humanity's technical and scientific knowledge. In line with these efforts, France will lend its support to the Software Heritage initiative.

As part of its government support for journals, France will recommend the adoption of an open data policy associated with articles and the development of data papers. A similar policy on these will also be implemented.

Roadmap:

1) Make open access dissemination mandatory for research data resulting from publicly funded projects.

2) Create the post of Chief Data Officer and corresponding network within the relevant institutions.

3) Create the conditions for and promote the adoption of an Open Data policy for articles published by researchers.

Accelerate:

– Suggest an ANR FLASH call to accelerate the adoption of FAIR Data Principles and the opening of research data access in France.

– Create a research data award to reward outstanding teams and projects in this field.

Coordinate:

– Create a network of contacting liaising with the Chief Data Officer in the institutions to respond to researchers' questions about research data.

– To ensure government support for journals, recommend the adoption of an Open Data policy associated with articles, the development of data articles and data journals.

Structure:

– Generalize the implementation of DMPs in calls for research projects.

– Develop subject-based and discipline-specific data repositories.

– Create a simple generic data hosting and dissemination service.

– Implement a certification process for data infrastructures.

Organize:

– Support the Research Data Alliance (RDA) and found the French chapter of the organization (RDA France).

– Support Software Heritage, the source code library.

CNRS 2019 Open Science Roadmap

November 18, 2019

Source: https://www.science-ouverte.cnrs.fr/

Released under a Creative Commons Attribution 4.0 International (CC BY 4.0) license

Section 2: Research data

Objective: data (raw data, texts and documents, source codes and software) produced by CNRS researchers or with means implemented by the CNRS must, as far as possible, be made accessible and re-usable according to the FAIR principles for a consolidation of knowledge essential to the development of a more efficient science. "Data should be as open as possible and as closed as necessary".

Action 1: Develop a culture of data management/sharing among all of the actors in the data lifecycle: researchers, engineers, computer scientists, documentalists, librarians, etc.

With the current massification of digital data produced during the research process, it is essential to develop and share good practices (FAIR) among research actors. By data, we mean raw or processed data, texts and documents, source codes and software. The OPIDoR services developed by Inist allow DOI (Digital Object Identifier) identifiers to be assigned to data sets (via DataCite) and support for the implementation of a DMP. DMPs are required when writing research projects by the European Commission and more recently by the ANR. The opportunity to identify resource persons is found in the concept of "Data stewardship". The *Mission pour le pilotage et relations avec les délégations régionales et les instituts* (MPR) has developed a methodological tool for data management that can help in the implementation of a data sharing and management policy. We will set up a network of resource persons, responsible for data in research structures and projects, trained in the use of specific services.

The principles will be implemented in different ways in different disciplinary contexts, without dogmatism and respecting established practices. The definition of data itself varies greatly from one scientific community to another. This includes in-depth discussion within communities on the lifecycle of data, its storage, access, archiving and reuse. The CNRS institutes and their communities are not all at the same level of progress in developing a culture of data management and sharing. The challenge is to raise the awareness of all research actors in order to implement the FAIR principles.

Action 2: Develop data publication (data papers), joint publication/data deposits and support researchers in the use of data management tools.

This objective is a way of making a concrete commitment to the issue of data sharing. The data on which publications are based must be made accessible and reusable as soon as possible. This requirement is already implemented in the European H2020 programme and must be applied more broadly to all data produced from public funds. It will therefore be necessary to facilitate the deposit of the datasets on which the publication is based in the open archive at the same time as the publication (this does not mean that the data should be deposited in the open archive). The datasets associated with the publications will be deposited in an appropriate data repository, if possible, a thematic repository that will best ensure the quality and dissemination of the data. More generally, the CNRS encourages the dissemination of all structured data by depositing them in thematic or general data repositories, possibly accompanied by the publication of data papers. To this end, the CNRS institutes, in conjunction with the DIST, may identify resource structures around them, such as university libraries and the MSH (*Maison des Sciences et de l'Homme*) in the humanities and social sciences, as well as resource persons who can assist scientists in these new practices. These "voltigeurs" in charge of data curation activities prefigure the effective recognition of "data stewardship". The institutes, which have a policy of supporting journals, have an additional lever and could include a component on data related to publications in the future.

Action 3: Support and accompany research infrastructures that produce data in defining and implementing data policies.

The CNRS is heavily involved with its partners in national and international Research Infrastructures (RIs), which are the places where research data are created and analyzed: analytical instruments, computing infrastructures, data infrastructures, observatories, etc. In order to roll out the application of FAIR principles in all disciplines, the CNRS will publish a charter for infrastructures, committing them to respecting FAIR practices and quality standards, by displaying data policies agreed upon with the scientific communities using the infrastructures concerned.

Some infrastructures (such as Progedo and Humanum at the Institute for Humanities and Social Sciences (*Institut des sciences humaines et sociales* [INSHS])) are already well engaged in this process, while others are in the process of being supported, such as the RIs in chemistry. The SOLEIL synchrotron has also initiated a data management policy.

There are many examples of this and they should become more widespread. These developments must be correlated with certifications (such as CoreTrustSeal) if the infrastructures themselves handle the distribution of their data.

Action 4: Support and accompany data infrastructures – Implement a coordinated service with the institutes to promote data deposits for all CNRS unit personnel. Thematic data infrastructures play a national or international role. Some are included in the national roadmap for research infrastructures.

This is in line with the structuring measure of the National Plan for Open Science, which recommends "developing thematic and disciplinary data centers". The CNRS will continue to support these infrastructures and the development of new thematic data repositories and services. This support will be conditional on an evaluation of their impact, their relevance to scientific needs and the quality of their management. CoreTrustSeal certification will be sought.

Data sharing is already a widely developed practice in some disciplines; thus, disciplinary repositories, generally international ones, have been developed for several decades, especially in astronomy. This is not yet the case for other disciplines for which the international structuring of research data is less obvious and/or established, and because the very nature of the data produced (size, heterogeneity, complexity, etc.) requires prior reflection on the nature of the data itself. Thus, many units may create a large amount of "small data" (in a data storage sense, as opposed to "big data"). This is called the long tail of data. The CNRS will study the opportunity to create a generalist data repository to house the so-called long tail data for which thematic repositories cannot be identified. This study will be conducted in the context of a national study on the handling of long-tail data and the measure in the National Plan "to develop a generic service for the reception and dissemination of simple data". Since the reuse of the data sets collected in this way can only be effective within a recognized framework of trust, a CoreTrustSeal certification mechanism will be implemented.

Action 5: Create and post a directory of data deposits and services that the CNRS is responsible for and participates in.

This repository would be an important element of the CNRS contribution to Open Science. It would bring together the data services of the mentioned research infrastructures set up under Action 3, the thematic data centers and services (Action 4) and the generalist data repository possibly created under Action 4.

CoSO 2019 data use and governance

October 2019

Source: https://www.ouvrirlascience.fr/usage-et-gouvernance-des-donnees/

Released under a Creative Commons Attribution 4.0 International (CC BY 4.0) license

Recommendations

Ideally, we would like to address these recommendations not only to the steering committee of the Open Science Committee, but also to the Open Science Committee in general, or at least to its "data" college, and especially to the "kit for institutions" and "Dataverse" working groups. Indeed, we do not pretend to propose definitive solutions, but we point out elements on which it seems a priority to us to develop a collective position, on the one hand, to advance open science in laboratories, and, on the other hand, to allow the sustainable opening of more data very concretely.

Recommendation A – define what should be retained

It is important to distinguish between different life spans and archiving periods for data, as is done for archives in general (whether or not they are science-related). It is not possible – and probably not useful – to keep everything.

It is therefore necessary to select the data to be retained. A good practice should then include a programmed destruction of a part of the data, which in return allows an appropriate treatment of the retained data. This reflection must be done from the beginning (when the DMP is drawn up), by providing for a life span by type of data, even if it means allowing a moment of revision just before the destruction. In the case of very massive data, samples can be kept (either random or not), as is already done for administrative archives.

Guidelines for this should be defined by discipline at the national level (at least): see recommendation B.

Recommendation B – classify open science by discipline

As a first step, guides to open science should be developed, presenting the motivations, principles and legal framework, more adapted to each discipline (or at least, to start with, a large set of disciplines; or even to large types of data), with adapted choices of examples and focus. The Open Science Committee could set up working groups within itself and/or work with representative bodies: sections of the CNU, the CNRS, learned societies (recently grouped into a federation), etc.

The establishment of bodies or persons mandated to give the point of view of a discipline on the major choices to be made regarding data – what exactly to open, to whom, when, for how long – could accompany the opening of data. Should this work be part of the mission of alliances (Athena, Aviesan, Allistene, etc.)? How can the various research and research support professions, as well as representatives of the public concerned by the reuse of data, be involved in the choices?

Recommendation C – provide legal training opportunities for researchers

Researchers have never been trained on the links that might exist between the results of research and the legal obligations/rights concerning them, their institution, or even the state. What about the ownership of data co-produced in collective projects between people of different status? What about doctoral and post-doctoral students? Are courses and other content related to teaching subject to the same regime as those related to research? What about data enriched by researchers, but coming from museums, libraries, publishing houses, administrations, companies, etc. (a frequent occurrence in the humanities and social sciences)? We therefore propose to:

– clarify the copyright status of different personnel;

– clarify the articulation between patentability and open science, and between GDPR and open science, working with research staff to define and publicize research exceptions to the GDPR;

– clarify the situation for data that are edited and enriched in the laboratories, but that were originally produced elsewhere and are therefore subject to other rights;

– highlight the need to license all shared content and develop clearer communication about possible and recommended licenses;

– manage the tensions between, on the one hand, legal guides drafted in such a way as to favor open science and, on the other hand, lawyers from universities/research organizations or data protection officers who, by virtue of their duties, often favor a more restrictive interpretation of the texts.

Recommendation D – provide researchers with training in research data curation

In order to allow researchers to take ownership of the issues related to data management and openness, it would be good to generalize very concrete training with work on specific cases, or even on the researchers' own data sets, rather than more general or theoretical training.

Such training should not take the upstream phases of open data archiving for granted. There is currently too little training on how to store data immediately after it has been produced, either for oneself or for a small project team. Some researchers, for example, store photos of texts because they do not know how to do otherwise. Training should also take into account the appropriation of know-how related to the establishment and implementation of DMPs, always based on concrete cases of projects carried out by researchers.

Open science will not progress without recognition of the corresponding work in the assessments of researchers. See the Open Science Committee's text on "Types of documents, outputs and activities valued by open science and eligible for evaluation".

More specifically, in terms of data openness, this would involve taking into account:

– training in data management and openness;

– the time spent to make its data durable and shareable;

– efforts to effectively open up data;

– efforts to learn about the practices of other disciplines, to understand what data could be reused or what data could be allowed to be reused by others. For example, this means encouraging specialists in the humanities and social sciences to attend conferences outside of the humanities and social sciences, experimentalists to attend theory conferences, and vice versa – something that is less valued at present than interdisciplinarity in the strong sense (joint projects).

Recommendation E – organize the human support needed to open up the data

For open science as for value creation, it is necessary for employees to know both their own job and understand the "tough" questions specific to each discipline sufficiently. This requires either twice as much training upstream (in one's job as well as one's discipline), or a professional workforce who can learn to understand these discipline-specific issues.

The issue of data openness requires coordination between staff from different professions (information systems, documentation, archives, law, data protection, even quality, etc.) rather than the invention of a new profession. We need to invent ways of getting these staff to work together, without systematically placing them in "poles" isolated from the laboratories, which risks distancing them from research practices. We could draw inspiration on these questions from the experiences – whether successful or unsuccessful – of development services, which pose similar problems in many respects; this would also be an opportunity to reflect on the link between development and open science.

In the current situation, the most urgent thing would probably be to provide researchers with a list of contacts. More precisely, a lexicon of data-related tasks should be created (understandable by researchers and therefore developed with them), and individuals and their professions should be indicated in each institution/department/large laboratory, opposite each task. For example, "if you want to know which parts of your data should be made public: go and meet an e-archivist -> name and contact details". The guides mentioned in our recommendation B could include this lexicon of tasks referring to the professions.

The development of a list of contacts in each institution could be a priority task for the data administrators who are to be appointed within the framework of the PNSO. Finally, legal support seems essential (see the paragraph above on "who owns the data"). It is thus a question of structuring a clear service offering for researchers by connecting the existing offering to the need.

Recommendation F – structure infrastructures to meet the needs of open science

The opening up of research data involves not only quantitative changes, but qualitative ones, too. At the institutional level, the infrastructures dedicated to the storage and availability of data are insufficient and often too restrictive, making it difficult to share data between members of a project belonging to different institutions.

Moreover, when the opening up of data has already been planned, the storage and opening up of data (in the framework of project funding) are designed for a limited time. For example, there are many websites designed to provide access to certain research data for a wide audience, but they often have a very limited lifespan. It is important to consider the risk in terms of recruitment for these functions if the funding is linked to a project: temporary staff (loss of know-how in the long term) or subcontracting with no guarantee of continuity.

Truly opening up data therefore requires infrastructure to host the data in order to make it available, but also to archive it sustainably. There are national centers such as the CINES, but we must ensure that they are able to increase their capacity at the pace of the expansion of open science. Storage seems to be something developed by institutions, generally, but this may pose problems linked to the duplication of effort, as well as retrieval (could each type of target audience really search efficiently in all of the repositories? This seems rather utopian, in any case expensive and time consuming to implement). Huma-Num, for the humanities and social sciences, appears to be a good model for a national infrastructure. But can the Huma-Num model be transposed beyond the humanities and social sciences? Can it be scaled up, or at least sufficiently so, to absorb national scientific production in all disciplines?

The infrastructures set up in the institutions often have limitations, particularly in terms of data storage and openness. They also do not offer archiving possibilities, unless an electronic archiving system is set up. The tools put in place are not designed for the long term and it happens all too often that the data made available are no longer accessible.

CoSO 2019 toward a data policy – strategic guide

November 2019

Source: https://www.ouvrirlascience.fr/pour-une-politique-des-donnees-de-la-recherche-guide-strategique-a-lusage-des-etablissements/

The Research Data College of the Open Science Committee has made seven recommendations to help formalize and implement a research data policy within research and higher education institutions.

Introduction

This guide identifies a number of fundamental objectives to be achieved, supplemented by proposals for additional actions (recommendations), which can be adapted according to the institutional ambition, resources and specificity of the research units.

The National Plan for Open Science published by the Ministry of Higher Education, Research and Innovation on July 4, 2018 has set itself the ambition of eventually making data from publicly funded research compliant with the FAIR principles (objective #2). To achieve this, a series of measures have been outlined, including the following:

– make the open dissemination of research data from funded programmes mandatory;

– create the conditions for and promote the adoption of an open data policy associated with articles published by researchers;

– build a network of correspondents around the data administrator in the institutions to answer the questions that researchers have about research data;

– roll out the implementation of DMPs in calls for research projects;

– develop thematic and disciplinary data centers;

– develop a generic reception and dissemination service for simple data.

This guide attempts to take into account the existing differences in the management of research data, both at the level of disciplines and at the level of MESRI institutions and operators.

This document does not deal with aspects related to publications, scientific integrity, nor the legal aspect (licenses, RGPD etc.), which will be the subject of further work by the CoSO.

Objective 1: Formalize an institutional policy

Open science issues are becoming more and more prominent in research practices. One of the reasons given for this is the evolution of public funding policies, which are gradually shifting from incentives to obligations. More broadly, the major objectives of open science are to share knowledge for the purpose of validation and integrity of scientific practices, encourage new collaborations, and enhance and reuse the data produced during research projects. Furthermore, all of these objectives must respect the production framework established during the project's framework agreements and take into consideration the regulations in force (Act 78-17 of January 6, 1978 as amended, Digital Republic Act of October 7, 2016 and Regulation 2016/679 on Data Protection).

Each research operator at the national level (university, research establishment, grouping, etc.) is encouraged to take up these issues and adopt a framework text at the highest level, defining the main policy areas and its ambition in terms of open science.

Recommendation 1:

Adopt a framework text on open science at the institutional level.

Recommendation 2:

Appoint an open science officer in charge of governance.

Recommendation 3:

Encourage the writing of data papers.

Objective 2: Implement the institutional policy

As soon as the principles of open science are adopted by governance, the first actions will focus on awareness raising and the progressive development of skills and good practices.

Recommendation 4:

Develop a culture of open science by raising awareness and training the various research actors.

Recommendation 5:

Implement a one-stop shop.

Recommendation 6:

Create a position for an institutional data administrator.

Recommendation 7:

Encourage the writing of DMPs in all research projects.

Conclusion

Integrating research data into a more general reflection on open science primarily means managing them better. An ambitious research data policy integrates the notions of reproducibility and reuse of research, based on the quality and validation of the data sets produced, whether or not they are intended to be open to the scientific community.

It is by taking into account all of the issues (legal, technical, scientific, etc.) relating to research data that we can enrich research and make it more collaborative; by preparing its archiving, we can ensure the preservation and future of our rich scientific heritage; and finally, by aiming for transparency of research and its results, we can make research honest and responsible.

INRAE 2019 guide to analyzing the legal framework in France on the opening of research data

December 2017 (v2)

Source: https://hal.inrae.fr/hal-02791224

Released under the Etalab Open License/Open License (version 2.0)

The guide "Ouverture des données de recherche. Guide d'analyse du cadre juridique en France" published by a group of lawyers from the Higher Education and Research sector, including INRA, specifies the terms of communication of data which, depending on the nature of the data, may be made compulsory, prohibited or subject to conditions.

This reference document also explains the principles to be respected in terms of data dissemination. It recalls the technical criteria to be met in order to qualify as "open data" and provides guidance on the delicate choice of the dissemination license and dissemination methods. Finally, it provides a decision-making flowchart and a series of practical sheets.

How to disseminate the data

The main principles

Technical aspects of Open Data

The recommendations drawn up in 2007 by the Open Government Data working group define good practices for data made available in Open Data. These data must be:

– complete and of good quality: raw data with metadata;

– directly accessible and usable: non-proprietary digital format, preferably open source.

Thus, to be considered "open" in the sense of the "Open Data" movement, public data must be, as far as possible and subject to certain choices, left to the discretion of public institutions:

– complete: all data are made available, except for data that are subject to limitations, for example, personal data;

– primary: data are open and collected at source, with as little modification and as much granularity as possible;

– timely: data are made available as quickly as necessary to preserve their value;

– accessible: data are accessible to the widest possible range of users and for the widest possible range of uses;

– usable: the data are computer-readable or machine-readable. The data are structured to allow automated processing;

– non-discriminatory: the data are non-discriminatory, that is, accessible to all, without any prior obligation or registration, and in principle, without cost;

– non-proprietary: the data are accessible in a format over which no entity has exclusive control. For example, non-proprietary text file format that allows easy reuse and does not require the purchase of a license;

– free of rights: the data are free of rights. They are not subject to copyright, trademark or trade secret law. Reasonable rules of confidentiality, security and priority access may be allowed;

– permanent: the data must be made accessible online with a system for archiving, tracking changes and indicating the last update.

The regulations echo some of these recommendations by requiring the dissemination of completed documents and by recommending that electronic dissemination is done in an open and freely reusable standard.

In addition, the regulations require administrations to disseminate:

– the databases they produce or receive that are not otherwise publicly available;

– data whose publication is of economic, social, health or environmental interest.

Of course, the application of purely technical recommendations is left to the discretion of the institution.

Legal aspects: the publishing license

If the control of the nature of the data has demonstrated the possibility of their dissemination in Open Data, there is one last point to consider: the choice of a license.

A data publishing license protects the data provider. Indeed, it makes it possible to limit the liability of the data provider during its reuse (limitation or exclusion of liability clause).

The Law for a Digital Republic of October 7, 2016 indicates that the license must be chosen from a list of licenses established by decree, or according to a license approved by the state (at the request of the institution).

Two main types of licenses are offered:

– permissive licenses (no or few constraints for the reuser): open license and for software: BSD, MIT, Apache, CeCILL-B;

– copyleft licenses (the reuser is obliged to share all or part of their work on public information when they redistribute): ODbL and for software: MPL, GPL, CeCILL. However, in order to use these copyleft licenses, the requirements of article L323-2 of the *Code des relations entre le public et l'Administration* must be met. These requirements are as follows: restrictions on reuse must be proportionate, dictated by reasons of general interest and may not have the purpose or effect of restricting competition.

Whether or not the institution chooses a license, the law states that every "reuser" must (unless the institution renounces it):

– respect the integrity of the data (no alteration, no distortion of meaning);

– acknowledge the source of the data;

– make sure that the date of the last update is indicated.

Thus, instances of commercial reuse cannot be prevented.

Free or paid license?

Since the so-called Valter Law of December 28, 2015, the principle of free reuse has been enshrined.

Paid access to data is now only possible for institutions that are required to cover a substantial part of the costs associated with the performance of their public service missions through their own revenues, for example, Météo France and INSEE.

List of Authors

Mark G. ALLEN
Strasbourg Astronomical Observatory
CNRS
University of Strasbourg
France

Hugo CATHERINE
Institut de Recherche pour le
Développement
Montpellier
France

Esther DZALÉ YEUMO
INRAE
Paris
France

Renaud FABRE
Professor Emeritus
Université Paris 8 Vincennes-Saint-Denis
France

Juan GARCÍA MORGADO
Elsevier
Amsterdam
The Netherlands

Françoise GENOVA
Strasbourg Astronomical Observatory
CNRS
University of Strasbourg
France

Wouter HAAK
Elsevier
Amsterdam
The Netherlands

Mark HAHNEL
Figshare
London
UK

Gabriele KLOSKA
Karlsruhe Institute of Technology (KIT)
Germany

Frédéric MERCEUR
Ifremer
Brest
France

Loic PETIT DE LA VILLEON
Ifremer
Brest
France

Stéphane POUYLLAU
CNRS – TGIR Huma-Num
Paris
France

Violaine REBOUILLAT
Claude Bernard University Lyon 1
Villeurbanne
France

Louki-Géronimo RICHOU
Sénat
Paris
France

Jennifer RUTTER
Elsevier
Amsterdam
The Netherlands

Joachim SCHÖPFEL
University of Lille
Villeneuve d'Ascq
France

David TUCKER
Elsevier
Amsterdam
The Netherlands

Sybille VAN ISEGHEM
Ifremer
Brest
France

Nina WEISWEILER
Helmholtz Open Science Office am
Deutschen GeoForschungsZentrum GFZ
Potsdam
Germany

Alberto ZIGONI
Elsevier
Amsterdam
The Netherlands

Index

Printed and bound by CPI Group (UK) Ltd, Croydon, CR0 4YY

27/10/2024

14580249-0002